D0078701

DESTINED TO BE WIVES

DESTINED TO BE WIVES

The Sisters of Beatrice Webb

BARBARA CAINE

CLARENDON PRESS · OXFORD
1986

HQ
1593
.C34
1986

Augustana College Library
Rock Island, Illinois 61201

Oxford University Press, Walton Street, Oxford OX2 6DP
Oxford New York Toronto
Delhi Bombay Calcutta Madras Karachi
Petaling Jaya Singapore Hong Kong Tokyo
Nairobi Dar es Salaam Cape Town
Melbourne Auckland
and associated companies in
Beirut Berlin Ibadan Nicosia

Oxford is a trade mark of Oxford University Press

Published in the United States
by Oxford University Press, New York

© Barbara Caine 1986

All rights reserved. No part of this publication may be reproduced,
stored in a retrieval system, or transmitted, in any form or by any means
electronic, mechanical, photocopying, recording, or otherwise, without
the prior permission of Oxford University Press

British Library Cataloguing in Publication Data
Caine, Barbara
Destined to be wives: the sisters of
Beatrice Webb.
1. Potter (Family)
I. Title
929'.2'0942   CS439.P/
ISBN 0-19-820054-4

Library of Congress Cataloging in Publication Data
Caine, Barbara.
Destined to be wives.
Bibliography: p.
Includes index.
1. Women—Great Britain—Social conditions.
2. Upper classes—Great Britain—History—19th
century.   3. Webb, Beatrice Potter, 1858–1943.
4. Potter family.   I. Title.
HQ1593.C34 1986   305.4'2'0942   86-8422
ISBN 0-19-820054-4

Set by Joshua Associates Ltd
Printed in Great Britain
at the University Printing House, Oxford
by David Stanford
Printer to the University

For Larry and Tessa

30991

Preface and Acknowledgements

I FIRST became interested in the Potter family while working through Beatrice Webb's diaries some years ago. Although my original object was to establish clearly Beatrice Webb's relationship to and ideas about nineteenth-century feminism, I found myself becoming more and more fascinated by the accounts she gave of the activities, the family life, and the problems faced by her sisters. Her description of Blanche's suicide, of Lallie's wretched final years, of Georgie's marital misery, and of Rosie's strange behaviour were graphic and compelling. They were both extraordinarily interesting in themselves and at the same time offered broader insights into the conflict, tension, and misery which could be hidden within overtly respectable, affluent, and comfortable family life. But while Beatrice's accounts were intriguing, the very distance between her and her sisters to which she so often referred, and her differences from them in outlook, made it clear that her record of events was written by a critical observer with a particular perspective of her own. Her diaries served to open up the subject and to indicate its interest but, at the same time, they pointed to the need to seek further information.

Enquiries directed to a couple of libraries and to descendants of the Potter sisters brought to light a great deal of additional material. The family has kept many records, and papers and sources for the Potter sisters are immensely rich. In part this is because various members of the family have contemplated writing its history. Beatrice Webb, the first to think of this project, made sure that many of the letters she received from her family were deposited with the Passfield Papers at the London School of Economics. She ensured that the papers of Kate and Leonard Courtney, including Kate's correspondence and diaries, went there too. The prominence of the sisters and their husbands was also a factor in ensuring the survival of their papers: thus Lallie Holt's letters are part of the large Durning–Holt collection held by the Liverpool City Libraries. In addition to these collections, there are many papers in private hands. I was therefore able to see the diaries of Blanche Harrison Cripps, the correspondence of Georgie Meinertzhagen and Maggie Hobhouse, and the autobiographical writings and correspondence of Rosie Dobbs. Some collections of papers have been destroyed: Mary Playne kept a diary, but apparently destroyed it before her death. Theresa Cripps's papers, although they were carefully collected by her husband after her early death, were destroyed by fire during the Second World War. Fortunately the sisters corresponded frequently with each other and this means that the existing collections contain letters from all of them.

The relationships of the sisters to each other, and the busy nature of their adult lives, have meant that much of the correspondence and many diary entries deal with particular rites of passages or crisis points in the sisters' lives. Coming out, marriage, childbirth, family problems bulk large in all of this, although they are often set against the tenor of everyday life. As a result I have organized this study in terms of the life cycles of the sisters, focusing on their childhood, education, entry into Society, marriage and family life, and old age. The very active involvement of several of them in public life suggested that a chapter should be devoted to this as well. This particular focus has allowed me to see the Potter sisters within the general context of late nineteenth- and early twentieth-century England. While dealing primarily with the experiences of the Potters I have tried to show the insights the Potters offer into the broader situation of the women of their class, and thus to combine a collective biography of the sisters with a social history of upper-middle-class women.

This work would not have been possible without the help and co-operation of many descendants of the Potter sisters. The interest and enthusiasm of several members of the family, and their willingness to discuss the project and to share with me their own recollections, have made the whole undertaking an immensely enjoyable one. I am particuarly indebted to Kitty Muggeridge for her unstinting generosity, and for the warmth of her enthusiasm. The project became a reality for me on the afternoon I visited her to seek information about her mother, Rosie Dobbs, and to find out if any of Rosie's papers were still extant. Kitty Muggeridge had herself once contemplated writing a book about the Potter sisters and she showed me not only all her mother's papers, but also the notes she had made towards this project. My approach is a rather different one from hers, but the meticulous notes and typescripts she had made from the various Potter collections proved invaluable, as did her correspondence with other members of the family concerning the whereabouts or fate of various sets of papers. I owe much of my own sense of the Potter sisters, particularly Beatrice and Rosie, to the long talks I had with Kitty and with Malcolm Muggeridge during the visits I made to Robertsbridge. The few days that I stayed there, to complete my work on Rosie, were both enjoyable and stimulating, and indeed formed one of the high points of my research.

I have received a great deal of help from other members of the family as well, and would like to thank Antonia Booth, John Booth, Belinda Norman Butler, Christopher Clay, Niall Hobhouse, Paul Hobhouse, George Holt, Elsie Lee, Daniel Meinertzhagen, Nicholas Meinertzhagen, Lord Parmoor, and Lady Theresa Rothschild, who allowed me free access to material in their possession—often accompanied by generous hospitality and useful and interesting conversation. I would also like to thank Ruth and Ernest Poisson for making my trips to London so enjoyable.

In my quest for material, I incurred a great debt to Dr Angela Raspin and Linda Bell at the British Library of Political and Economic Sciences for their help while I was working through the Passfield and Courtney Papers. I also received assistance from the staff at the Gloucester Record Office, the Liverpool City Libraries, and the University of London Library. I am very grateful for the help which the staff at Virago offered to me in locating members of the Potter family and in my quest for illustrations.

The assistance I received while doing research in England was augmented by family, friends and colleagues in Australia who provided support and help of many kinds in the writing of the book. Hilary Weatherburn provided invaluable assistance at every stage of the research and writing and in producing the family trees and the index. Peggy Caine, Diana Caine, Robyn Cooper, Margaret Harris, Judith Keene, and Martha Vicinus all offered enthusiasm and critical comments on earlier versions of the work. Rhona Ovedoff helped me with the original synopsis and with the index. The secretarial staff of the History Department at the University of Sydney have not only typed several drafts of this work, but indicated an interest in the book which has been very heartening. Kathy Boyd and Diana and Louise Caine provided both theoretical and experiential insights into familial relationships, particularly those of sisters. I can only offer my heartfelt thanks to Larry Boyd for his willingness to assume my domestic and familial responsibilities while I went away to do research or retired to my study to write. This book would not have been possible without his constant affection, interest, and support. My daughter Tessa has shown considerable equanimity at having her life constantly interrupted by my absorption in the Potters and her enthusiasm about the book has added immeasurably to the pleasure of writing it.

I wish to thank Ivon Asquith for his help during both the research and the writing of the book. He has been an ideal editor, unfailing in his interest, efficiency, and preparedness to offer assistance and advice when needed, while allowing me complete freedom in the actual planning and writing of the book. His expression of interest in the project at the very beginning of my research provided the necessary incentive to transform my vague ideas into a detailed plan and then into a book. I would also like to thank the editorial staff at Oxford University Press for their help.

For permission to quote from manuscript collections in their possession, I wish to acknowledge the British Library of Political and Economic Sciences for the Passfield Papers, the BLPES and the Potter family for the Courtney Papers, the Liverpool City Libraries for the Durning-Holt Papers, and the University of London Library and the Booth family for the Booth Papers. I wish to thank Virago Press for permission to quote from Beatrice Webb's Diaries. Some of the passages I have quoted from the Diaries can also be found in Norman and Jeanne Mackenzie (eds.) *The Diary of Beatrice Webb*, 4 vols., London, Virago, 1982–5. I have indicated in the notes when this happens and in which volume of the published *Diary* the quotations can be found. I am grateful to Christopher Clay, as the literary executor of Rachel Clay, for permission to quote from the Potter Papers in his possession; to Paul Hobhouse for permission to quote from the Hobhouse Papers at Hadspen House; to Elsie Lee for permission to quote from the Diaries of Blanche Harrison Cripps; to Daniel Meinertzhagen for permission to quote from the Meinertz-hagen correspondence; to Kitty Muggeridge for permission to quote from the papers of Rosie Dobbs and the other Potter family papers in her possession; and to Lady Theresa Rothschild for permission to quote from Beatrice Mayor's autobiographical sketch, 'One Family of Ten'.

For permission to reproduce photographs, I would like to thank Lord Parmoor for the many pictures I have used from Theresa Cripps's photograph Album, Paul Hobhouse for the pictures from the Hobhouse Collection at Hadspen House, Elsie Lee for the Harrison Cripps family portrait, Nicholas Meinertzhagen for the Meinertzhagen family portrait and for the portrait of Georgie Meinertzhagen, Kitty Muggeridge for the pictures of Rosie Dobbs, and the President and Fellows of the Royal College of Surgeons for the illustrations done by Blanche for William Harrison Cripps's *Cancer of the Rectum*. I would like to thank Kitty Muggeridge for permission to publish the cover photograph and Virago Press for supplying me with copies of it.

B. C.

Sydney,
January 1986

Contents

List of Plates

Between pages 144 and 145

Note: Theresa Cripps's photograph album is now in the possession of Lord Parmoor: Plates 1, 2, 3, (ii) and (iii), 4 (i) and (iii), 5, 11, 12.

1. (i) Martha Jackson, in Beatrice's words 'the family saint', who was nurse to all the Potters except Rosie
   (ii) Richard and Lawrencina Potter and little Dickie, *c.*1864
   Photographs from Theresa Cripps's photograph album

2. Page from Theresa Cripps's photograph album

3. (i) Kate Courtney outside Westminster, *c.*1885
   (ii) Mary Playne, 1883
   (iii) Blanche Potter, 1876
   (iv) Georgina Meinertzhagen, date unknown
   (i) Photograph from the Hobhouse collection, Hadspen House. (ii) and (iii) Photographs from Theresa Cripps's photograph album. (iv) Photograph in the possession of Nicholas Meinertzhagen

4. (i) Theresa Cripps, mid-1880s
   (ii) Maggie Hobhouse, *c.*1916
   (iii) Beatrice Potter, early 1880s
   (iv) Rosie Potter, 1889
   (i) and (iii) Photograph from Theresa Cripps's photograph album. (ii) Photograph from the Hobhouse Collection, Hadspen House. (iv) Photograph in the possession of Kitty Muggeridge

5. Family group at Standish, 1883
   Photograph from Theresa Cripps's photograph album

6. (i) and (ii) Kate and Leonard Courtney, dates unknown
   Photographs from the Hobhose Collection, Hadspen House

7. The Meinertzhagen family, early 1890s
   Photograph in the possession of Nicholas Meinertzhagen

8. Blanche Harrison Cripps with Fanny Hughes, her housekeeper, companion, and children's nurse, and three of Blanche's children, *c.*1883
   Photograph from Theresa Cripps's photograph album

9. The Harrison Cripps family, 1895

   Photograph in the possession of Mrs Elsie Lee

10. Illustrations made by Blanche from microscopic slides for William Harrison Cripps, *Cancer of the Rectum: Its Pathology, Diagnosis and Treatment* (London 1880)

    There is no acknowledgement to Blanche in the book itself. The original drawings, however, are now in the Library of the Royal College of Surgeons in London. Attached to the volume of drawings is the following note: 'The original drawings direct from the microscope to illustrate the first edition of my Jacksonian Prize Essay (Royal College of Surgeons, 1877) published in 1884. The whole of the drawings were done by my wife Blanche (nee. Potter). The success of the book was chiefly due to these beautiful and accurate illustrations.' (Willie was incorrect about the date of publication of this book.)

11. The Cripps family, 1889

    Photograph in Theresa Cripps's photograph album

12. Margaret Hobhouse with Stephen and Rachel *c.*1883

    Photograph in Theresa Cripps's photograph album

13. The Hobhouse family, *c.*1892

    Photograph from the Hobhouse Collection Hadspen House

14. (i) Dyson Williams and Rosie Potter, 1889 (the year of their marriage was 1888)
    (ii) Rosie and Noel Williams, *c.*1896. Rosie is in mourning for Dyson

    Photographs in the possession of Kitty Muggeridge

15. (i) Portrait of Rosalind Dobbs painted by Frank Carter and exhibited at the Royal Academy in 1903. Rosie left this painting to her son Richard in her will
    (ii) George Dobbs exhibiting his prowess as a skier, a sport he was instrumental in introducing into Switzerland

    Picture and Photograph in the possession of Kitty Muggeridge

16. (i) The last of the Potter sisters. Kate, Beatrice, and Rosie taking tea together in the mid-1920s
    (ii) Rosie and George Dobbs, shortly before George's death in 1946

    Photographs in the possession of Kitty Muggeridge

I

Introduction

I

WHILE working through her diaries in the early 1920s as a preparation for writing *My Apprenticeship*, Beatrice Webb referred on several occasions to her desire to write a book about her eight sisters. She wanted 'to give an account of *the Potter Sisters* and their husbands and children—illustrated by accounts from my diaries, to be published after my death as a description of a bourgeois family'.[1]

As *My Apprenticeship* makes clear, Beatrice Webb was fascinated by the way in which her own family exemplified the rise of the commercial and professional middle class in England in the course of the nineteenth century. Her grandfathers, Richard Potter and Lawrence Heyworth, were 'men of initiative and energy' who 'rose rapidly to affluence and industrial power, one as a Manchester cotton warehouseman, the other as a Liverpool merchant trading with South America'. Her father, also named Richard Potter, moved beyond his forebears in wealth and in his range of business interests by becoming an entrepreneur, investor, and speculator on an international scale, holding directorships in railway companies in Canada, the United States, and Europe as well as in England.[2] Several of his daughters took the next step in this rise, marrying men who added social standing to the wealth they shared with Richard Potter. Lallie, the eldest, married Robert Holt, a member of one of Liverpool's wealthiest and most established commercial families. Holt was a philanthropist and an active figure in local and national politics. He crowned a long career in the Liverpool Corporation by becoming Liverpool's first Lord Mayor in 1892.[3] Kate, the next daughter, married Leonard Courtney, a distinguished Member of Parliament who was made a peer in 1906.[4] Most of the remaining sisters married men who had distinguished careers and whose activities ranged across the spectrum of upper-middle-class professions, including merchant banking and medicine as well as law and politics. One of the sisters, Maggie, rose above the others by marrying into the gentry. Her husband, Henry Hobhouse, was a member of an extremely distinguished landed family, who became the first Chairman of the Somerset County Council.[5] Beatrice chronicled this rise, noting as well the decline in wealth experienced by her sisters' children. Even more disturbing to one with her pronounced eugenicist sympathies was the reduction in fertility and, in her view, in intellectual ability which she noted amongst her nephews and nieces. After the triumphant rise of this bourgeois family in the nineteenth century it seemed fated to a decline in the twentieth.[6]

The proposed history of the Potter sisters was never written. Although Beatrice's tale of the fortunes of her family would have been a fascinating one, it no longer seems to provide the most appropriate framework for looking at the Potter sisters. But her diaries do serve to point to the Potters as an interesting subject for historical investigation. It was rare for a family visit to take place without Beatrice commenting on her siblings: on their situation, their family circumstances, their way of life. The affluence of their material surroundings was often described in detail, and it contrasted sometimes with the spiritual disquiet which Beatrice was so acutely aware of as a family trait. Hence the diaries offer a wealth of information about the married life and domestic circumstances, the social activities, political beliefs, and changing fortunes of the Potter sisters. Because she saw her sisters infrequently, especially after her own marriage, Beatrice concentrated on the crisis points in their lives. Illness, difficult childbirths, marital tensions, familial discord, misfortune, and death figure prominently in her account. In this way, she alerts one to some of the intense misery, suffering, distress, and even violence which occurred within this large, established, and successful family. At the same time, her knowledge of these details indicates something of the way in which the family functioned and offered support to its various members. Beatrice was very interested in the relationship between the sisters, the more so because of her own sense of distance from most of them. She noted the changing relationships amongst the others: the closeness of some; the ways in which sisterly ties were affected by marriage, by changes in fortune, and by political differences. She was acutely aware of the way in which the fact that they were all female affected her siblings and gave them a sense of belonging to a 'sisterhood'. The nature of this broad concept, and the ways in which it changed from adolescence through adulthood and into old age, was something Beatrice commented upon often.

The Potter sisters were women of strongly marked and interesting personalities. Several of them were women of exceptional ability. One of the major purposes of a study of them is to make known this interesting and able group, Beatrice Webb's sisters. For Beatrice herself, the struggle to establish an identity and gain respect and recognition from her domineering and bossy older sisters was one of life's major battles. She is better able to be understood if seen within this familial context, for it explains much about the complex and contradictory nature of her values. It also enables one to see how hard she fought, and what she lost, in her struggle to establish an independent career and a life free from familial constraints.

At the same time, many of the other sisters deserve recognition for their own sakes. Mary Playne, the third sister and the one who ranked second to Beatrice as a public figure, was a major force within her own community and county as a philanthropist, a woman prominent in local government, education, and politics. In a similar way, the philanthropic and political work of Kate Courtney and Lallie Holt also deserves some recognition. Along slightly different lines, Georgie Meinertzhagen is noteworthy for her charming and entertaining histories of her own and her husband's families.[7] Moving to the opposite pole, the life of Rosie Dobbs, the youngest of the Potters, is fascinating because of its extreme unconventionality and because of her unusual range of sexual and social experiences.

No study of the Potters would be adequate if it failed to do justice to the different experiences and the different personalities of the sisters. But a detailed knowledge of them also offers insights into the broader question of upper-middle-class women in the late nineteenth and early twentieth centuries. All the sisters went through some, if not all, of the stages and rituals of young women of their class. Their education, entry into Society, marriages, family lives, and public activities are thus particular variants of the general pattern of life of upper-middle-class women. This is not to suggest that the Potters were 'typical' in an ordinary sense. But many of their experiences were the common ones for women of their class. Their particular stories show us how one family of women experienced courtship, marriage, childbirth, motherhood, family life, and old age. Their experiences can be set within the context of recent historical discussions of nineteenth-century women, but at the same time they serve to extend and sometimes to question the broader discussions as they enable us to see how one group of women coped with, attempted to manipulate, and suffered from the very restrictive conventions of upper-middle-class Victorian womanhood. Though Beatrice expressed ambivalence about them and Rosie, for a time, flouted them completely, the Potter sisters for the most part did not question the conventions or the social and familial expections which established the framework for their lives. They accepted the need to fit within the conventional pattern and devoted themselves to society, to family life, and to an approved range of philanthropic and public causes. The detailed study of the lives of the Potter sisters shows us how difficult a task it was for some of them and how well or badly they managed it. We know already the ways in which legal disabilities and familial structures limited the scope of action for women, but a detailed family study enables us to see how these formal restrictions operated in day-to-day life. In some cases one can see how personality, inner strength, and marital or familial compatibility enabled women to gain both influence and satisfaction within marriage and family life. In other cases, one can see the reverse of this as some of the sisters proved ill-fitted for family life while in turn their family responsibilities prevented them from exercising their notable talents in the public sphere. In all cases we are able to see the complex interaction between legal restrictions, social norms, and individual personalities, and can thus broaden our understanding of the general situation of Victorian women.

II

There were nine Potter sisters, widely separated in age, which makes them a particularly useful family for exploring the general experience and situation of women of their class. The lives of the sisters span just over a century, from the birth of Lallie in 1845 to the death of Rosie, the youngest, in 1949. The sisters thus experienced slightly different epochs, with the oldest ones growing up and marrying in the 'High Victorian' period while Beatrice took advantage of the expanding interest in social questions in order to establish herself as a social investigator in the 1880s. Rosie, by contrast, was widowed and then remarried during the 1890s, a decade renowned for its rejection of much of the solemnity associated with the very term 'Victorian' and one which saw the emergence in literature of a 'New Woman', whose attitude to marriage and sexual behaviour was very much more experimental than was that of earlier Victorian heroines.

The century which the Potter sisters spanned was not only one of massive political and social change, but also one in which some of this change was extended to women. The granting of a measure of women's suffrage in 1918, the admission of women to universities and to professions, and the granting of legal rights to married women were all developments which occurred within their lifetimes. Their activities and their attitudes reveal much about the ways in which these legal changes were perceived by and integrated into the lives of actual upper-middle-class women. Through the Potter sisters one can see very clearly the changing mores and moral norms which determined the framework in which women lived, but at the same time, one can see the very strong thread of continuity which not only encompassed them, but extended backwards to their mother and forwards to their own daughters. This continuity points to the very limited nature of the changes in the situation of women which were occurring in the later nineteenth century.

One example of this can be seen through Rosie. She received her education during the 1870s, by which time the Oxford and Cambridge local examinations had been opened to girls. Hence whereas the education of her older sisters was entirely arranged and organized by their mother, with the help of a variety of governesses, tutors, and finishing schools, Rosie was educated in accordance with a formal syllabus which was structured on somewhat tighter lines. She did not manage to complete this, however, being unable to withstand the stress which serious study imposed on her health. Her sisters too were all very critical of the strain which the heavy programme involved, and felt that their mother was misguided in attempting to apply it to Rosie. No one ever seems to have thought that this education would direct Rosie in any other way than towards the traditional vocations of women of her class: Society, marriage, and the raising of a family. Important though the admission of girls to university locals and entrance exams, to improved and academically oriented schools, and to women's colleges attached to the universities was, it could not and did not in itself revolutionize any aspects of the lives of women. Like so much other reforming legislation and administrative procedure, it was essentially permissive rather than prescriptive. It allowed more scope for that small number of women who were interested in and able to take advantage of the increasing number of occupations and activities,[8] but it did not bring about substantial changes in the outlook of women, or of the families in which they lived.

All of the Potter sisters lived through the start of the campaign for women's suffrage as well as the campaigns to improve the legal situation of married women and to extend the range of both paid and unpaid employment open to women. The sisters were on the whole interested in very few of these campaigns. Women's suffrage was not a matter of great interest either to Lawrencina Potter or to her daughters. Some of them were actually opposed to women's suffrage, while others only evinced any interest in it as a result of marrying men who regarded the matter as a serious one. Nor did the Potters indicate any interest in the rights of married women to their own inherited or earned property. They were all provided with marriage settlements which secured them a small income 'for their own use' under the control of trustees. They were not themselves ever faced with the problem of either being denied anything by their husbands, or of having those husbands attempt to commandeer their property and income, and so took no interest in any of the questions of basic principle or justice which reform of the married women's property laws involved.

While the Potter sisters did not take much interest in any of the various campaigns to extend the rights of women of the late nineteenth century, they were affected by some of these campaigns and by some aspects of the changes in the situation of women. The most noticeable one was the extension in the range of unpaid public work and public service which was becoming available to women in the second half of that century. After the pioneering efforts of philanthropists like Louisa Twining and Mary Carpenter, and the widely publicized work of Florence Nightingale, the participation of middle-class women in many of the organized forms of philanthropy became widely accepted. It was not the involvement of such women with charitable work which was new: the wives and daughters of local squires and landowners or of wealthy businessmen had for generations dispensed good advice along with broth and baby clothes to tenants and other impoverished people in their neighbourhoods. What changed in the mid-nineteenth century was the scale of this work and the ways in which it was organized. There were quite new forms of philanthropic work, like Workhouse Visiting, or the many Friendly Societies established to help train and place as domestic servants the girls who had been born and brought up in the workhouse. There was also a whole range of domestic visiting for the purpose of giving advice to or collecting rent from those living in the dwellings of charitable trusts. There were many societies set up to deal with the 'sanitary question': the problems pertaining to health and hygiene within new industrial cities. The reforms in local government, and the extension in the range of activities incorporated into local government along with the inclusion of women rate-payers as voters and as candidates for some local office, also increased the range of unpaid work available to women, particularly in areas like education. Finally, the 1880s saw the advent of a range of women's groups affiliated to the major political parties, and designed to assist in the electioneering and the general work of those parties.[9] Most of the Potter sisters became involved in some of these activities—and those who did so demonstrate convincingly how very important it was for late Victorian upper-midle-class women to have a range of interests and activities outside the sometimes oppressive confines of their family.

At the same time, the very involvement of the sisters in these areas and the immense interest and competence which some of them displayed there points to a central problem. The Potter sisters, for all the various kinds of change around them, were born into and grew up in a society with a very narrow range of options for women. Girlhood, Society, marriage, child-rearing, was the intended pattern of their lives, and the one which most of them followed. This could be expanded slightly, by periods of philanthropic work for single young women, or by engaging in a range of public activities for married ones. But outside this there was very little. Theoretically, and this was another new departure of the late nineteenth century, there was the possibility also of a 'celibate working life', involving either unpaid philanthropy or engagement in teaching or one of the few other poorly paid occupations open to women. Two of the Potter sisters chose such alternatives for a time. The elder of the two, Kate, has left diary accounts and letters which show the extent to which the decision to embark on the life of an unpaid charity worker was the result of family tensions and dislike of the pressures of the Season. She has also left records which show how hard it was to decide to do this and to carry out the decision. Parental disapproval and distrust, echoed sometimes by sisters who shared more conventional beliefs about the appropriate behaviour of a young lady, made the attempt to set up an independent life into a battle for respect and recogniton—and one which had to be fought against familial disbelief and constant undermining. The other, Beatrice, has left a vivid and moving account of the emotional problems, including sexual deprivation, which were attendant on taking the decision to defy convention and engage in activities other than those of Society.

Theresa also had a strong desire to enter into some form of

independent celibate life, but recognized that she lacked the strength and determination which enabled Kate and Beatrice to withstand criticism and family pressure. Maggie in particular commented on the emptiness of a life geared for many years around the social Season, but not being of either a studious or a philanthropic cast of mind, she saw nothing for it but to wait until marriage liberated her from this stage and introduced her to the next.

All the Potter sisters married, and it is clear that all of them wanted to do so. Most of them also had children and devoted the larger part of their lives to the care, or at least to supervision of the care, of their families. Some aspects of marriage and of motherhood were fulfilling and enjoyable for them, although they responded to motherhood in very different ways. All, except Rosie and Blanche, seem to have had great skill in the administrative abilities required to organize large families and often more than one house. All, again with these two exceptions, enjoyed an active and busy social life, entertaining friends as well as a whole host of the social, business, and political contacts who were important for their husbands' careers. Most were, as has often been noted, women of great intellectual and organizing abilities, known for their outspokenness—and their lack of the gentler feminine virtues. Yet despite that they had little articulated inclination—and even less opportunity—to venture outside the 'female sphere'. Hence the framework for their lives remained the typical one for women of their class and they tried, often to their cost, to confine their lives properly within this.

Beatrice Webb is obviously an exception to this general pattern: she married late, having already made a name for herself, she had no children, and she married into a working partnership. But impressive though her achievements are, she remains in many ways a case-study of the high cost women had to pay for breaking the bounds of convention in the interests of personal achievements.[10]

III

While the similarities in their general situation far outweigh any of the differences in the experience of the Potter sisters in the early years of their lives, this is not true of their adulthood. The span of their lives meant that the younger sisters, Beatrice and Rosie in particular, experienced whole historical epochs which were outside the knowledge of the others. Indeed, there is a sense in which the sisters might almost be seen to have lived through different historical periods. Lallie's life, for example, spanned most of the Victorian period, beginning in 1845 and ending in 1906. Rosie, by contrast, was born in 1865, just as the great boom period of mid-Victorian England was coming to an end. She bore most of her children in the Edwardian period—and lived to see one killed in the First World War and another taken as a Japanese prisoner of war in the Second. As a self-conscious and in some ways introspective woman, she lived through such changes in outlook and ideas that she spent agonizing months thinking about what psychoanalysts would say about her own upbringing, and more particularly about the ways in which she had applied certain Victorian norms and standards to her own children.

The sisterhood falls into three groups or stages in terms of this general question of their historical experience. A large group died before the First World War, with their experiences centring on Victorian England. Theresa died first, in 1892, making the first painful breach in the sisterhood. But the end of a phase in its life came with the death of Blanche in 1905 and perhaps more significantly with the death of Lallie, the oldest and sometimes the fiercest of them all, in 1906. Georgie died next in 1914, just after the outbreak of the war. For these sisters there were still many changes to contend with: Lallie lived to see the motor car and the telephone—to say nothing of having her eldest daughter complete her education at Cambridge. Georgie lived through a terrible marriage, punctuated constantly with unplanned—and often unwanted—pregnancies from a husband who believed in keeping his professional and recreational life entirely separate from his wife and children. But when she was freed from this relationship by widowhood, she found in the movement for women's suffrage an absorbing interest which gave her a quite new outlook and indeed a new lease of life.

For the remaining sisters, an experience more catastrophic than they had ever imagined came with the First World War. There had been much concern and agitation within the family over the Boer War, but the scale of that war, as of their involvement, was dwarfed by the First World War. For Kate, who with her husband Leonard was adamantly opposed to the war, it was hideous and wrong. She also saw the war in a way that was common to many intellectuals, writers, and activists, as bringing an end to civilization. Her views were not shared by her sisters, although Beatrice regarded the war as quite outside the scope of her philosophy or understanding. However, the participation of some of their sons, and the loss of two of them, made the war an event of terrible anguish to the Potters. Kate was right in many ways: the war did bring an end to the world she had known and in which she had participated. Her husband died in 1918, and although Kate lived for another ten years, those years were in a sense an epilogue. For two other sisters this was also the case: Mary and Maggie both saw the war as putting an end to much of their lives, and both of them died within a very few years of its end.

Beatrice and Rosie were the only two to live through the inter-war years, and at least into the beginning of the Second World War. Although Beatrice kept commenting on how old she felt, she watched with great interest. These years were not just an extended period of observation, tacked on to her active life. She remained very busy with her writing and research during them, and found the answer to the problem which had preoccupied her since her late adolescence: the loss of faith in Christianity or in any other organized form of religion. The pursuit of spiritual values and religious certainty which had accompanied all her historical research, political involvement, and social life was finally ended with the discovery of Soviet Communism. This 'new civilization', in her—perhaps misguided—view, combined all the civic virtues which she endorsed with an active set of ideals and beliefs which were quite independent of theology.

For Rosie, these years provided a solution of a slightly different kind. Unlike her older sisters, Rosie had never been a public-spirited or fully integrated member of any community. Through a combination of predilection and circumstance, hers had always been a somewhat peripatetic life, moving from one place to another in search of health for one husband and of occupation and pleasure for another, and as a way to avoid paying income tax. The scope for a wandering life became much greater in the inter-war period, as improved communications and her more mature age gave her the freedom to move around Europe and the world, sketching all the time and indulging a passion for varied scenery. Between trips she visited her children, attempting in some peculiar way to expiate a long-lasting sense of sin by giving them money and providing manual help in the cleaning of their homes. She did not exactly find peace; it was rather that the values and the kinds of behaviour in which she had always believed and indulged were now becoming acceptable, and she ceased to be, or see herself, as an outcast. Beatrice and Rosie shared a fascination with changing moral standards, particularly those involving sexual behaviour. But whereas Beatrice deplored the decline in sexual morality and the advent of a belief in the merits of sexual relationships independent of procreation, Rosie had the satisfaction of seeing her views on sexual relationships become the generally accepted ones.

II

The Potter Family

I

THE most noticeable thing about the Potter family is the sheer scale
on which they lived. The size of the family and its enormous wealth
entailed massive organization and vast dwellings. The nine sisters
grew up in a series of huge houses rented by their father or belonging
to members of their family or to friends. They moved from one place
to another in large carriages, accompanied by troops of servants.
When they were in the country, they lived in houses situated in
spacious estates which provided them with fruit, vegetables, and
game—as well as allowing them to stable their horses and to exercise
their skills on horseback. In London, they lived in fashionable parts of
Kensington and engaged in the paying of calls and the giving and
attending of the balls, parties, and dinners which made up the activity
of the social Season. They always had stables in London too, and rode
regularly in Hyde Park. The fact that there were so many children,
with ages ranging over twenty years, meant that establishments often
had to be kept up in a number of different places. The younger children tended to remain in the country with governesses, housekeepers,
and maids while the older ones were introduced to the social Season.

Beatrice Webb frequently commented on her family background and
took a certain pride in belonging to the new ruling class which had arisen
out of the industrial revolution. But when she analysed her background
she insisted that the first distinctive feature of which she became aware
was that of belonging to 'a class of persons who habitually gave orders,
but who seldom, if ever, executed the orders of other people'.[1] It was this,
rather than the family's wealth, that impressed itself upon her mind, she
argued, because the existence of servants and of a whole external world
which responded to her parents', her sisters'—and then to her own—
demands was an irrefutable reality. By contrast, the 'discriminating
penuriousness' of her mother, with her constant quibbling over expenditure, resulted in the Potter girls all being brought up to 'feel poor'.

Lawrencina Potter clearly believed in thrift and kept a tight rein on
family expenditure. But her natural puritanism and inclination

towards a simple life were probably increased by her uncertainty for many years about the size of the family income or the state of Richard Potter's fortunes. Richard Potter had inherited a 'modest competence' from his own father, estimated at £2,000 per annum by his youngest daughter. This income, which was quite sufficient for a comfortable, leisured life, was drastically reduced by the depression and the financial crises of 1847–8, which left an income of only £700 per annum.[2] In subsequent years, his income fluctuated wildly in accordance with the fate of the many speculations and investments in which he was involved. His changing circumstances were replicated elsewhere in the family. In 1858, the year of Beatrice's birth, Lawrencina Potter noted in her journal that her father Lawrence Heyworth had lost half of his property through the collapse of the railway company in which it was invested and that 'our own affairs have been somewhat unprosperous'.[3] By the early 1860s their affairs were looking up. In 1864, she notes that 'my dear husband has doubled his property',[4] and for many years after that the family standard of living continued to rise.

In the absence of his account books, it is impossible to estimate the actual size of Richard Potter's income. One can get some sense of it though from the odd comments scattered in letters. In 1879, for example, his income from the timber company, Price Potter and Walker, was close on £13,000.[5] In the early 1850s this had provided the major part of the family income,[6] but by now it was only a small part in comparison with what came from his many other investments. A few years later, when Beatrice was keeping house for him, her domestic expenditure was £3,700 per annum, and this presumably did not include the cost of leasing the house, stabling horses in London, carriages, or any of the other appurtenances of fashionable living.[7]

Richard Potter's money came from a variety of different sources. When he lost the greater part of his inheritance, he was invited by a close friend, W. E. Price, to join his firm. Potter agreed to do so and in 1849 became a partner in the firm of Price and Co., timber merchants. The business was initially based in Gloucester, but branch houses were soon established in Grimsby and Furness. Potter had a very substantial share in these. Shortly after this, he was instrumental in setting up the Wagon Works in Gloucester. He was chairman of its board of directors from 1860 until 1863 and then again in the mid-1870s. But Potter certainly did not confine himself to local industries. In the year that he first joined Price and Co., he was also offered a directorship of the Great Western Railway by his father-in-law,

Lawrence Heyworth. Subsequently, when the Great Western and Midland railways amalgamated in 1863, he became chairman for two years. His railway interests were particularly extensive, and took him out of England to North America and to Europe. In 1862, he became a director of the Grand Trunk Railway of Canada and was president of it from 1869 to 1876. In addition to these posts, Potter was also for some years a director of the Hudson's Bay Company and one of the English Commissaries of the Dutch Rhenish Railway. He had a large range of other financial and business interests, including a substantial investment in the South Wales Coal Company, the Ruabon Coal Company, and the Severn Bridge Railway Company.[8] The diversity of Potter's business and financial interests meant the family income was always variable. Charles Macaulay, Potter's brother-in-law, often referred to his recollection of 'hearing Richard Potter say that nothing was so easy as to make money, and nothing so difficult as to keep it'.[9]

The nature of Potter's interests, the fact of his having so many directorships and of his wishing to supervise some of the concerns in which he had large holdings, meant that he and his family led an ambulatory and unsettled life. 'The restless spirit of big enterprise dominated our home life', wrote Beatrice and indeed it did, causing the family to be almost continuously on the move from one house and locality to another. Both the constant movement and the varied and often international nature of Richard Potter's investments meant that the family never established close ties with any locality or any community.[10]

As if to underline his own desire for freedom of movement, and his status as a capitalist entrepreneur rather than a landowner, Richard Potter did not buy houses but usually rented them. The family rented a large furnished house in London every year for the Season. Even Standish House, where they were based for more than thirty years, was rented from Lord Sherborne.[11] In subsequent years, other houses were also rented. In 1865 he bought a house called The Argoed, a Jacobean farmhouse in Monmouthshire, where the family could go for short holidays and where they tended to stay for some weeks every year. In the late 1870s another house was rented near Windermere. Rusland Hall, as it was called, was a convenient base from which Richard Potter could oversee the timber yards at Barrow-in-Furness in which he was involved, and it provided a suitable spot for the family to retire to after the London Season.

The Potters moved from one part of the countryside to another in accordance with the social seasons and with Richard's business needs. In addition there were many visits to Liverpool, the home of Lawrencina's father, and later also of Lallie, the oldest Potter daughter. Other trips, on business, for pleasure, or to see family were frequently made: to Wales, northern Scotland, and to a variety of seaside resorts. The size of the family and of the household made it impracticable for everyone to move together all the time. Besides, Richard's business sometimes necessitated solitary trips, and Lawrencina clearly enjoyed breaks away from her large family. Often two or three children would accompany the parents while others remained at Standish or Rusland Hall, or went on visits to family or friends. During the London Season, the girls who were not yet 'out' remained at Standish and some of the daughters spent quite long periods there while others moved about far more.

Richard Potter's business interests did not only require frequent travelling within England. His period as chairman of the Grand Trunk Railway of Canada inolved him in yearly visits there. Throughout the 1870s, he spent two to three months of every year visiting Canada and the United States. He also had on occasion to visit Holland in conjunction with railway interests there. Two daughters usually accompanied him on these visits and were thus initiated into the ways and the wealth of American capitalism.

Richard Potter was in many ways a most unusual father. As one recent biographer has said, parental roles were largely reversed in the Potter household: it was Richard who had a close, affectionate, and confidential relationship with his daughters while Lawrencina remained largely distant and aloof from them.[12] The love the daughters all felt for their father is amply attested to not only by Beatrice, but also in several other unpublished autobiographical fragments or memoirs. And indeed one can well see why this was the case in reading through the many letters which passed between father and daughters. He wrote frequently to any absent daughters; daily to Rosie when she was sent away to school in 1883, and almost as often to Beatrice when she went on a brief holiday the following year. After the death of his wife, he wrote to at least one of his daughters every day.

Potter's letters make it clear that he took an interest in every aspect of the lives of his daughters. Those few that survive from the girls' school-days show his concern about their health, their lessons, and their school progress, as well as their general states of mind. Unlike Lawrencina, he sometimes wrote simply to say he was thinking about a particular daughter and wanted to send love. As the girls grew up and married, his letters deal with their social activities and friends, their successes at particular occasions, and then with their married life and children. He was often taken into confidence and was fully informed about the various domestic problems his daughters faced. Sometimes he assisted, particularly when there were financial problems, or when his renowned negotiating skills could be of use. And he was an exemplary and enthusiastic grandfather.

Potter's open and affectionate relationship with his daughters extended also into the realm of his business and financial affairs. Here, however, one sees something of the wily diplomat at work for, while he kept his daughters very fully informed about his affairs and even asked for their advice, they had very little capacity to influence him. Many of his letters to them contain accounts of the precise state of his business undertakings, or the detailed breakdown of a particular financial deal. He welcomed their comments and asked for their views. But it is clear that he let them talk, and then did precisely what he wanted. On one occasion, he went to discuss his plan to give up the timber business with Maggie, one of his main family business advisors. Subsequently, he wrote to Rosie of this visit. 'I talked much and long with Maggie about this Barrow business and the change of habits and residence which it might bring about and though she wished me to be guided I stand by my own personal wishes and instincts.'[13] His wife, however, did influence him in matters of business and, in Beatrice's view, generally in unfortunate directions. But his daughters could not get him to give up hare-brained schemes, like that for importing live cattle from America, with which he flirted for years, nor could they get him to retain positions or investments which they thought were in his interests. Even after his stroke in 1886, Beatrice only managed to stop him speculating in shares by going over his head and insisting that his brokers disregard his demands.

As a result of his closeness to his daughters, and of his habit of taking one or two of them on his long trips to America, the Potter sisters knew and wrote about Richard Potter's weaknesses. On some of the trips his excessive indulgence in food and wine resulted in ill-nesses that involved changing plans and itineraries. Maggie wrote confidentially to Beatrice in 1874, to explain one such change. 'The truth is we have been rather disarranged by dear Papa being rather knocked up through too great a profusion of champagne lunches and speechifying, at both of which things he excels.'[14] On another occa-

sion, when Richard had just gone to America, she wrote asking him to take care of himself and to 'avoid the hospitality of your friends, who so kindly try, through a treatment like that given to those unfortunate pate de foie geese, to feed their guests off the earth'.[15] Whether or not her advice was heeded one cannot say. Neither Beatrice nor Kate, who accompanied him on this particular visit, made any comment about it. Subsequently, however, Beatrice wrote at some length about 'the French chef; the overabundant food; the extravagantly choice wines and liqueurs' which were all part of travelling through America on board the cars reserved for the chairman of the railway company.[16]

Despite the obvious affection which existed between Richard Potter and his daughters, many of them agreed that it was almost impossible to know him. Although Lawrencina Potter chose to present her husband even in her private journal as a man of unquestionably noble and upstanding character, whose success was due to his 'firmness, truth and liberality', his daughters portray him in a rather more equivocal way. Beatrice, whose carefully balanced portraits of him are masterpieces of description and of social analysis, accepted that ultimately it was impossible to understand or to come to terms with him. She wrote at length of his outward character: his personal loyalty and almost childlike religious faith, and the strange way in which this was combined with a genius for the duplicity of industrial diplomacy and lack of any fixed moral values. In her view he managed his difficult wife and strong-willed daughters with the same skill he applied in business, but perhaps as a result of this, he remained intensely reserved while outwardly spontaneous and genial. '"We do not know whether Mr Potter is very simple or very deep," said one Gloucestershire lady to another. Which of his daughters could count on his actions; could lay bare the secret intentions of his heart? He told all; left all untold. Who can read the paradoxes of Father's nature?'[17]

But indeed the paradox presented by Richard Potter is a more complicated one than this contrast between the simplicity of his faith and the subtlety of his business dealings. For the pictures of Potter available from different sources seem to have nothing in common with each other, and the affectionate and laudatory picture presented by his wife and daughters is substantially undermined by others. In her *Apprenticeship*, Beatrice Webb explained that her father's conduct was governed by friendship and personal loyalties rather than by any fixed or general principles. 'Hence he tended to prefer the welfare of his family and personal friends to the interests of the companies

which he presided, the profits of those companies to the prosperity of his country, the dominance of his own race to the peace of the world.'[18]

This view of Potter is endorsed and expanded by others who knew him through business dealings. Sir Daniel Gooch, the man who followed Richard Potter as chairman of the Great Western Railway, regarded him as both incompetent and dishonest. In Gooch's view, Potter and his friends were all men 'little guided by the usual principles that govern gentlemen of honour'. Whereas the Potter daughters tended to argue that it was his entry into the world of railway expansion and financial speculation that turned Potter into a sharp bargaining man, Gooch argues the reverse case, and insists that it was the advent of men of Potter's ilk who brought a deterioration in the standards of conduct and ethics which governed business dealings. Gooch had several altercations with Potter, all of which served to increase his sense of Potter's insincerity and duplicity. He went beyond general criticisms and attributed some of the financial strains and weaknesses evident in the Great Western during Potter's chairmanship directly to Potter's double-dealing. Gooch was particularly appalled by Potter's support for a new railway line in South Wales. This line offered little to the Great Western Railway, but a great deal to Potter himself as he had substantial investments in a colliery in South Wales which would have been served by this line. Gooch provided a final damning summary of Potter as chairman of the Great Western Railway: 'had Potter remained in the chair a few years longer he would have brought ruin on the company and wiped out all the original capital and much of the preference. He was reckless in expenditure and a vain, soft headed fool, blown about by any wind.'[19] Although recent histories of the two railway companies of which Potter was chairman do not endorse quite so negative a view of him as this, it is clear that he lacked the capacity either to carry out his own grandiose schemes for these companies or to deal adequately with all the various financial and political problems which had to be faced. His departures from both the Great Western and the Grand Trunk Railways were taken in moments of heated dispute and attended by unpleasantness.[20]

Unlike their mother, the Potter sisters acknowledged the fact that their father was shrewd, crafty, and even questionable as a business man. Rosie, who idolized him, noticed his capacity for 'being diplomatic to the verge of dishonesty' and his ability to 'drive a bargain as hard as any man'. But she, like the others, tended to argue that this

side of Potter was evident only in his business dealings and contrasted with his genial and affectionate behaviour within the family.[21]
But other members of the family point to the way in which Potter
carried his business ethics into family affairs. His brother-in-law,
Charles Macaulay, wrote on several occasions of his absolute distrust
of Richard Potter and of his wish to ensure that Potter had nothing to
do with the financial welfare of his immediate family. Some of
Macaulay's reasons for this mistrust are made evident in a letter he
wrote to his daughter, Mary Booth, in 1875:

I have just stumbled upon an awkwardness with R. Potter. In consequence of
grandma's death a sum of £2,500 comes to the trustee of your marriage settlements. Having heard nothing about it, I wrote to Janson—my attorney & the
attorney to the Trusts—to ask about it. He wrote to say 'I presume that Mr
Potter has accounted to you for the interest from the date of Mrs Potter's
death.' Why, you ask, should he do so?—Because, says Janson, 'the money
remains secured upon the Argoed Estate—though at present there is only an
equitable deposit of the title deeds. It would I think be more regular that there
should be a mortgage in the ordinary form'—So that Richard—without saying
a word to us—he being one of our Trustees—has kept the capital in a security
which is not strictly regular—and has moreover never sent us a word to
intimate to us either the nature of the investment, or that he was our debtor for
the interest, of which we have not received one farthing.[22]

Macaulay's letters to his daughter also provide a very different
picture of Richard Potter's behaviour to his family. From these, Potter
emerges as a harsh and even violent man, brutal and unfeeling in his
treatment of his mother, his dogs, his nephew, and even, on occasion,
his daughters. In the course of several visits to Standish, Macaulay
detailed incidents in which these aspects of Potter came to the fore.
He wrote of his own and his wife's horror when Potter told the
assembled family about how he had beaten his dog until it was covered
with blood because it had disobeyed him in running after another dog.
He noted several times the neglect Potter showed towards his mother
when she lived in a cottage close to Standish—acknowledged only
when the Potters had too many guests and sent some to stay with her.
Macaulay was particularly critical of the way in which Potter treated a
young nephew, who was also his ward, bullying and humiliating the
boy and exploiting his financial dependence.[23] But the most surprising
picture presented by Macaulay was one of a breakfast scene during
which Richard Potter

spoke to Maggie before everybody so brutally that even she—not a melting girl by any means—got up from the table, and rushed out of the room in tears. Richard then turned to me and said—have you observed, Mac, what an injurious influence the example of America has exercised over all our domestic relations: formerly children were obedient to their parents—but now it seems to be expected that Parents should submit to their children . . . I wish I could give you an idea of the awful solemnity with which this was said.[24]

Macaulay had little reason to care for Richard Potter. He had been more or less inveigled into marrying Potter's slightly disturbed younger sister and had, some years before, appealed in vain to Potter to help the family during one of his (Macaulay's) absences.[25] Macaulay's wife, Mary, had apparently regarded Richard Potter as a hard and cruel bully during her youth—and found no reason to change her views.[26] The Macaulay and Potter adults were never close. Their daughter, Mary Booth, however, was a close friend of several of the Potter girls and had spent much time at Standish with them. In the light of her quite intimate knowledge of the Potter family, it seems unlikely that her father would have exaggerated or given anything other than a truthful account of events as he saw them.

While there is never any suggestion from his daughters of their father behaving as cruelly as Macaulay describes, this may well be the result of a desire to protect him and his memory. It does seem that some aspects of his behaviour were not talked or written about, and his propensity to violence and occasional harshness may have been among them. It is clear that the daughters sometimes tried to protect each other from Richard Potter's vagaries and that, although they all succumbed to his charm, they did not think him always either reliable or even stable. He certainly indulged in moods and hysteria and made his own state of mind a very central part of family gatherings. This was particularly the case after Lawrencina's death. When Richard was threatened by the possible loss of Beatrice as his housekeeper and companion, he became quite impossible. He did not like Joseph Chamberlain, the man in whom she was interested, and set himself strongly against the match. Thus over the Christmas holidays of 1883, when Chamberlain was expected to visit Beatrice, Richard became 'irritable and hysterical. He broke down at the Xmas dinner and his excitable allusions to Mama and sudden transition from joviality to unhappiness were most trying.' Mary Playne, who had remained at The Argoed in order to distract her father and leave Beatrice free to concentrate on her own situation, subsequently wrote to her older sister about their father. 'When one is much in Father's company, delightful as he is to talk to sometimes and brimful of kindness, one turns instinctively to the calm and sensible Holt way of looking at things for comfort and repose.'[27]

The other area where it seems that a decorous cloak is being drawn by the daughters is that of Potter's sexual behaviour. There is nothing to indicate that Potter was unfaithful to his adored wife, although the suggestion that he was tempted in this direction is made by Beatrice. In her view, Richard Potter's 'insistence on his daughters' company whenever he went abroad was, I think, partly due to a subconscious intention to keep out of less desirable associations. In his struggle with the sins of the devil and the flesh ... he had two powerful aids—his wife and his God.'[28] But after Lawrencina's death, Potter seems very rapidly to have developed and expressed an interest in other women. There is a suggestion that he proposed to Bessie Belloc, one of the founders of the English Women's Movement and a friend of Barbara Bodichon and, for a time, of George Eliot.[29] Gossip amongst the Potter descendants also links his name with that of Mrs Eustace Smith, the woman at the centre of the Dilke scandal, and with several other London neighbours.[30] The really interesting question here is how much the daughters knew and what part they played in it all—and one wonders whether there was not a quiet conspiracy to prevent Richard's remarriage.[31]

In any event, Richard Potter only enjoyed a few years of activity after his wife's death. He suffered a stroke in 1886, four years after Lawrencina died, and was increasingly incapacitated after that time up until his death in 1892.

The apparent ease and closeness which existed between Richard Potter and his daughters was not paralleled by the relationship existing between the girls and their mother. Although the extremely stilted nature of the childish letters to her may well be explained by late Victorian notions of correctness, and by the careful scrutiny exercised over these communications by governesses, even the adolescent letters make clear the need constantly to placate a very difficult and arbitrary woman which was felt by her daughters. Again it is Beatrice who seems to encapsulate her mother best in the analysis she provides in *My Apprenticeship*. Here she stresses the great difficulties Lawrencina faced in her 'pilgrimage through life', in coping particularly with the dual pulls of a desire for faith on the one hand and a critical and rationalist intellect on the other. Beatrice's own life-long struggle with this same duality made her extremely sympathetic to her mother here. She points also to her mother's own upbringing in a family of men, all of whom spoilt and adored her—an unfortunate preparation for the mother of nine daughters, none of whom showed the least inclination to the scholarship to which Lawrencina turned in her spare time and which increasingly filled the days in her later years.[32]

In many ways Lawrencina's own life, particularly after her marriage, was a series of disappointments. When she had met and then married Richard Potter, she had envisaged their future as a life of shared interests in political and religious questions, which would bear fruit by Richard becoming a Member of Parliament. His financial loss brought an end to all of this—and although Beatrice saw it as a stroke of good luck for him, for Lawrencina it was quite different. The roving life of a capitalist entrepreneur which so suited Richard left her at home, bearing and then supervising the large family of daughters. Her journal shows how her pregnancies became increasingly debilitating, and suggests, not surprisingly, that it was the combination of continuous pregnancy and ill health which prevented her from accompanying Richard abroad. She agreed to his constant expansion of interests and to his becoming chairman first of the Great Western and then of the Grand Trunk Railway—as her daughters frequently pointed out in their letters, which served as more or less gentle admonitions to her to cease complaining about his regular and prolonged absences from her. But it is hard to see how she could really have refused or in any way have altered his activity. The family 'lived where it suited him to live, and he came and went as he chose'.[33] Lawrencina had no real choices and apparently became increasingly embittered as a result. Her imperiousness and much vaunted strength of will did not, as in the circumstances they could not, ever produce anything but bad feeling. Lawrencina is one of the few mid-Victorian women who can be shown to have refused to surrender to maternity and family duties with a good grace. The surrender was inevitable, but she retained at least the power to do this gracelessly.

It is at the same time hard to see how Richard Potter could ever have provided Lawrencina with the marriage of her choice. Although constant reference is made in biographies of Beatrice to his wide range of intellectual associates, this view of him is rather an overstated one. Herbert Spencer was his close friend, but this was because Spencer succumbed immediately to Potter's charm rather than because they shared either intellectual or any other interests. As Spencer himself records, the lengthy discussions he enjoyed at the Potter home were chiefly with Lawrencina. She 'was scarcely less argumentative than I was, and occasionally our evening debates were carried on so long that Mr Potter, often playing chiefly the role of listener, gave up in despair and went to bed.'[34] It was Lawrencina who kept up their contacts with political and intellectual figures, like the Chevaliers, with whom she could discuss free trade. Spencer certainly introduced the family to other intellectual and scientific friends, whom some of the girls took up. T. H. Huxley, Francis Galton, and John Tyndall became friends of Kate, Georgie, and Beatrice but never of Richard Potter. Indeed, when Beatrice took over as his housekeeper after the death of Lawrencina, he wrote to his youngest daughter Rosie of a dinner Beatrice was giving for the Huxleys and the Leckys adding, rather ruefully, 'Beatrice decidedly inclines towards the intellectual, scientific grandees & masters and not towards people of fashion as much'.[35] Potter was an eager follower of political developments and his letters are filled with comments on particular Parliamentary debates or the state of play in regard to questions like Home Rule. But he does not ever discuss other questions. He was, as both Beatrice and Rosie pointed out, passionately fond of poetry. He constantly reread Dante, and bought a copy of Milton so that he could reread 'Lycidas' on a train journey. He spent much of the early 1880s reading and rereading Carlyle's letters and his memoir of Jane Carlyle and was constantly moved by them. But his range of intellectual interests did not extend far beyond this. Rosie insists that 'outside his business career and his family life, my father had not a great many interests. His knowledge of literature and art were limited to standard writers and he had little or no ear for music. . . . He had little or no appreciation of modern books and was completely out of touch with modern thought.'[36]

Richard Potter thus had neither interest in, nor particular sympathy with, his wife's religious and spiritual yearnings. He had neither her sceptical and rationalist intellect nor her sense of need for some deep and fulfilling religious communication. He did not read the Bible in the obsessional way she did, and her attempts at translating it into different languages, like her attempts to learn as many languages as she could, were activities in which he took no part. Herbert Spencer's ideas were, in a similar way, of little interest to Potter and they made no impact upon him. He pitied Spencer, for his lack of instinct and his incapacity to enjoy life, and he felt that Spencer's materialism and denial of divine authority were all related to this. In 1884, Spencer stayed for some weeks with Potter in the Lake District. He was particularly gloomy and weak at that time and Potter felt sure he could not last much longer. As Spencer got into his carriage, Potter said '"God bless you my dear fellow" and he responded by a look of despair at the sound of the words so foreign to his innermost aspiration. I almost expected a mild rebuke for the use of such an expression and I mentally ejaculated Thank Heaven I am not a disciple of the Spencerean philosophy.'[37]

In regard to Lawrencina, while there is much evidence both of her involvement in intellectual activity and of the respect in which her intellectual attainments were held, it is hard to find written records which give any real insight into this. From her journal, as from her letters to her children during their infancy, the thing that is most noticeable is her rigid sense of duty and her lack of any sense of humour. She felt very strongly about the need to supervise the children's education. 'It is absolutely necessary in order to ensure regular progress', she wrote in her journal, 'that I should weekly or at least fortnightly examine all their copy and exercise books and if they do not make further progess change their teachers. For childhood is a precious time which profitlessly wasted can never be afterwards redeemed.'[38]

In an attempt to establish an independent area of intellect and literary activity for herself, Lawrencina published one novel, *Laura Gay*.[39] She was uncertain about fiction as her *métier* and thought she would take another tack, should a 'more eligible' one present itself. And indeed her hesitancy was more than justified. Although her older daughters read it, and dutifully wrote to her of both their progress through it and their enjoyment of it, few others responded in this way. The book was unfavourably reviewed by those few papers which noticed it, although one reviewer did foresee the posssibility of better work in the future.[40] It contains a mixture of political and social satire, unjust and therefore repulsive, in the eyes of the *Sunday Times*, alongside the love story of Laura Gay and Charles Thornton.[41] After a series of difficulties, this young couple eventually marry and lead a life of affection and true intellectual companionship. The love plot was seen by one reviewer as 'a thin one, woven out of a single incident', but it was apparently intended as an idealized version of the relationship between Lawrencina and Richard Potter. The whole book is excessively moralistic and sententious. The characters never emerge beyond the sets of adjectives which describe them. Laura herself is beautiful, blooming, graceful—and knowledgeable. She knows Latin and French as well as having a 'solid grounding' in history, art, and literature. She is practical, and can manage money and deal with all the organization that is required for a European trip. She finds lodgings in Italy and acts as both companion and courier to her aunt. Needless to say, she is also original, and, despite her lack of conformity to organized forms of religion, 'truly religious'. Two men are attracted to her. One, Charles Thornton, is an honourable and handsome young man, with a sound intellectual training gained from having used his years at Oxford properly, original views on politics and economics, and a strong sense of duty. The other, Redford, is quite the opposite of this. He is 'both a cynic and a sybarite', and, of course, a man with only the smallest smattering of knowledge to match his thin veneer of social graces. No one ever converses in the novel in anything less than a full paragraph—and Laura's charm is certainly not evident to us the way it appears to be to her friends and admirers. When Thornton tells us that he fears that his nature is 'too balancing and scrupulous' to achieve a distinguished position in the House of Commons, Laura argues that lack of distinction does not signify

if you do your best. We are not gifted for self-illustration, but for the good of our fellows and the glory of God. We may not hide our light under a bushel, and bury our talents in the earth; we are bound to work while it is day, keeping ourselves pure and unspoiled for the whole world as it may be. Ours is no passive faith, it demands action, glorious action; and there is One who stands ever nigh to ease our path in the daily struggle.[42]

Thornton is convinced by this and embarks upon a parliamentary career.

The only place where one sees another side of Lawrencina is in the entries in her journal dealing with her much beloved and short-lived son. In 1862, four years after the birth of Beatrice, her eighth daughter, Lawrencina gave birth to a son, Richard—or Dicky, as he was always called. This long-awaited event seems almost to have transformed her. The difference between the announcements in her journal of the arrival of Dicky and that of Beatrice shows clearly how she felt about having a son, as compared with daughters. The only notice of Beatrice is the following: 'Unfortunately for my children my strength has been much impaired by bearing little Beatrice, my eighth daughter and now again I am enceinte but I think that during this pregnancy I may

venture to do more than I did last time.'[43] Presumably this pregnancy
ended in a miscarriage as Dicky was not born for another few years.
Shortly after his birth, the journal contains this entry:

A son has been given to us now 8 days ago of most promising appearance,
exceedingly healthy, strong full sized and like his Papa and placid too beyond
all my former infants. May we have wisdom and self-denial enough to train the
child in the way he should go, always setting his religious and moral culture
before any other, and carefully guarding him from insidious evil influences.[44]

Later, on 2 October 1864, we read the following: 'It is more than two
years since the birth of our little Richard and all things have prospered
with us.' Still later in that year comes the heart-broken account of the
death of this cherished son. 'Sorrow such as we have never known
before overwhelms our hearts for our dear lovely little son, our
Darling Dicky, has been removed from us after seven day's great
suffering by a severe attack of scarlet fever.'[45]

   Lawrencina had to bear not only the loss, but also the knowledge or
at least the strong feeling that she had participated in a system of treatment which had both harmed the child and increased his discomfort.
As the fever increased, little Dicky wanted only to drink water, but the
doctor had insisted that he should not be given water but that he
should be fed. He ate, with difficulty and to please his mother, but the
food only increased the fealing of nausea and of stomach pain. After
three or four days, he became increasingly drowsy and unable to talk
or take notice of his surroundings. He was in pain for much of the
time, with sores in his mouth and on his lips and having difficulty in
breathing. Finally, on the seventh day after the illness began, he died.
Lawrencina remained with Dicky throughout his illness, trying to
sleep in his bed, talking to him and caressing him. Up until the very
end, she wrote, 'he seemed to like me near him and to feel my hands'.

   His death was an incomparable loss to her. He was unquestionably
her favourite child and, as a boy, the one on whom she had pinned all
her hopes for achieving greatness vicariously. Her final comment on
him, after his death, shows the sense both of immediate personal loss
and defeated ambition.

It is an inexpressable comfort to us that from the earliest dawn of his very
remarkable intelligence he had grown day by day more in charity, love, truth
and duty. To all he seemed a remarkably gifted boy, but his constant health,
his robust appearance and his cheerfulness did away with any sense of
precocity. We fondly hoped that a character so rare combined with such a

bright intelligence and such excellent health marked him out as one formed to render a long lived service on earth to God and Man.[46]

It must be remembered that the intelligence and character being described were those of a little boy who died at the age of two years and six months!

There are a few records available to indicate what happened to Lawrencina after Dicky's death. At that stage Lallie, the eldest daughter, was already in charge of the housekeeping. Moreover, Lawrencina herself was pregnant at the time of Dicky's death and seven months later, in July of 1865, she gave birth to her last daughter, Rosalind. The announcement of Rosalind's birth in the Journal harks back strongly to the earlier loss and to the disappointment of having yet another daughter.

We were very much disappointed that she was not a son, for it seemed that a little son might have in some measure consoled us for the angel that we have lost. Alas! my darling no present infant could withdraw my mind from dwelling most constantly on your dear life and your untimely death. May it please the Lord to unite us all together hereafter.

May our dear little babe walk in your loving steps and yet be spared to close our eyes if ever we live to old age.[47]

Despite the fact that the new baby was a girl, she apparently did go some way to filling the gap left by Dicky; at least she became the favourite and pet of both her mother and her father.

As Lawrencina's favourite, Rosie spent much time during her childhood in her mother's boudoir and thus experienced to the full Lawrencina's adulation of her lost son and her own particular cult of mourning. Long after the death of Dicky, Rosie later recalled, Lawrencina 'cherished the memory of all his little ways, his baby sayings and doings. I can still remember the beautiful inlaid cupboard which contained the precious relics which had belonged to my brother; his little shoes, the hat he had last worn, many of the toys he used to play with. These were all kept in a cupboard with glass door, which stood in a corner of her boudoir.'

Rosie's recollection of her mother in this particular setting points also to the fact that after the death of little Dicky, Lawrencina became more and more withdrawn from social and family life and more and more engrossed in her private theological studies. The older daughters could now relieve her not only of housekeeping responsibilities, but also of the care of the younger children. She continued to supervise the education of her youngest daughter—to the horror of some of her older ones, who deplored the excessive strain which was constantly being imposed on Rosie and under which her health deteriorated rapidly. But the day-to-day running of the large household was something she gladly relinquished.

Lawrencina seems to have become rather closer to her grown-up daughters during these years. She managed to sympathize with their experiences, especially once they were married and dealing with families of their own. She was concerned, sympathetic, and generous to her adult daughters in a way she had been incapable of when they were young. The shared experiences of marriage and motherhood provided a firm basis for this, and she no longer carried the burden of having to bring up girls in place of the boys she wanted. She played an active role as a grandmother, having grandchildren to stay, especially when confinements made their mothers very grateful for her help. In these years, she even grew closer to Beatrice, the once rejected and disparaged daughter. It is indeed interesting to note that while Richard Potter filled the lives of his daughters with his own vitality, after his death few of them referred to him or felt any sense of his continuing presence or influence. By contrast, for several of the daughters Lawrencina became more central to their lives after her death than she had ever been during her life. Her interests, her religious conflicts, her struggles were ones which some of the daughters underwent themselves in later years and the sense of her having been through these experiences before them gave them strength and reassurance. It was fitting that this should have happened, for despite their veneration of Richard, the Potter sisters were very much the daughters of Lawrencina.

III

The Early Years of the Potter Sisters: Childhood and Adolescence

I

SHORTLY after their marriage in 1844, Richard and Lawrencina Potter moved to Gayton Hall, a rambling old manor-house in Herefordshire. It was here that their first six daughters were born. Lallie arrived first, just a year after the marriage. She was followed within the next seven years by Kate, Mary, Georgie, Blanche, and Theresa. During those years the family lived on Richard Potter's inheritance, and faced severely straitened circumstances when the financial crises of 1848 drastically reduced his income. This period of modest living was, however, quite short-lived. In 1853 the income which Potter received from the timber company in which he had recently been offered a share enabled him to rent Standish House, the enormous and imposing country residence of Lord Sherborne.[1] It was here that the remaining three daughters were born, Maggie in 1854, Beatrice in 1858, and Rosie in 1865. It was here too that little Dicky, their long-awaited and cherished son, was born and where, two and a half years later, he died.

Standish, nestling in the Cotswold Hills outside Gloucester, was the place where the girls spent the major part of their childhood and the one they loved most and recalled most frequently in later years. Rosie in particular wrote warmly about the pleasures afforded her by the extensive gardens and grounds which surrounded her home.

The part of my life which stands out most vividly is the long summer days spent in the beautiful Standish garden, exploring its glades and hidden pools. Alert in mind and body I roamed what seemed to me an earthly paradise. I climbed its tall trees and spent hours in an old boat on the great round pond surrounded by huge clumps of pampas grass, whose great white feathery heads swayed in the breeze. How I loved to explore that wonderful water world, and its mysterious depths whence the great trout my father had imported from some northern stream grew fatter and larger in the clear but almost stagnant waters.[2]

The garden provided all the sisters with a multitude of secret places in shrubberies and trees, the most favoured of which was a large oak-tree under which the girls sometimes gathered to listen to their father's stories.

Beatrice, looking back on her family life in later years, insisted that Standish and the Potters' life there was entirely representative of the behaviour and beliefs of the social class to which they belonged. Standish was 'in all its domestic arrangements typical of the mid-Victorian capitalist'.[3] In a period during which housing design for the wealthy was coming increasingly to separate employers from servants, children from adults, and the necessary activities of housekeeping and housework even from the view of those engaged in the pursuit of wealth and leisure, Standish provided a perfect model of such segregation.[4] The large and rather institution-like building was divided into front and back premises. The front, which contained the sitting rooms and the bedrooms of Richard, Lawrencina, and 'honoured guests', were all carpeted, comfortably furnished, and provided with a splendid view over flower-gardens and the Severn Estuary. The back premises, with their sparse furnishing and their view over kitchen gardens, stables, and servants' yard, contained the hierarchically arranged living and sleeping quarters for the servants as well as the day and night nurseries, the bare schoolroom, and the bedrooms of the older daughters and their governesses. The particular structure of the Potter family was perhaps demonstrated by their failure to follow the trend towards having an 'increasingly large and sacrosanct male domain'[5] situated in an attractive location. It was Lawrencina's boudoir which was placed in the front of the house, and furnished more ornately than any other room, while Richard's billiard and smoking room was tucked away in the back of the house.

The daughters lived in the back premises, visiting the front for family meals, to use the library or, for her favourites, to have time alone with Lawrencina in her boudoir. This location was appropriate because, like most upper-middle-class children of the period, they were looked after mainly by paid domestic staff. For most of them there was a succession of nurses and nannies who gave way to the 'nursery governesses' who taught the girls reading, sewing, and the rudiments of composition. The nursery governess would in turn be succeeded by the German, French, or English 'finishing governesses'. Here, as in many other aspects of their lives, maternal favouritism determined the variety and the quality of care. Thus Rosie, the youngest daughter, was provided with a wet-nurse who remained to look after her until, at the age of 4 or 5, she came under the care of Miss Mitchell who 'grounded me in the three R's'. Miss Mitchell was replaced when Rosie was 12 by Miss Brown, a recently graduated student from Newnham who was employed to prepare her for Oxford Junior local examinations.[6] Beatrice, by contrast, had neither special nurse nor governess, but had to make do with whatever attention was spared to her from the staff employed for her older sisters or the general household servants.

The children's special staff took their place alongside a range of other servants: housekeeper, cook, maids, gardeners, and farm and stable hands. Over all of this presided Martha Jackson, the 'household saint' who had been Lawrencina's companion and attendant from childhood and who remained with her until her death. Martha brought what there was of calm and serenity to the household, counselling and advising Lawrencina, soothing domestic storms, and providing much of the warmth and affection which the children received. She was essentially the head servant, although her distant kinship to Lawrencina and her long service to the family gave her a privileged position. Her role in the lives of the daughters was recalled by Mary many years later.

Dear, dear old Dada, what a good woman she has been all her life and what a blessing to others! How much *we* owe her! ... My first remembrance of happiness was being rocked in her lap when I had that brain illness and I never got a smacking or a snub from her without feeling how just it was and how richly deserved. . . . we could always depend on her sense and kindness. In our intimate child life she was our real mother on whom we could depend for daily comfort and discipline. Our own mother never near to us, at least never to me, and never seemed quite natural.[7]

But Dada was merely the closest amongst a number of servants and governesses with whom the girls had affectionate and important relationships. In contrast to these people, their parents were remote beings, and their mother particularly a rather difficult one. Beatrice later recalled her early view of her mother.

Throughout my childhood and youth she seemed to me a remote personage discussing business with my father or poring over books in her boudoir; a source of arbitrary authority whose rare interventions in my life I silently resented. I regarded her as an obstacle to be turned, as a person from whom one withheld facts and whose temper one watched and humoured so that she should not interfere with one's own little plans.[8]

Even the favoured daughters commented upon the remoteness of their mother and on their difficulties in dealing with her. Theresa, the gentlest of all the Potter sisters, and an especial favourite of Lawrencina's, did not feel quite the same way about her mother as did Mary or Beatrice. She later recalled her feelings of closeness to her mother at the age of ten, 'when I worshipped her with the ardour of child worship, and clung to her as a true mother'. But, as she was forced to concede, although Lawrencina 'loved all her daughters, [she] sometimes forfeited their sympathy through showing too little tolerance for their natures'.[9]

Lawrencina did not provide her daughters with a model of tactful or nurturant womanhood any more than she provided them with the experience of being mothered. For all Dada's care and kindness, this lack remained. Some years later Mary Booth, a cousin of the girls and a close friend of several of them, commented that 'what all those girls have wanted in life is a mother's influence. They are all that women can be who have never had that side "developed" to borrow one of Bee's favourite new terms.'[10] Richard Potter, for all his much-vaunted closeness to his daughters, never made up for this lack.

The Potter home functioned, as did most other middle-class homes, as the central socializing agent for daughters. It provided their basic understanding of the sexual division of labour and of the many ways in which gender determined the opportunities open to them and familial and social roles.[11] The home was presided over by Lawrencina and she supervised the domestic work, almost all of which was done by female servants. She was frequently pregnant or looking after small babies, and hence, despite her private studies, was often immersed in domestic cares and responsibilities. Richard Potter offered a complete contrast to this. He spent his days engaged in business matters away from home, returning either at night or at weekends and bringing news of the outside world as well as many treats. The Potter family may have differed from the Victorian stereotype in the personality make-up of its adult members: Lawrencina was domineering, imperious, and wilful, while Richard was genial, affectionate, and outwardly compromising. But this only served further to underline the differences between male and female roles and powers. The girls were very well aware that the family worked along the lines determined by, and designed to meet the needs of, their father. At the same time as they shared with their father the need to cope with and to manage the difficult temper of Lawrencina, they entered into a supportive relationship with Richard Potter, sympathizing with his aims and desires, and criticizing Lawrencina when she made any complaints about being left so long alone while he was away on business. Lawrencina probably found all of this very galling, but there was nothing she could do about it.

Richard Potter distributed largesse and contributed much in the way of good fellowship to his daughters in the way which was very common to the Victorian paterfamilias. He had, however, little to do with the day-to-day running of his home or the organization of his family. It was Lawrencina who designed and directed the education and other activities of her daughters. This division had the advantage of ensuring that it was her range of interests, rather than her husband's narrower one, that formed the basis for the girls' education. Hence at least some amongst the daughters received an unusually broad and stimulating education. Lallie was the chief beneficiary of this, writing home from her London boarding-school in some surprise that 'no one here learns Latin and no one knows anything about it'.[12] Even before their teens, she and Kate had begun basic training in classics and mathematics usually reserved for boys. They and their younger sisters were supplied with specialized tutors, employed not only to teach classics, but also music, history, and geography. All the girls began their education at home under the general supervision of a governess. But the proximity of Standish to Gloucester Cathedral and the friendship between the Potters and Bishop Elliot meant that they had access to a steady stream of young clergymen and minor canons who were only too willing to augment their stipends by offering private tuition. In London, other tutors were found so that the girls' education was not interrupted during the Season, and when the family was staying at the seaside Lawrencina herself gave them lessons.

Lawrencina took her supervisory role in the education of her daughters very seriously. She regularly heard their exercises and examined their notebooks, commenting in her journal on their progress. In June 1858, she noted that the children had been provided with a music teacher,

but without much success. They have also had Mr Clarkson twice a week to teach them classics and mathematics. Lallie has made some progress in arithmetic, Latin and Greek, but I find that in music, history and geography she has not progressed. Kate has progressed in Latin and to some extent in arithmetic. Mary has made little progress of any kind, Georgina still less. Blanche has improved morally. She and Theresa have made some progress in reading and sewing but far too little in other directions.[13]

The fact that the Potter girls were given tuition in mathematics and classics did not mean that they were allowed to ignore or to neglect feminine accomplishments. Sewing was learnt early: Blanche and Theresa were 6 and 7 respectively when their progress in this field was noted. All the girls were expected to do both plain and fancy sewing, and dutifully reported on their progress at working screens and other household ornaments when Lawrencina was away from home. Singing lessons, with an emphasis on carriage and deportment, followed on from piano lessons, as part of the standard instruction of a young lady. Sketching and painting were also taught to the girls, and followed up by sketching holidays and by trips to see the European 'great masters'. Although the Potters were not as a family renowned for their artistic talents or interests, Blanche and Rosie were exceptions. Both had a passionate interest in painting and made it their major activity in adult life.

Despite her own interest in scholarship, and the efforts she made in regard to her daughters, Lawrencina did not succeed in imbuing any of them either with any sympathy for her own intellectual pursuits or with serious intellectual interests of their own. Indeed Beatrice never ceased to wonder at the fact that her family was so intelligent, but so very unintellectual. However, all but two of the daughters had a very firm grasp and understanding of literature, politics, and many of the major intellectual and social developments of their day, and this probably owes much to their early training.

Lawrencina's surveillance extended towards matters of discipline and in this sphere too her daughters were aware of the contrast between her severity and their father's 'more lenient treatment'. Rosie later recalled the way in which Lawrencina had constantly supported her governess when the latter had resorted to punishments as a way of controlling her unruly pupil. 'At one time it was the exception for me not to be under sentence of some such punishment as extra tasks, or early to bed. Once I remember being kept in bed all day as the result of a fit of temper.' Rosie regarded the sending of children to bed as a favourite punishment of her mother's because 'it combined the intolerable ennuie of solitary confinement with the disgrace of not appearing at meals'. She felt that this punishment fell on her with particular force: 'When my older sisters were sent to bed they generally passed the time playing at pillow fights, but being a solitary child no such mitigation of my sentence was possible.'[14]

Lawrencina Potter saw her role in regard to her children primarily in the form of a duty. This sense of maternal duty did not, however, prevent her from having very different feelings towards her daughters and from treating them in markedly different ways. Rosie, as we have seen, was one of her favourites. Beatrice, by contrast, was a child whom Lawrencina did not like, nor was much care taken for her welfare. She was, as she has recorded in her autobiography, very much neglected as a child. This neglect was made all the more painful when compared with the attention which was heaped upon her baby brother. The discrepancy in their treatment forms the subject of her earliest recollection. The first scene she could remember was of

finding myself naked and astonished outside the nursery door, with my clothes flung after me, by the highly trained and prim woman who had been engaged as my brother's nurse. What exactly happened to me on that particular morning I do not recollect. The French and English governesses who presided over the education of my sisters decided I was too young for the schoolroom. Eventually I took refuge in the laundry . . . under the voluntary but devoted care of the head laundrymaid.[15]

The fact that Beatrice was followed by the son for whom Lawrencina had waited so long emphasized the difference between her treatment and that of the next child. However, it was not just the difference in sex which explains her neglect. After Dicky's death, Lawrencina transferred much of her devotion to Rosie, and lavished care, attention, and special staff upon this last baby daughter. Moreover, Beatrice's rejection by Lawrencina was only the best-documented in a set of mother–daughter relationships, all of which involved either pronounced favouritism or rejection. Mary, the third of the daughters, was greatly disliked by her mother, not only throughout her childhood but also into adult life. In her case there was not the later recognition of being kindred spirits or the growing closeness which developed between Beatrice and her mother in the last couple of years of Lawrencina's life.[16] Indeed, even as Lawrencina lay dying and the sisters gathered to nurse her, it was felt that Mary should not actually go to her mother for fear of distressing her. She and Beatrice were recognized by all as being two of Lawrencina's daughters whom she particularly disliked. By contrast, Theresa, Maggie, and Rosie were particularly favoured.

This marked differentiation evident in Lawrencina's attitude towards her children was also evident in Richard Potter, but in a very reduced form. He had special sweethearts amongst his daughters whom he petted and caressed, in contrast to others who were his confidential business advisers. But there were no daughters who were or who felt rejected by him. The strong affection from him may have gone some way to counteract the lack of warmth from Lawrencina for Mary, who was always one of her father's great favourites. It was Beatrice's particular tragedy that, while admired by her father, she was no more a favourite of his than she was of her mother.

It would be quite inaccurate to see the Potters as experiencing a childhood composed of misery and gloom. Beatrice was lonely and depressed most of the time, but she was herself aware that her situation and experiences were not the same as those of her sisters. The very tone of the few surviving letters written by Theresa as an adolescent illustrates the differences between her feelings about her family and those of Beatrice. This letter, sent to her father shortly after Theresa went to school, is a particular case in point: 'How very kind of you to write us such a nice long letter; we read it aloud, and then we had a general huggation, and thought what lucky girls we are to have such dear affectionate parents.'[17] Theresa was at school with Georgie and Blanche and this companionship clearly played a major part in her greater sense of ease and comfort.

Apart from the companionship of each other, the girls found much to keep them amused at Standish House itself. The building lacked charm, but none the less it contained much that was interesting. Rosie later recalled many happy hours spent playing in the bathroom with a young relation. In this room, 'there was a sort of gymnasium with swings, rope ladders and trapezes, and here we loved to disport ourselves on wet days, and became quite expert gymnasts, climbing ropes and hanging head downwards from the swing. We thought ourselves very courageous and like boys, and we had an institution called "Chink a ring Clids" for inflicting pain on each other and bearing it stoically.'[18] And like most other large country estates, Standish had extensive and beautiful grounds where the girls could play, learn to ride, and generally feel both free and at home.

The grounds of the estate offered not only opportunities to play, but also a whole separate farming life. Many of the girls became intimately acquainted both with the farming families and staff and with various agricultural activities. Beatrice kept hens and sold the eggs, initiating

Rosie into this activity by giving her a pair of bantams as a present. The curious correspondence between Beatrice and her mother, as they negotiated who would pay for the feed of Rosie's hens, shows yet again Lawrencina's concern for economy and for the proper use of experience. (In the end it was agreed that Lawrencina would pay for the feed until the hens began to lay, at which point Rosie, then aged 5, would pay for it herself.)[19]

The social network of the Potter family provided ways of increasing the pleasures the girls derived from Standish. Their carefully regulated days involved long walks and frequent excursions into the countryside. Under the influence of Herbert Spencer, these soon became scientific expeditions. In 1859, Spencer noted in his diary that during his last visit to Standish 'I initiated my little friends there . . . in Natural History by establishing an aquarium and giving them lessons in the use of the microscope. Hitherto our afternoon walks had been walks simply; now they became expeditions in search of interesting objects.'[20]

Spencer's visits were of particular significance for Beatrice as he soon singled her out for special attention, and was the first person to take any notice of her intellectual abilities. She later wrote that what she had learnt from Spencer had nothing to do with his interest in natural history: she disliked looking at objects under a microscope and could not feel any interest in them. Moreover she soon realized that he had nothing to teach her as regards objective or scientific observation. He selected only those items which confirmed his hypothesis and totally ignored all the rest. But by this very means he provided her with an immensely useful education, not in ways of establishing the truth, but in ways of assessing 'the relevance of facts', and of marshalling evidence to support a case.[21] But even before Beatrice developed the interest in Spencer's methods which dominated some years of her teens, she took part in the specimen- and fossil-collecting expeditions to which he had introduced all the Potter girls. Beatrice described one such expedition in a letter to her mother.

We started at around 11 o'clock and as Walters had a fit of going round the country in search of turnpikes, we did not get there very soon ... After spending a delightful day we came home at half past five, as we came the right way it took only one hour; Maggie found some lovely fossil seaweed, one piece grey and the other red; for our walk yesterday we went to Boveron Hill where we found some pretty clay fossils they are so finely marked and so easy to break that Theresa broke one beauty just in picking it up, and we went to the same place today, and found some more of the same kind. I collect for Maggie, and Blanche collects for Theresa, and Miss Baker and Georgie divide theirs between the two.[22]

In addition to teaching them about natural history, Spencer initiated the girls into some of the tenets of his extreme individualism, criticizing the abilities and methods of their governesses, and inveighing against the rules and regulations of the school room. 'Submission not desirable' was one of the slogans he constantly repeated. With the enthusiastic acquiescence of their governess, the Potters sometimes put Spencer's ideas into practice while they were on walks with him. Not only did they refuse to submit to his authority, but they even attacked him, pinning him to the ground and pelting him with decaying leaves. Their refusal to submit to his wishes was not appreciated, and several of them recalled the way in which he stalked into Lawrencina's boudoir on their return, expostulating on the rudeness and bad manners of her children.[23]

The great enjoyment which Standish afforded the girls became a source of grief when they were forced to go away from it for lengthy periods of time. The family was frequently on the move, going to London for the Parliamentary Session and the social Season, spending the summer months at holiday resorts, and visiting relatives in Liverpool and elsewhere. In their early years, both Beatrice and Rosie hated to be away from Standish. London was for them a place of limited interest and restricted activity, as they were merely observers of their sisters' social life while being kept away from the world they loved. Lawrencina's devotion to her father and brothers meant that she was often away from Standish, visiting them in Liverpool. But she also sent the girls there for quite extended periods. For some, especially Lallie who was immensely fond of her grandfather, this was a great treat. But for others it was real hardship as they found little that was congenial in Liverpool. One little letter written by Beatrice, aged about 7, from her grandfather's home, is quite pathetic in its tone of supplication: 'Dear Mama, I hope you will grant our wish. We have not seen Standish for seven months and are dying to be there and I think it will be convenient to you, but I do not know how the trains go, but Georgie will tell you that.'[24]

Although some of the family's travelling was determined by the illnesses or weaknesses of particular daughters, who were considered to need a change, or a spell of sea air, in general their wishes were no more consulted on this issue than they were on matters of education. Prevailing notions of parental authority meant that Richard and Lawrencina decided what would happen and the girls simply went away or stayed at home as they were directed. Decisions could be extremely arbitrary and very sudden. Beatrice in particular was often left in a state of complete ignorance as to whether she would join the family in London, or at a holiday resort, or not. Whether or not she did so was always the result of other people's convenience and never of her own. On one occasion, when Beatrice was 12, and had thought she was going to join her parents and two sisters in the north of Scotland, she was suddenly whisked off to visit some family friends who wanted a companion for their own daughter. Several letters to her parents point to her lack of ease or enjoyment of this visit. One to Lawrencina, explaining that although she liked the adults and the little boys, she did not get on with the little girl for whom she had been intended, elicited this response: 'you know that Mr. and Mrs. Menzies are anxious that Rosalie should have a companion, that they will be disappointed if you neglect her for the boys, and it will be very selfish to do so.'[25] In due course Beatrice came home—but only when it suited Richard Potter to come and fetch her.

II

There is very little information available about the transition of the Potter girls from childhood to adolescence or about the age at which they reached puberty. Puberty itself was not referred to in correspondence, nor is there any discussion of other physical or psychological developments. Beatrice and Rosie are the only two sisters who seem to have written about their adolescence at all, and in both cases it was a difficult stage of life, beset with emotional and physical problems. Rosie, whose autobiographical writings are strongly confessional, was very much more frank than Beatrice, even in her private Diary. Both of these sources make it very clear that the experiences of the younger sisters were heavily dominated by the fact of reaching puberty at the very time that several older sisters were 'out' and actively seeking or being sought by marriage partners. Hence the world in which they lived was one dominated by sexuality, romance, and marriage. Rosie was apparently quite open and at ease about this. 'Puberty came upon me early at about thirteen, and from that time on my thoughts were largely occupied with the other sex. I was secretly violently in love with all my sisters' admirers, and also with the heroes of the novels I read. A strange glamour seemed to surround nearly all the young men I knew. But all who came to the house looked upon me as still a child.'[26]

This easy acceptance of her own developing sexuality, at least from the vantage-point of middle age, is very different from Beatrice's agonized diary entries dealing with exactly the same preoccupation. Beatrice's diary from her adolescence is constantly filled with self-criticism, especially of her vanity and of her tendency to dishonesty. Like Rosie, she was constantly 'making up love scenes or building castles in the air'. But unlike Rosie, she took herself severely to task for doing so. At the age of 15, she felt it necessary to give herself a stern warning. 'You are really getting into a nasty, and what I should call an indecent, way of thinking of men, and love, and unless you take care you will lose all purity of thought, and become a silly vain self-conscious little goose. Do try and build no more castles in the air: do try to think purely and seriously about love.'[27]

For Beatrice, personal fulfilment and self-indulgence were always weaknesses to be fought against. One can almost see the subsequent battle, fought entirely within herself, over her intense sexual attraction towards Joseph Chamberlain, as a particular instance of a long established war against desire and self-gratification, in the interests of a higher moral purity made up of renunciation and asceticism. Beatrice, on more than one occasion, likened herself to Rosamond Vincy in *Middlemarch*, with her obsessive vanity and self absorption. But one could, with equal justice, argue that she exhibited something of Dorothea's enjoyment in 'giving things up'.

The difference in attitude between Beatrice and Rosie when confronting their own adolescent sexuality is interestingly paralleled by the later statements made by both of them concerning their state of knowledge in regard to sexual questions. Beatrice maintained that the extensive library at Standish, combined with her father's belief that 'a nice-minded girl can read anything, and the more she knows about human nature the better for her and for all the men connected with her', meant that she had no real curiosity about sex, 'my knowledge of the facts always outrunning my interest in the subject'.[28] Rosie, while acknowledging this 'open door' policy as regards the library was less inclined to avail herself of its benefits, and consequently did not feel at all well informed on the subject. Her immense curiosity clearly outstripped her very rudimentary knowledge.

In those days most girls were brought up in almost complete ignorance of the facts of life, and the function of sex, and although I was allowed to read books which would have been forbidden to the majority of my companions, yet I was more or less innocent as to nature's methods for the reproduction of the race ... That is not to say that I was not curious on the subject; rather the reverse; and my imagination wove strange fantasies as to how babies originated. I had too many small nephews and nieces not to know the main facts of the actual birth of babies, but of what happened beforehand to start life in the mother I had the most elementary ideas.[29]

In the Potter family, as in most other Victorian families, the experience of sex, pregnancy, and childbirth was available to women only once they were themselves married. Rosie was enlightened, with brutal frankness, by her sister Maggie on the eve of her first marriage, but the accumulated knowledge of her sisters was not made available to her prior to that.[30]

While Beatrice suffered more acutely than Rosie from the sexual preoccupations of adolescence, she did not undergo the same difficult physical developments. Rosie, like her older sister Theresa, 'became, shortly after puberty, extremely thin and emaciated, grew hysterical and refused to eat'. Both remained very delicate throughout their adolescence and were a constant source of concern to the family. It is curious that it was perhaps the two most highly favoured of the daughters who should have developed these symptoms. It certainly resulted in their getting even more attention as doctors were constantly consulted, and the family's movement and holiday plans were centred around their need for alternating mountain and sea air. Theresa had never been strong, but in Rosie there seems to have been a very marked contrast between an active, healthy, and adventurous girlhood and an ailing and problem-ridden adolescence. She connected her collapse with the period of concentrated study which she had begun, at the age of 12, in order to prepare for the Oxford Junior Locals. In order to prepare for this examination, Rosie was tutored in English, mathematics, Latin, French, and divinity. Her lessons occupied six hours each day and involved her in an unusual amount of work—to say nothing of curtailing her freedom to roam around the garden. 'Shortly after this period of somewhat concentrated study (whether caused by it or not it is difficult to say) my constitution seemed to undergo a change: my monthly periods became irregular and finally stopped. I became highly neurotic, and was attacked by the first of these curious manias which have haunted me from time to time throughout my life.'[31] Rosie evinced no interest in scholarship and all her sisters were agreed in their criticism of Lawrencina for forcing this course upon her.

Rosie continued to suffer from amenorrhoea until she became involved in a regular sexual relationship. Subsequently she developed other symptoms, particularly sore and cracked lips, which also left her as soon as she began engaging in sexual activity. The desire to get rid of these symptoms, without having to cope with the strains of marriage, later became one of the reasons why she embarked on a series of sexual liaisons.

Life did not really change much for the Potter sisters with the onset of adolescence. It was only in the last couple of decades of the nineteenth century that adolescence as a separate distinct stage in life became a subject of interest in educational and medical literature—and even then it was in relation to boys rather than to girls that the matter was discussed. Adolescence was increasingly coming to be seen as the transitional stage for boys between childhood and adulthood, during which a sense of independence and of responsibility needed to develop. For girls, whose future was seen as involving only the shift from dependence on fathers to dependence on husbands, such a stage was unnecessary and problematic.[32] This was particularly so in the case of middle-class girls. Their working-class counterparts had often had to leave home and become financially independent even before they entered into their teens. But for middle- and upper-middle-class girls, childhood lasted well on into adolescence; indeed, it was ended only when a girl 'came out' into Society and was thus seen as ready to embark on a courtship and marriage. Prior to this, the protected life of the schoolroom under the supervision of a governess served to minimize the sexual and emotional changes now associated with adolescence. There were some small changes in the routine and in the activities of the Potters as they neared the end of their childhood: it was at this time that they had their brief period of schooling and hence their first lengthy separation from family. In these years the girls also came to participate more and more in the social activities of the family, especially in London where even those who were not yet 'out' became involved in family theatricals and in small dances and dinner parties. This all provided a small preparation for the years in Society which served as the transition period between childhood and adult life.

It was during their adolescence that the Potters seem to have become particularly close companions of their father. The occasional childhood games and stories which stood out in their memories gave way to regular companionship as they began to take an interest in his business activity and to share his literary tastes. Visits to London added an additional focus. Like many provincial families with some religious interests, the Potters took advantage of their visits to the capital to sample all the various different churches and religious services. Richard Potter and his daughters attended sermons at a range of churches extending from Westminster Abbey to Frederic Harrison's Positivist Sermons at Newton Hall. All these services were discussed at length and formed a strong bond between father and daughters. This closeness was cemented for some when they accompanied him on his business trips abroad, thus becoming closely immersed in all the details of his daily life.

III

There are few more telling indications of the difference between the way boys and girls were brought up in Victorian England than the place of schooling in their lives. For the Potter sisters, when they married and had children, establishing their sons in major public schools was an essential part of their parental duty and the schools in turn formed an important core of their son's experiences. For their daughters, as for themselves, schooling was a very minor and peripheral part of both their childhood and their education.

The range of schools available for girls was still very limited during the 1860s and 1870s. The reform of secondary schools for girls and the admission of women to colleges and to universities did not take place until several of the Potter girls had finished their education.[33] The Schools Inquiry Commission which was set up to investigate the provision of education for the middle class only began in 1865, by which time Lallie was already 20 and Kate, Mary, and Georgie all over 15. The reform of girls' schools, and the establishment of schools with a high academic standard like the Cheltenham Ladies' College, were only in their initial stages during this decade. The opening of the Oxford Junior Locals and of the Cambridge Higher Local Examinations were also developments of the mid to late 1860s and hence, although they could have been made available to Beatrice, as they were intended to be to Rosie, they were of much less use to several of her older sisters.

The schools which were available, then, were the small, select, and fashionable establishments in London, Brighton, and Eastbourne which were patronized by Society. That none of these was ever quite satisfactory seems to be clear from the number of different ones that were tried. Lallie went to two schools, one in Brighton and one in London. Theresa, Georgie, and Blanche went together to another, Beatrice to yet another, and finally Rosie was sent to school in France.

Exactly what the Potters sought in the schools to which they sent their daughters is hard to ascertain. It is made even more difficult by the different reasons for which the daughters were sent to school. Lallie and Kate, and later Georgie, Theresa, and Blanche, were all sent as part of their total education and, particularly in Lallie's case, in order to acquire the 'finish' which would come from regular music and dancing lessons. Beatrice, by contrast, was sent to Bournemouth in the hope that a few months governed by the regularity of school life would 'prove favourable to your complete restoration to strength and health'. In her case, intellectual provision was apparently not considered. Richard Potter commended her chosen schoolmistress, Miss Tapp, as 'a very kind and sensible woman' who 'seems to give you every consideration and a considerable amount of affection. I do not believe I ever heard of a school life more free from petty constraints and more full of healthy and judicious kindness.'[34] The very marginal role of school in the education of the girls is perhaps made most clear in the case of Rosie. For her youngest daughter, the one over whose education she took most pains, Lawrencina seems not to have planned any schooling. Rather she chose specially qualified governesses to teach her at home. Rosie did go to school for a few months, but only after Lawrencina's death—and as a means of separating her from her father. After Lawrencina's death, the close affection between Rosie and Richard Potter developed in ways which the other sisters saw as dangerous and disturbing. In order to deal with this, they decided to send Rosie away to school in France, choosing Fontainebleau as much because of its distance as for its reputation as a sound and humane establishment.

The records of the experiences of the Potters at school reflect as much the personality differences between the sisters as they do the different kinds of schools to which they went. This is particularly noticeable because the most detailed records of school life were left by Lallie, Beatrice, and Rosie whose positions in the family and whose different personalities and interests present extreme contrasts. Lallie, as the eldest sister, and one who assumed considerable pre-eminence as a result of this, showed already in her school letters the assurance and the 'managing disposition' which were so much a part of her adult personality. Beatrice, by contrast, confided her extreme diffidence and personal unease to her diary. Her thoughts were occupied alternately by religious conflict, and by the uncomfortable sense of intellectual pre-eminence and moral and social inadequacy which made her social contacts always something of a trial. Rosie in turn presents an interesting picture in her own school letters of a somewhat docile individual, modelling her opinions on family views, while at the same time doing her best to fit into the school and its social framework. The differences evident in these records are emphasized further by the form of the records themselves. Lallie's school experiences are recorded in letters to her mother which are intended to provide precise information about her tuition and social life at school. This was the more necessary as Lallie herself had to do much of the negotiating about particular lessons and teachers and needed both to establish her mother's view and to explain what she had decided. Rosie's schooling took place after her mother's death and her letters were addressed entirely to her father. It is clear from their surviving correspondence that banishing her to school in France did nothing to break the close tie between them. Richard Potter wrote to her every day while she was at school and his letters overflow with warmth and intimacy. She replied three times a week—making up for the relative infrequency of her letters by their much greater length. She commented occasionally on her lessons, although she was not impressed by the standard of the school and seems not to have addressed herself to lessons with any zeal. Instead she wrote at length about the activities of the school: their quiet routine and occasional social evenings, their walks, picnics, church attendance, and visits to the opera. She told him about all the other girls and about all her conversations and friendships, working quite hard at making each letter both affectionate and amusing and using them to integrate her father as fully as possible into her school life.[35] In contrast to the other two, Beatrice recorded her school life in her diary, as always confiding her loneliness and private anguish to the 'other self', the only recipient available in her solitary world.

Lallie's letters to her mother provide an interesting picture of the organization and tuition of an English girls' school in the 1860s, and one which questions some received notions on this subject. She attended a school run by Miss Leatherdale at 78 Hamilton Terrace, Regent's Park, for two years. Initially she disliked the school very much indeed, complaining on her arrival that 'Mr. Smith told Papa that there were very few rules but it seems to me that the rules are numberless'. She was particularly incensed at the prohibition of letter-writing on a Saturday afternoon, one of the few times in her busy schedule for this activity. She also disliked Miss Leatherdale herself, regarding her as 'very good and pious but most horribly full of fads'.[36] Miss Leatherdale in turn took against this most outspoken of the Potter sisters, writing to her parents to complain of her ill manners and general want of conduct. Lallie accepted the need to humour this rather difficult woman and wrote to say that both she and Kate, who had accompanied her to the school, were doing everything they could to please Miss Leatherdale, 'even to paying attention to her Bible classes and learning hymns most industriously all Sunday'.[37] The intense emotional bonds which apparently existed in some Victorian girls' schools in which 'ties of affection, dependence and close personal obligations might be relied upon to secure discipline' were not evident in this establishment.[38] In Miss Leatherdale's school rules were clearly articulated and enforced. Far from even trying to manage the girls merely by indicating that certain behaviour would make her cease to love them, Miss Leatherdale attempted to marshal parental disapproval as a disciplinary weapon. Lallie was much too strong and self-confident to be cowed by affection given or withdrawn, or by parental disapproval. She made her own dislike of Miss Leatherdale's approach quite plain. 'I do wish Miss Leatherdale would be a little more frank with us. She gives us no chance of defending ourselves or of changing anything in our conduct of which she disapproves. We have been careful not to make offensive remarks and will be still more so now.'[39]

It was perhaps the ease and self-assurance which had always enabled Lallie to cope with her mother which finally won her campaign to tame Miss Leatherdale. By her second year at the school, Lallie's relations with the mistress were very good, and she was managing to combine her school life with an active and varied social life composed of dinners out, visits to friends and relations, and expeditions to art galleries and to the theatre. The school itself, in comparison with many other girls' schools, offered a fairly broad-ranging education. Latin, to Lallie's surprise, was not taught there, but English composition and history were, as well as French, German, and Italian. The school had a resident staff of governesses who gave some of the lessons, supervised homework, and read with the girls. In addition a number of 'masters' were employed for special subjects. Thus Lallie learnt algebra with a Mr Reiner, history and composition from Mr Graham, and singing from Signor Perugino. The choice of subjects and sometimes also of teachers was left to the girls and their parents. Lallie and Kate, who accompanied her to this school, were part of a very small algebra class; the music master, on the other hand, was in such demand that he had to have a deputy. Some lessons were taken outside the school: dancing, for example, was practised at Madam Michaud's academy, which the girls attended once a week.[40]

Within this general framework, the quality of the tuition and the learning experience varied. History occupied one hour per week, during which Mr Graham dictated the notes from which the girls learnt. Lallie rather enjoyed history lessons, although one senses that they were composed of lists of discrete facts and events which had simply to be remembered. This is certainly the impression given by her description of the examination. 'We had 70 questions on French history during the 17th and 18th centuries, and English history during the 18th. Kate and I came off without any faults and I hope we do the same next Saturday when our examination will be on German, Spanish, Dutch and Portuguese history.'[41] But at the same time, she read right through Macaulay's *History* with one of the governesses, and liked it 'better than reading detached pieces from various books'. She also commended Mr Reiner as a maths teacher because he was nice to his students and 'explains the reasons of everything he shows them'. Lallie found some of the masters stimulating in their approach. Mr Masters, one of her music teachers, had 'a very dry, sarcastic manner of notifying you of your mistakes which, although disagreeable at the time, impresses them upon your mind very effectually'. Mr Graham was 'rather amusing in his criticisms but not very severe'.[42]

Lallie's easy conquest of school life was matched by the ease and success with which she dealt with her family. Her letters to Lawrencina Potter are not only very assured in tone, but also contain information about the family home (for example where the keys to the hall closet were located) which indicate that she was already taking a major role in running it. She used her time in London to refurbish her wardrobe, arranging for either schoolmistresses or her parents to be available when she wished to be taken to purchase gloves or underclothes or to try on new riding habits and formal dresses. In a similar way, it is clear that she was already a valued part of the extended family

circle, spending a lot of time with her mother's family, and frequently
having to decide whether to spend her weekends with members of the
family or with friends. Lallie had a pronounced stammer at this time,
as indeed she did in moments of tension or excitement throughout her
adult life.[43] But it does not seem to have made her in any way self-
conscious or socially awkward, nor did it impede the way in which she
established herself in Liverpool society shortly after leaving school.

None of the other Potters dealt quite so easily with the family or
with their school life as did Lallie. Georgie and Maggie managed fairly
well, but both family and school life seem to have been more difficult
for Kate, Mary, Theresa, and Beatrice. Theresa, for example,
managed only one term at school before collapsing with an unknown
and debilitating ailment which made the family fear for her life and
caused her instant withdrawal from the school.

Although Beatrice was never able to develop quite so interesting an
illness as Theresa, her entire early life was marked by ill health and
unhappiness. In her case schooling was looked to as a possible remedy
for this. But her school-days were no happier for Beatrice than were
her earlier experiences at home. Whereas Lallie arrived at her school
with a strong sense of her own abilities and a sense of surprise, even
shock, at the intellectual deficiencies of the other girls, Beatrice went
to school after only the most rudimentary of home-based educations.
Her mother had a very low opinion of her intellectual abilities, and her
ill health combined with this not only to mar her childhood, but to
make it barren as regards any extended education. Her life at Stirling
House followed the same pattern of isolation as she had known at
home, with an intensity of misery added to this by the fact that it coincided with her first major period of religious doubt. Beatrice spent her
days there in lonely contemplation of the religious questions that had
come to dominate her adolescence. She sought a secure foundation for
her personal conduct in religion, only to find herself quite unable to
accept certain fundamental tenets of Christianity. Like George Eliot
and T. H. Huxley, two of the Victorian intellectuals in whom Beatrice
took a particularly close interest, she had ethical objections to certain
aspects of Christianity. Like them, she objected most strongly to the
doctrine of Atonement. 'The idea that God demanded that some
innocent person should die for the sins of men, and that, by the
voluntary death of that just man, wicked and damned men, who would
not otherwise have been saved, are saved, is repugnant to me.'[44]

In her quandary, Beatrice wrote several letters to Theresa, the only one of her sisters for whom religious and spiritual questions were a constant preoccupation. But Theresa, although sharing some of Beatrice's disquiet about this doctrine, was prepared to believe that it was an issue of historical rather than essential importance and had been incorporated into Christianity because of the practice of sacrifice among the ancient Egyptians and Israelites. These peoples would not have accepted the new religion unless it incorporated practices and symbols with which they were already familiar.[45] Beatrice could not accept this, and it served, alongside her general scepticism and her interest in Spencerian and other materialist theories, to undermine entirely her religious beliefs.

Beatrice's anguish over religious questions was exacerbated by her sense of inadequacy and of sin. The incisive and detached critical spirit which makes her diaries such a pleasure to read was already in the process of formation. But Beatrice had not yet come to enjoy it and constantly berated herself for her critical views and for her lack of sympathy and compassion. 'Oh that I had more charity, true charity, so that I might see and reverence and not sneer at and despise what I do not understand. God only give me help. I am so weak, so vain, so liable to fall into self-confidence.' Whereas Lallie was openly critical of the other girls she met at school, Beatrice became ensnared by her own transparently false attempts at humility.

I must also above everything endeavour not to think myself superior to the other inmates of Stirling House, because I have been brought out more by circumstances and encouraged to reason on subjects which other girls have mostly been told to take on faith. Both systems have their advantages and disadvantages. But perhaps the mistake I felt most was joining gossiping conversations. And this is certainly most difficult, because it in a great way necessitates keeping aloof from the girls.[46]

Social life and contacts never became easy for Beatrice. Even in the years when she and Sidney were people of note, entertaining and being entertained by vast numbers of more or less prominent people, her lack of really intimate friends and the state of her relationships with those few to whom she was in any way close remained a preoccupation in her diary. Indeed, it is to a great extent the habit of isolation to which she was forced to become accustomed as a child which made her seek her closest companionship in the diary.

School life, then, although it apparently brought about the desired improvement in her health, did not produce any other changes for

Beatrice. It did not increase her ease or self-assurance, nor did it provide her with much intellectual assistance. She was a 'parlour boarder' at school for only a few months and hence did not undertake any formal curriculum. Indeed, it is hard to regard this brief period as really involving serious schooling, and certainly it does not rate a mention in Beatrice's actual education. For her, as for her other sisters, it is important to see the continuity between their home life and their school. For girls, unlike boys, school did not provide a world of its own with its own rituals, hierarchy, power structures, and so on. School was permeated constantly by family life and demands and was merely a very temporary break from them.

IV

Coming Out and the Social Season

I

THEIR brief period at school marked the end of childhood for the Potter sisters. It was followed almost immediately by the 'coming out' into Society which formed the transition between childhood and adult life. This social début was both carefully planned and expensive. It was, as Beatrice Webb pointed out, 'regarded by wealthy parents as the equivalent for their daughters, of the university and professional training afforded to their sons'. Society life would subsequently become the main focus of the activity of the Potter girls as for other girls of their class. In this early stage it provided a training in the requirements of that life while offering the opportunity to make 'that marriage to a man of their own or a higher social grade [which] was the only recognized vocation for women not compelled to earn their own livelihood' in Victorian England.[1]

While Beatrice stressed constantly the importance of the business of marriage as the focus of the London Season, she was well aware of the complex interweaving of business, political, and financial interests which formed the basis of Society. The many dinner parties, dances, and evening and afternoon assemblies of the Season were not only the means whereby one's daughters could be introduced to eligible young men, but also provided ways in which business and political ties could be strengthened through hospitality and shared social activities.[2] The Season, which lasted from April to July, coincided with the Parliamentary Session, which points very clearly to the complex interactions between political and social life for the English upper- and upper-middle classes. This conjunction of political, business, and social interests is nicely illustrated through the Potters. 1864 was the first year in which they took a London house for the Season. This was the year in which Lallie made her début. It was also the year that Richard Potter became the chairman of the Grand Trunk Railway. In this capacity, he needed constant access to Parliament in order to lobby for the legislation on which his plans for railway expansion depended. Lawrencina noted in her journal that the family had gone to London 'in order that my dear husband might not be left alone all through the parliamentary session'.[3] The family thus 'entered modestly into society with Lallie acting as housekeeper'. Almost as an afterthought, she noted that Lallie 'also took lessons in English, drawing, dancing and music. And she was presented at Court.'

It was the presentation at Court that formalized the entry of a girl into Society. This took place at one of the four Drawing Rooms held by the Queen expressly for the purpose of receiving débutantes. Admission to the royal presence was accorded by the Lord Chamberlain to those with the necessary credentials and social contacts. It illustrated very clearly the role of the Court both as head of Society and as the arbiter of who should be admitted to it. Preparation for this presentation bore a striking resemblance to preparation for marriage—for which in a sense it was the first step. The clothes and accessories which were needed were not just bought, but rather were presented as a 'coming out' trousseau. For the Court appearance, despite the fact that it took place in the afternoon, a white ball gown was mandatory, finished off with a head-dress consisting of three plumes and a veil. Lessons in how to approach the Queen, how to curtsey, and how to walk backwards were a necessary preliminary, as each girl had to be able to retire gracefully from the royal presence without either turning her back on the Queen or tripping on her long train. The brief moment of presentation was thus the climax of much lengthy preparation.[4] It was either preceded or followed by a large celebratory ball given by the girl's parents.

'Coming out', although it was in a sense a recognition of sexual maturity, occurred some years after puberty and during the later part of adolescence. It was made immediately visible to all onlookers by the fact that when a girl came out, she ceased wearing her hair loose and began to 'put it up'. A sophisticated coiffure thus became the sign of a girl who might be invited to dance. In some situations this change of coiffure slightly predated the presentation at Court. Just before Beatrice went to Stirling House in 1874, the family had a large dance and she was allowed to put her hair up for it. She waxed lyrical over the whole event. 'The dance; oh! how I did enjoy that. It was the first dance I had ever been at as a grown-up young lady, and I felt considerably satisfied with myself, as I had two or three partners for each dance.' It would not have been Beatrice had she not followed this ecstatic outpouring with self-recrimination: 'Ah vanity! vanity! Unfortunately for me my ruling passion.'[5]

There is no information available about the presentations of the

Potters, or about who it was who introduced them at Court. It is clear that following on from Lallie, each of the other girls was presented at the age of either 17 or 18 and that they then took their place in Society. Beatrice was the only one who even thought of refusing to do this. During her intense period of religious doubt and study at school, she planned to eschew society, at least for a time.

I hope when I return home I shall not lose the little earnestness I have gained; that I shall be diligent in the study of religion. I do not want to 'come out', and I hope I shall have enough determination and firmness to carry my point. The family does not want another come out member; there are almost too many as it is. I wish my aim in life to be the understanding and acting up to religion. Before I can enter society with advantage I must conquer two great faults, love of admiration and untruth, and I must become a little more settled in my religious belief.[6]

She did not have the firmness to carry this point, however, and subsequently noted that 'at the conventional age of eighteen I joined my sisters in the customary pursuits of girls of our class, riding, dancing, flirting and dressing-up'.[7]

The lives of the Potter sisters were not entirely given up to pleasure during the Season. 'Coming out' had a particular significance for them as it formed the prelude to their taking a turn at housekeeping. Lallie began this in 1864 and subsequently each of the other sisters, except Blanche and Rosie, had to take their turn. A 'turn' was of a variable length of time, depending on the availability of a younger sister to take over. Kate, Theresa, Maggie, and Beatrice, all had two or more years of the somewhat onerous task of running a home which was not their own, and which had to be organized in accordance with the ideas of their mother. In addition some of the girls had lessons during the Season. Serious academic subjects were given up but music, drawing, dancing, and deportment continued. These lessons, like regular attendance at art exhibitions, were all designed to give the girls added polish.

As Beatrice's comment suggests, the life of the Potters during the Season conformed to that of most other families engaged in the same pursuit of pleasure and social recognition. Balls, dinners, concerts, and amateur theatricals made up the evening entertainment, while the days were spent in paying calls, shopping, riding in the Row, picnics, and excursions. Occasionally there was a day of rest to prepare for another round of activity. The Potters attended the whole array of private, semi-private, and charity balls. Theresa found the number somewhat excessive and commented on the time it took her to recover from

Three balls in a week particularly [for] one so little accustomed to dancing as I am. I did not enjoy the two last the 'Self Help' and the Hospital Ball, the air was so horrible and the dancing so crowded but the Somersetshire ball was a very good one. We went with some cousins of the Tinlings, Mr. and Mrs Elton, Somersetshire people & met Cap'ts Gulton, Beading, Mr. Leigh Smith and Mr. Broadmead & were introduced to some rather ordinary new partners. Mr. Broadmead is a friend of the Tinlings and is going to call on us: he is very attentive to Maggie, but I'm afraid she does not return the attentions.[8]

For the most part the girls preferred private dances and balls given in people's homes to public ones. The Potters were always very conscious of their exact social standing. Theresa in particular felt most at ease with others of similar status. 'Maggie and I were at a large ball the other night at the Dobrees (a new acquaintance): they are immensely wealthy & seem to have a very nice position, not among swells but in our own class, substantial but not fashionable.'[9]

The Potters were not among the first rank of fashionable people, but they certainly paid attention to all the formality and the ceremony which fashion required. Every Season began with the ritual of calling on friends and acquaintances and leaving cards. They had a regular 'reception day' each week, to which friends and acquaintances could come for a short visit which was less formal than a dinner or a dance. The large reception provided the means whereby new acquaintances could become better known, or by which those with whom acquaintance was desired could be brought into the family home. The importance of the Season as a means of extending the family's range of acquaintance is constantly spelled out in letters to those absent from the festivities. Often the names of new people or of new dance partners are listed and information provided about anyone of particular interest. As time went on and some of the sisters settled or set up house for themselves in London, the Season provided the occasion for introducing their friends to the rest of the family. In 1883, the first year that Beatrice played hostess to her father in London, she took over the role of paying ceremonial visits. Richard Potter explained the process to Rosie: 'tomorrow Beatrice begins calling on our acquaintances simply leaving cards, and Kate accompanies her, so that some of Kate's particular friends shall be placed on the list of our acquaintances'.[10]

Although the Potters sometimes found balls exhausting, there were other popular pastimes which they relished. Riding in Hyde Park and organizing amateur theatricals were pre-eminent amongst these. Amateur theatricals had long been an activity in which the family took a keen interest. During their early adolescence these had been staged just for the family at Standish. Now they became much more lavish undertakings in which friends were involved as actors and to which quite a large audience was invited.

In their productions, the Potters of course supplied all the female roles, with Theresa, Georgie, and Maggie being the most enthusiastic actresses. Friends had to be inveigled—or dragooned—into taking the male roles. The whole undertaking was both time-consuming and expensive. There were days of rehearsals often supervised by Mrs Stirling, a friend of the family with theatrical connections. Rehearsals took place both during the day and in the evenings, in which case the cast was given dinner. Finally, for the performances, cards and invitations were sent to large numbers of friends and acquaintances and seating and supper had to be provided for between 60 and 100 people. Throughout all of this activity, family letters indicate the continuing preoccupation with the ways in which the theatricals extend the family's range of acquaintances. Writing to Beatrice about the forthcoming production for 1873, Theresa indicated that Mrs Tom Hughes, 'wife to the man who wrote *Tom Brown's Schooldays*', would be there.

Altogether we shall have several new people as the actors have been allowed each to ask a few friends; Mrs. Charles Dickens the novelist's wife will be there & one of her daughters. Last night we had such a noisy party even poor little Trish Dickens became demoralised; lost command over his company & himself, & ended by joining in a general disputaton & skirmish among actors and actresses; at last I had to threaten to distribute a cup of hot tea over them if they were so giddy.[11]

A few days later, she reported that

the invitations to the theatricals are going on famously. About 80 people have accepted for the first day . . . & 70 for the second day . . . Charles Macaulay knows Mr. Tom Taylor, the author of 'Helping Hands,' & we shall persuade him to send him an invitation. Then Mrs. Stirling will be present at one representation & the great actress that was, Mrs. Theodore Martin is very likely coming too. So we are in for some very decided critics among our audience & I do hope they will have nothing to do but applaud.[12]

Looking back on this social life many years later, Beatrice insisted that it was 'an existence without settled occupation or personal responsibility, having for its end nothing more remote than elaborately expensive opportunities for getting married'.[13]

II

The London Season involved three months of hectic activity. It formed a very marked contrast for the Potters to the rest of their time, which was spent in a very quiet way at Standish or at their other houses in the country. In the 1860s there had been a great deal of family visiting and many large house-parties to engage the attention of the family during the summer, autumn, and winter months. Increasingly throughout the 1870s, however, Lawrencina withdrew from social life and devoted herself to private studies. Richard Potter was away more often during this decade than during the previous one, making the home party a smaller and a less convivial one. Several of the sisters commented on the dullness of home life and on the difficulties they experienced in having to spend long periods at Standish or Rusland Hall with their mother. 'If only one might divide one's life more evenly and, instead of the absolute stagnation of Standish and the rush of London, have an even tenor', life would, in Maggie's view, have been much more enjoyable.[14]

The long months in the country were made less pleasant than they would otherwise have been by family tensions. Lawrencina Potter bitterly resented her husband's increasing immersion in business and his ever more frequent absences from home. Her daughters were not only subjected to her depression and displeasure when they remained at home with her, but also seem to have been used rather unscrupulously by both parents to argue out the matter of their differing needs and desires. Thus when Richard Potter was in Montreal with Maggie in 1874, it was she rather than he who had to reply to Lawrencina's reproaches.

Of course we all feel how disagreeable it must be to you to be so much alone at home. Papa feels it very keenly and he would do anything to make it better, but you yourself would hardly have wished him just in the middle of the battle to give up the Grand Trunk, and perhaps to lose success, or at least to lose all credit. It is a great trial to you, and to us in a way a disadvantage to be so much without his care at home. But having once undertaken the concern with your approval, he seems almost forced to continue. And then, I think, the suddenly breaking of all intercourse with the railway life and this continent, and retiring entirely to private life with no career left, would be dangerous to his health and spirit and very unsatisfactory to you in the end. So I hope dearest mother, you won't allow yourself to be so miserable.[15]

At this particular time, Lawrencina wished to have nothing to do with Society at all, and had even to be coaxed by Lallie to persuade her to continue to take a London house in order to allow the girls to enter into the Season. Her own interests turned more and more to religion, and this in turn made her a somewhat difficult companion. After spending some months alone with her in 1878, Maggie wrote to Beatrice telling her how much she looked forward to Beatrice's return from a visit to Germany, 'for we do not see a soul; and although I am very fond of Mamma and always get on perfectly with her, yet we are hardly real companions, being stopped on so many subjects by a fundamental difference of opinion, which in Mamma is of a proselytising nature, so we must often agree to differ.'[16]

The only break from this routine was that provided by travel. Each year one or two of the sisters spent a few enjoyable months in North America with their father. Occasionally there were also trips to Europe: to Germany to study the language, or to Italy to see the Great Masters. In 1878, Kate and Maggie also had a long and rather enjoyable trip to Egypt—marred only by the very cantankerous behaviour of Herbert Spencer, who accompanied them.[17] But these visits, while enjoyable in themselves, sometimes pointed very strongly to the contrast between this active pleasure and the tedium of being at home. Just before she returned from Egypt, Maggie wrote to Beatrice telling her how much she had enjoyed the trip, but refusing to see this enjoyment as the basis for changing the normal tenor of her life. 'This life here is very delightful now, and calm but it will only be a sweet episode to which I shall always look back with pleasure. It cannot alter things at home, and the difficulties there must be overcome in time.'[18]

In addition to trips abroad, there were also a number of visits to relatives and friends in England. Lallie was settled in Liverpool after 1867 and several of the sisters visited her there. Kate in particular spent many months with her older and favourite sister. The other married sisters, Mary, Georgie, and, after 1874, Blanche, also received visits from their single sisters. In some cases these were for pleasure, but more often they were in response to the need of the married sisters. Georgie in particular was in almost constant need of the company and support of her sisters. Right from the very start, her marriage offered the unpleasant combination of no companionship and constant pregnancy.

In the years between 'coming out' and marriage, the Potter sisters lived the life so feelingly described by Florence Nightingale in 'Cassandra'.[19] They were constantly at the beck and call of others and had neither settled occupations of their own nor any recognition that they needed one. No thought was given to their personal needs, or their desires for privacy and time to pursue independent activities— and indeed they had few such activities in mind. When Beatrice was in the United States with her father, Maggie wrote despondently about the little progress she was making with her private studies, and of the problem of trying to pursue knowledge with no idea of the use to which it might be put.

I am not getting on with German as much as you may expect, somehow or other I have rather come to Faust's opinion, that mere learning is not worth much unless it has some particular aim which alas! poor women can hardly have, unless they could have some idea of their future; Blessed spinsterhood or holy matrimony are equally on the cards, including every description of states between.[20]

The only new activities which seemed to have entered the family routine during the 1870s were those which followed from Theresa's interest in spiritualism. She prevailed upon other members of the family to engage in seances with her. As well as sittings with a spiritual medium, much time was devoted to the favourite Victorian forms of tapping spiritual energy through table turning and spirit rapping. Most of the Potters were prepared to try these activities just for fun but as Beatrice wrote, 'We quite came to the conclusion that as far as our experience went Spiritualism was nothing more than a kind of semi-conscious action of the brain.' Georgie was equally sceptical. On a visit she made to Standish in 1876, she wrote to Daniel about the new enthusiasm:

Theresa has just returned from staying with Florence Jeffreys and is holding communion with the invisible world in darkened chambers all day long, and as the process seems to agree with her appetite, there can be no harm in it. She persuaded me to sit on a table for half an hour yesterday in the hope of raising or turning it, but nothing happened except our hands went to sleep and pricked with pins and needles most frightfully, which Theresa declared was the first sign of a spiritual manifestation.[21]

This unsettling and rather pointless cycle of activity was the lot of the Potter sisters for several years. Even Lallie, Mary, and Georgie, who married in their early twenties, had four or five years of it. Blanche, Theresa, and Maggie had to live through it for almost ten years until their marriages, during their late twenties, enabled them to escape. Beatrice and Kate, neither of whom married until their mid-thirties, contrived escape by other means, establishing lives which were independent of their family and of Society, and devoting themselves instead to philanthropy and social investigation.

III

Kate was unusual amongst the Potters because of her unequivocal rejection of the social life and of the general routine of the family. As the second sister, she grew up in the shade cast by Lallie's somewhat overbearing personality. At the same time, the fact that both Lallie and Mary, the third sister, married quite young gave Kate a particularly long stint as housekeeper. It was a difficult one because most of the girls were still unmarried during this time, so the family was still a very large one. Kate had a difficult time at home, being a favourite of neither parent. She hated the Season and the constant matchmaking that it involved, and finally resolved to leave it: 'After a particularly difficult year, during which many mistakes had been made, much trouble endured and some lessons learnt, I made up my mind to leave home and go to Miss Octavia Hill to be trained for her work in London. That had not been a happy year but for two things I shall never cease to be thankful: one that I did not marry either of the men who proposed to me during that troubled year and another that the pain drove me into a life of independent thought and action.'[22]

The family was not whole-hearted in its support for this endeavour. Its senior members, with Richard and Lawrencina ably seconded by Lallie, all gave vent not only to their disapproval of Kate's course of action, but also to their refusal to believe in her ability to organize and run her own life. Richard Potter, however, did not act on this disapproval and gave Kate an allowance which enabled her to take small but comfortable rooms in Great College Street, and to work in an unpaid capacity for the Charity Organisation Society.

The Charity Organisation Society had been founded in 1867 to co-ordinate charitable effort and to reform the indiscriminate alms-giving which its founders saw as the true cause of pauperism. It made extensive use of the unpaid labour of single women in its research and in its social work.[23] Kate acted as a rent collector at one of the buildings set up by the COS to provide accommodation for those poor families whom they believed amenable to help. She also ran a number of boys' clubs, giving lessons and arranging excursions for many young lads from the East End of London. Kate loved this work, enjoying the company of her fellow charity workers and, more particularly, of the poor amongst whom she worked. She arranged social gatherings for them—and the rest of the family were sometimes forced to attend one of Kate's 'poor people's parties'. They did so briefly, retiring at the earliest possible time to tea at fashionable houses close by.[24] But Kate enjoyed them far more than she did the balls and dances attended by her family. She also established her own social circle, composed largely of liberal political families and philanthropists. Beatrice had long envied Kate 'that way she has of drawing clever people out and making them talk to her as if they were talking to their equal',[25] and Kate's sociability developed in circles which were congenial to herself. Her new life made stringent demands on her time, enabling her to limit contact with her family as well as to reject their social life. She often had her sisters to stay, but she rarely allowed anyone to interfere with her routine.

Kate showed a great deal of strength of mind in leaving home and setting up her own life. She was supported by her younger sisters, particularly Theresa, but she had fundamentally to depend on her own self-assurance and determination. Lallie proved a particular obstacle as she was very outspoken in her disapproval and made no secret of her lack of faith in Kate's ability. This was made the harder to bear because she was the sister to whom Kate was closest. Kate persevered, but the opposition she met does go some way to explaining why Theresa, who shared to the full her interest in philanthropy, and also some of her dislike of Society, was unable to follow suit. Theresa spent much of her early adulthood dreaming of establishing a celibate sisterhood which would nurse the poor and engage in other charitable works. She devoted some of her time to teaching Rosie, but that left a considerable amount of both time and energy which she wished to devote to worthy causes. Several of the sisters sympathized with her. Beatrice noted in her Diary for 1874 that 'Theresa is very anxious to go and nurse at the hospital; I think she is right. If only she would have enough self-denial to take care of her health, I believe she would do much better to have settled work and a little discipline. I shall do what I can (which is very little) to persuade mother to let her go.'[26] Her pleas were unavailing and the assertiveness required was too much for Theresa. She could not follow Kate's lead, managing only a temporary stint as Kate's replacement when the latter went to Egypt in 1878.

Maggie's case is in some way more interesting than Theresa's. She had nothing of Theresa's gentleness or diffidence and indeed she was one of the most competent and forthright of the sisters. Beatrice regarded her as intellectually the most gifted. Maggie was very critical both of home life and of the lack of purposeful occupation available to herself and her sisters. But she never did anything about this. She differed from Kate and Theresa in the immense enjoyment she gained from the Season, and probably recognized that Society life was her true *métier*. At the same time, her recognition of the imperfections of her current existence was not accompanied by anything remotely resembling a feminist criticism of the situation of women. On the contrary, Maggie believed strongly that she and her sisters should become less strong-minded and more conventional in their behaviour and opinions. Finally, Maggie faced a rather more difficult problem than Kate's because there simply was not anything available which met her interests. Philanthropy was the only avenue available to women of her class. The few poorly paid occupations open to middle- and lower-middle-class women, like teaching or nursing, involved an unthinkable loss of caste. But Maggie had no interest in philanthropy whatsoever and certainly no inclination to devote her life to it; there was really nothing for her to do but stay at home and wait for the marriage which ultimately came her way.

IV

The three months spent in London each year for the Season were not always the same for the Potter sisters. For one thing the Season itself underwent some changes during the late Victorian period, becoming more and more elaborate and including an increasing range of sporting and leisure-time activities until it reached its pinnacle in the 1890s. During the course of the 1880s, for example, breakfast parties, luncheons, and visits to clubs outside London were added to the earlier list of balls and dances, afternoon receptions, and evening entertainments in theatres or private homes.[27] But the Potters experienced changes other than those which were intrinsic to the

Season as an event. Marriage, while it did not necessarily bring an end to involvement in the London Season, necessarily changed the nature and purpose of that involvement. During the late 1860s and the 1870s, four of the sisters married (first Lallie in 1867 and then Mary, Georgie, and Blanche). The early 1880s saw the marriages of Theresa, Maggie, and, after Lawrencina Potter's death in 1882, that of Kate to Leonard Courtney. Once married, Georgie, Blanche, and later Theresa, Kate, and Maggie all had London homes or came to London for most of the Season. Lallie and Mary visited occasionally. They continued, therefore, to engage in this round of social activities, which was directed now not towards gaining a husband, but rather towards pleasure, extending their social circle, and keeping up regular contacts with their family. The married sisters seem to have dined, had tea, or visited the theatre with their own family of origin at least two or three times a week throughout the Season. In 1883, the year after Lawrencina's death, it was rare for Richard Potter to dine at home without one or more of his daughters visiting.

Lawrencina's death brought the other great change in the orientation of the Potters to the London Season—as indeed it brought a change in their orientation to family life. When Lawrencina died Beatrice, as the oldest sister still living at home, took over the role of housekeeper and hostess and of companion to Richard Potter. Beatrice had run the house before, but the scale of her involvement and activities changed considerably. No longer was she there simply to supervise the servants and ensure the smooth running of things on a day-to-day basis. Rather, in the first London Season after her mother's death, she

realised that the pursuit of pleasure was . . . an elaborate and to me a tiresome undertaking, entailing extensive insignificant matters. There was the London house to be selected and occupied; there was the stable of horses and carriages to be transported; there was the elaborate stock of prescribed garments to be bought; there was all the commissariat of paraphernalia for dinners, dances, picnics and week-end parties to be provided.[28]

The ambivalence about Society which had made Beatrice determined that she should refuse to 'come out' remained throughout her life. It was powerfully present throughout the years she acted as her father's hostess. She found Society enervating and exhausting, and it led to a continuous need for new excitement and constant activity while depriving her of the capacity to undertake the disciplined reading and study which she felt to be so necessary for her to establish a career for herself. Despite this she enjoyed being fêted and courted, and found dinners and balls often both stimulating and exciting. She ran her father's large London home, York House, with efficiency and ease. Indeed she was for a time a noted London hostess, giving regular dinners and evening parties. She even extended her activities to the provision of large garden tea-parties for nephews and nieces and for the children of friends. Nor was her much vaunted carelessness of appearance in evidence. Members of her family—who showed little concern about sparing her feelings—commented frequently on how beautifully dressed she was at social gatherings. It was perhaps an example of the personal vanity which she regarded both as an 'occupational disease' of Society and as a particular constitutional weakness in her own case which made the appearance of her new riding habit (for which she had had six fittings) a major event.[29] At times Beatrice eschewed balls, and she certainly courted the intellectual members of society rather than the fashionable ones—sometimes to her father's discomfort. But there is no doubt that Society life absorbed much of her time and energy during the late 1870s and early 1880s and that she enjoyed to the full the power she exercised in it. This enjoyment was constantly counterposed to feelings of regret and remorse as she noted her diminished capacity to work, and reproached herself for the very pleasure she derived from Society.

For Beatrice this was a time of acute personal and emotional stress. She had begun to realize the extent of her ambition to make a name for herself in the wider intellectual world. At the same time she had a strong sense of familial obligation, especially to her father. In 1883 this was further complicated by her meeting with Joseph Chamberlain, then President of the Board of Trade, with whom she fell passionately in love. Her family's often expressed desire that she would make a brilliant marriage coincided with her own desire to marry Chamberlain, who was a man of considerable wealth and a rising political figure—although she realized that such a marriage would be a disastrous one for her.[30] Her emotional conflicts during these years resulted in periods of severe and prolonged depression. At the same time, her health improved—as if the need for her to exert herself in many directions enabled her to use fully the nervous energy which was such a problem to her for the rest of the time.

One of the tasks that fell to Beatrice in her new role was the supervision of her youngest sister, Rosie, as she emerged from the

schoolroom and into society. It is evident that this happened some
time during the mid 1880s, as Rosie was present at formal dinners and
dances in those years and, at one of them, met the man whom she subsequently married. There is no reference to this occurrence, however,
in any of the Potter diaries or letters. Rather the papers of the other
sisters indicate that Rosie continued to be considered a difficult child
throughout these years and that decisions about her welfare and her
whereabouts were made by the others with no reference to her.
Whereas Theresa recovered from the nervous ailment and the
inability to eat which had afflicted her as an adolescent and took her
turn at running the family, Rosie continued to be painfully thin, and,
in the view of her older sisters, to require supervision. That this supervision came mainly from Beatrice was a major tragedy for Rosie and for
Beatrice herself. Beatrice, with the acuteness of insight which makes
her diaries so compelling, acknowledged that she was 'not the best
possible person for her [Rosie]; too complicated in my thought and
feeling and too active in my life'.[31] She found the charge a difficult and
unrewarding one. But neither she nor any of the other sisters could
fully comprehend the underlying jealousy and bitterness which
poisoned Beatrice's relationship with Rosie. This jealousy, while only
too easy to understand in view of the way Lawrencina had neglected
and underrated Beatrice, while lavishing every care and attention on
Rosie, made Beatrice incapable of appreciating or caring adequately
for Rosie. Beatrice recognized her own failings to some extent. 'Poor
incapable Rosie, with her heavy face and irritating ways. I cannot be
loving with her: I can only be dutiful. My relationship to her is the blot
on my life, which in spite of personal failures—has been especially
successful in relationships.'[32] But she could do nothing about it.

Beatrice's task was made the more difficult by the fact that Richard
Potter relinquished all serious parental authority after his wife's death.
He was not able to advise his daughters and neither did he seem to
have any very clear idea himself about what his youngest daughter
needed. The other sisters sent her to school to break up the obsessive
relationship which developed between Richard and Rosie. But on her
return from school it continued and Rosie's jealousy, as she later
admitted, was such as to make it very difficult for any of the other
daughters to continue their ties with their father. Beatrice had thus to
contend with a very difficult situation which became even more complicated when Richard Potter had a stroke in 1885. Then, as after their
mother had died, the sisters agreed that the only way to deal with

Rosie was to send her away. She was banished to Sicily in the care of an old family doctor—only to return after a few months, still wretchedly thin and very unhappy.

These years were equally wretched for Beatrice and for Rosie. But while Beatrice was at least using them to wrestle with herself and to establish the directions which she wanted her life to take, Rosie was alternately banished and relegated to the status of a child. The years which, for the others, served as a period of transition from childhood to adulthood, were for her ones which saw the transference of dependence on parents to dependence on sisters and which left her quite unprepared for adult life, for marriage, or for motherhood.

V

Courtship and Marriage

I

THE Potters were unusual amongst upper-middle-class English families in size and in consisting only of daughters. They were even more unusual in that all the daughters married. In other families in the same social class it was common to have one or two daughters remain single in order to look after their parents in their declining years. Often one girl was specifically selected for this purpose by the parents or by the family as a whole.[1] None of the Potters was chosen for this fate, nor was there any desire expressed by Richard or Lawrencina that one of their children would remain with them. The fact that Beatrice assumed full domestic responsibility after her mother's death was not seen by her family as precluding the possibility of her marrying. Even when her father suffered a severe stroke in 1885 and needed constant care and supervision, marriage was not ruled out. Indeed throughout his last years and as his powers declined, he frequently told her that he wanted one last son-in-law before he died.

Amongst the Potter daughters there was considerable pride not merely in the fact that they were all married, but also in how successful they had been in attracting wealthy and distinguished husbands. Even Beatrice, who despised most of her brothers-in-law, was impressed by their positions. Members of the family still recall Kate in her last years repeating the comment 'we gels all married very well', perhaps as an admonition to nieces who seemed unlikely to continue this highly desirable family tradition.[2] Marriage certainly did raise the standing of the 'R.P. family', bringing into it barristers and Members of Parliament as well as connections with county, mercantile, and banking interests. Listing the various husbands by their professions or connections would be doing no more than the Potters did themselves: in a family of daughters connection with the professions or with parliamentary and business circles was only possible through marriage. Theresa's engagement to Alfred Cripps, a successful young barrister, was considered 'most satisfactory' by her sister Mary Playne: 'We want an Attorney General or even a Lord Chancellor in the family and Theresa won't make a bad Law Peeress.'[3] In a similar way, Kate's engagement to a distinguished Member of Parliament, Leonard Courtney, was welcomed by Blanche because 'we just wanted a political character to represent fairly all the professions in our various husbands'.[4]

Family tradition accorded Richard Potter a substantial role in the successful marrying of his daughters. Beatrice regarded his ability to ensure that 'his daughters married the sort of men he approved, notwithstanding many temptations to the contrary' as one illustration of the subtle but powerful control he exercised over their destinies.[5] The role of a father in the marriages of daughters was necessarily an extensive one in the late nineteenth century. In legal terms, marriage was very much a case of the exchange of a woman between two men. This was of course embodied in the very marriage ceremony itself, with the father actually giving his daughter to her husband. But prior to this the father was integrally involved in all arrangements. Middle- and upper-class fathers had their lawyers draw up marriage settlements through which they provided money for their daughters and ensured that some similar provision was made by the prospective husband. Richard Potter gave most of his daughters an annuity of £250 with a promise of £5,000 to be paid within six months of his death.[6] This money was provided for the daughter's own use, and hence could not be taken by her husband. It was not paid to her directly, but went instead to the trustees of the marriage settlement who paid her in small quarterly amounts.

Potter's wealth and his extensive business contacts enabled him to take a particularly important role in the forwarding of certain marriages amongst his daughters. When Georgie became engaged to Daniel Meinertzhagen in 1872, Potter was delighted. The match between his charming daughter and a talented merchant banker with whom he did business was one he had himself fostered. At the time, Daniel worked for Huth and Co., the bank in which his father had been a senior partner, but where he was still a junior employee. Richard Potter took it upon himself to interview the Huth partners, asking them to admit Daniel to a full partnership. They refused on financial grounds. Exercising some of that diplomacy which was almost his stock-in-trade, Potter went straight to another bank with which he had extensive dealings and asked them to take Daniel as a partner. Hearing this, Huth found the means to offer Daniel a partnership, thus enabling him to set up a comfortable home for a young wife.[7]

Even in cases where he was not especially enthusiastic about his prospective son-in-law, Potter was prepared to provide assistance. In 1882 Kate announced to her family that she and Leonard Courtney had entered into a 'special friendship' which was not quite an engagement. Leonard felt unable to undertake so formal a commitment in view of the uncertainty of his parliamentary pay and his lack of a personal fortune. He proposed that they wait until he had saved a sufficient sum to ensure Kate's future before they even begin to think about marriage. Richard Potter did not much relish the thought of his daughter marrying a man of 50 whom he regarded as somewhat rough and unrefined. Rosie added that he disliked the thought of having a son-in-law so close to his own age—and one who was more distinguished than he. At that time, however, Kate herself was 35 and thus unlikely to make a more desirable match. She had moreover given ample evidence already of her strength of purpose and was unlikely to be dissuaded from following her inclinations. Richard gave in gracefully, and showed both wisdom and generosity in providing the money which would enable the couple to marry without a long and uncertain engagement. He arranged to settle £10,000 on Kate immediately, thus reassuring Leonard about their financial security.[8] But for all this, Richard Potter did not have complete success in determining the kinds of men his daughters married. Blanche married a man whom he disliked and distrusted and, after his death, Beatrice married a man who epitomized all that he would have rejected. Indeed what is particularly interesting about the Potters is the substantial role which the girls themselves took in forwarding their own or, in one or two cases, their sisters' marriages. Lallie, as one might have expected, orchestrated the way in which her family dealt with the Holts and engineered the visits to Standish which she believed necessary in order for her and Robert Holt to sort out their religious differences. Kate went considerably further than this, eliciting a proposal from Leonard Courtney by inviting him to her lodgings and there confessing the intensity of her devotion to him. Beatrice too, in her long, distressing, and unsuccessful relationship with Joseph Chamberlain, arranged for some of their meetings and certainly established the emotional tone of the whole affair.

In a rather different vein, it is interesting to see how important the independent activities of the Potter sisters were in providing husbands. Kate and Beatrice both met the men they married in the course of their work. Kate also introduced Henry Hobhouse, whom she knew through various charitable committees, to her sister Maggie—and as Kate's diary notes, there was a 'sudden fancy and after a week or two they are engaged'.[9]

II

The whole of the Potter family tended to become involved in the process of courting and particularly in the engagements and marriages of each of the sisters. The girls were for the most part living with their family throughout these years and confided much in letters to their parents or to each other if they were away. In some cases, those of Lallie and Georgie, for example, the sisters worked together with parents to make marriages. In others, like those of Theresa and Rosie, although the family was not directly involved in each stage of the rela-tionship, they were fully informed as soon as it became serious and their views were necessarily taken into account. Beatrice and Kate were the only two who negotiated relationships without any familial involvement, although in Kate's case family pressure—and family assistance—turned a 'special friendship' into a formal engagement. Beatrice's life also shows two very different approaches to the family. In her first serious relationship, that with Joseph Chamberlain, the family was closely involved. Her sisters offered advice and support, arranged meetings between her and Chamberlain, and came to stay at Standish with Richard Potter in order to allow her to concentrate on her own affairs. In the later relationship with Sidney Webb, however, they knew nothing until formally notified of her engagement.

Lallie's easy relationship with her parents is as evident in the years of her courtship by Robert Holt as it was in her school-days. Here too she not only kept them informed, but offered advice as to how she thought they should behave. Lallie met Robert Holt in 1865 when she was staying with her grandfather in Liverpool. The Holts were one of Liverpool's wealthiest and most respectable mercantile families, with extensive interests in shipping and cotton. They were also well known as one of the Unitarian families whose philanthropic contributions made Liverpool a pioneering city in certain aspects of social welfare. Robert followed his father by becoming a cotton broker and was, when Lallie met him, already a man of considerable wealth and standing in the community. He and his family were old acquaintances of Lallie's grandfather, Lawrence Heyworth, and visited him at his home, although by this stage Heyworth felt too old to go to their dinner parties. It is not clear exactly where Lallie met Robert, but during the many months which Lallie spent in Liverpool in 1865 and 1866 she referred frequently to having seen Robert at balls and dances. Her parents were also told of the gentleman's visits to Lallie and to those of her sisters who joined her from time to time at Yewtree House. She wrote too of his conduct at balls at which they met and about the visits made to her by his mother and sister. Richard and Lawrencina met the young man and, believing that his attentions to their oldest daughter were serious, proposed that they write to his mother to establish the relationship between the two families on a more precise footing. Lallie demurred. She wanted rather to make the Holt family take the initiative, and made sure that they knew when she would be in Liverpool in order to see whether or not they chose to include her in their social arrangements. At the same time she insisted that her mother took 'too serious a view of Mr. R. Holt'. He 'most evidently likes the family and the society of us girls in particular he has never said or done the least thing to show any partiality for me'. She in turn thought him 'a nice sensible industrious man but I am sure I have no feeling for him at all approaching "being in love"'.[10] Lallie's want of romantic fervour occasioned some criticism from her mother. It did not, however, prevent Lallie herself from wanting to clear away any obstacles to a possible union between herself and this sensible young man. The main problem she foresaw was the religious one: the Holts were Unitarian, while Lallie still followed the Anglican faith of her father. This was not an insuperable obstacle, but it did need to be discussed, and in her view the best place for such a discussion was Standish:

> It is almost impossible in the way one meets people here [in Liverpool] to have any discussion on those kind of subjects so that is one reason why I think it would be a good thing to ask them [the Holts] to Standish soon because as you say if by any chance he were to take it into his head to flirt or to make love it would be impossible then to ask him without leading him on in a very unfair way if after all I did not care about him.[11]

Unfortunately Lallie's extant correspondence is all addressed to her mother, who was at Standish when the Holts visited, so there is no record of the outcome of this discussion. It must have been successful, however, as Lallie married Robert Holt in 1867.

The next two marriages within the family were both acceptable to the Potter parents and took place with their help. In 1869 Mary married Arthur Playne, a local landowner and a long-standing friend of the family. Although Arthur was a man without notable talents and with few interests beyond hunting and fishing, he became an integral part of the family and was always regarded by Richard Potter as a son rather than a son-in-law. In 1873 he accompanied Richard Potter on one of his journeys to the United States and Canada and, although his ill temper and bad behaviour annoyed Kate and Beatrice, who were also on that trip, they did nothing to interrupt the harmonious relationship between Arthur and his father-in-law.[12]

Georgie's marriage to Daniel Meinertzhagen was, of all the Potter marriages, the one in which their parents took the largest role. Daniel, who was a merchant banker known to Richard Potter through business associations, was actually invited to Standish by Richard in 1872 and there introduced to his daughters. Daniel was a remarkably handsome man who showed to good advantage on horseback. Georgie, like many of the other Potters, was a noted rider herself and an accomplished sportswoman. In the best Victorian story-book tradition, the romance between the two of them blossomed while Daniel was laid up after a sporting accident and Georgie nursed him back to health. It is not quite clear how this accident occurred or even what kind of accident it was. Their son, Richard Meinertzhagen, subsequently wrote that Daniel had had a bad fall while out hunting. Charles Macaulay, Georgie's uncle, however, referred instead to a fishing accident in the course of which both Georgie and Daniel fell into the water. In his view, Georgie had taken a very active role in the whole affair. 'She has played her game boldly and deserves to win. The adventurous angler is often obliged to go into the water in order to secure his fish. Georgie, like a true sportswoman does not hesitate between the risk of playing into the stream, and the charm of losing her bite.'[13]

Georgie was one of the most handsome and certainly the most dashing and charming of the Potter sisters. Unlike Lallie and Mary, whose engagements had a sober and business-like quality about them, hers was a most romantic affair. After she had nursed Daniel back to health she continued to meet him in town, often riding with him in Hyde Park. During one such ride, when they were caught in a fierce storm and isolated from the rest of her party, Daniel proposed and was accepted.

Richard Potter, as we have seen, went out of his way to forward the marriage and to enable the young couple to set up house in comfort. Lawrencina was thrilled by this engagement, which probably appealed to her own romanticism. Her habitual gloom and her sense of despair about the girls' futures seem temporarily to have lifted with its advent, prompting Maggie to comment that 'Georgie's engagement seems to have set up a new order of things which I trust will continue altogether'.[14] The sisters, however, were rather less enthusiastic; Charles Macaulay visited Mary Playne shortly after it was announced and noted Mary's comments that 'none of the girls—except Georgie like him; that he is morose and ungenial; that he takes no interest in them—and that she does not think he will be a great acquisition to anyone but Georgie'.[15] Unfortunately for Georgie, the assessment of her sisters was rather more accurate than that of her parents and, as Kate later noted, this intensely romantic relationship had no place for friendship within it and proved ill-suited to weather the trials of married life.[16]

The next engagement, that of Blanche to William Harrison Cripps, broke abruptly with the earlier pattern of marriages for the girls being made amongst family friends, neighbours, or business associates. It was also different in being disliked by Richard and Lawrencina Potter. The response of the Potters to Willie and to Blanche's engagement to him offers insights into the social hierarchy of the professions in the late nineteenth century as well as revealing some of the assumptions underlying the approved marriages. Willie Cripps lacked both charm and polish. He was, in Beatrice's view, 'at first sight repellant, almost unclean looking, with the manners and conversation of a clever cad . . . Father, who had an extraordinary instinct about men, always disliked him, and, in spite of his eventual success, never believed in him.'[17] This dislike, which turned out to be quite justified, was clearly an important feature in the family's response, more especially as some of the other sisters also initially disliked Willie. But at the same time, it is probable that there were also other factors involved in the family's disapproval of this marriage.

The other married sisters, Lallie, Mary, and Georgie, had married respectively a wealthy cotton broker, a local land and mill owner, and a merchant banker: all men of impeccable family and respectable occupation. Blanche, by contrast, was proposing to ally herself with a surgeon. In the mid nineteenth century, the medical profession was just beginning to establish its claims to social respectability alongside its professional pre-eminence. By the 1860s and 1870s physicians were coming to be regarded as gentlemen, with whom one might mix socially. Surgeons, however, had not yet attained this status and the older traditions of the barber–surgeon, a tradesman of many skills but of few social pretensions, died hard.[18] The difference between the two categories was symbolized by the fact that in the 1870s physicians were admitted to gentlemen's clubs, while surgeons were not.[19] Surgeons were not slow to demand recognition and, within a short time, the Royal College of Surgeons had established its eminence and the claims of its fellows and members to respect. But at the time of Blanche's marriage this was not yet the case. Where the other brothers-in-law were welcomed into the family in terms of the way in which their professions could add to the family's range of skills and honours, Willie was never referred to in this light. (This fact is somewhat ironic as several of the sisters subsequently owed much to his skill as an abdominal surgeon and to his interest in obstetrics; a couple indeed may well have owed their lives to his care and attention.)

But Willie's offence was compounded by the fact of his not yet being a successful surgeon. All the family marriages prior to this one adhered to the conventions involved in the 'spread of gentility' of the second half of the nineteenth century. In all of these marriages the husband earned enough—or nearly enough—to enable the young couple to 'start married life at the level of living which their parents had reached'.[20] Willie, by contrast, had not only to carry the burden of an ungentlemanly profession, but he was still very much a struggling young man. He had a small income, he had not yet made his name in his profession—and he could not even offer his young bride a home. That all of these problems would be temporary seemed very likely, in view of his close family connections with Sir William Lawrence, one of the most prominent doctors at Saint Bartholomew's. Immediately after graduating Willie had been appointed house surgeon, and shortly after he became Surgical Registrar and then Assistant Surgeon at Saint Bartholomew's.[21] But his large income and wide reputation were still in the future and he broke important conventions by marrying while this was so.

The extent to which Willie was regarded as unacceptable was made evident by the slighting comments heaped by the Potters on his family. Indeed it was simply accepted that his was a family requiring no consideration, and they were treated very shabbily by the Potters over all the arrangements for Blanche and Willie's wedding. There was no basis in fact for this snobbishness from the Potters. Willie's family, while not one of great national importance, was certainly not inferior in any way to the Potters. His father was a Queen's Counsel with a distinguished public career. He was the first Chairman of the Buckinghamshire County Council and served also as Chairman of the Buckingham Quarter Sessions and as Recorder of Litchfield.[22] Indeed a few years after Willie and Blanche married, the Potters recognized that they had to make amends and did their best to do so.

This recognition came about not specifically in relation to Willie and Blanche, however, but rather as a result of a later engagement, that of Theresa to Alfred Cripps in 1881. Theresa had met Alfred, who was Willie's younger brother, while staying with Willie and Blanche. Alfred was immediately captivated, although Theresa herself took a considerable time to respond to his attention. But Alfred was welcomed with open arms by the Potters and shown all the respect and affection which they could muster. He was already a very successful advocate, clearly marked out for leadership in a most respectable profession. He was also a man of considerable charm, warmly liked by all his prospective in-laws, although the more acerbic of the sisters disliked the gushing way in which Theresa expressed her adoration of Alfred after she had finally fallen in love with him. Mary wrote to Beatrice that Theresa 'would have liked to bore me to death with never ceasing accounts of his perfections—according to her he is the best, the cleverest, the most perfect man that ever lived—altogether he is great enough to be the first in the land, but not quite too good to accept worldly honours'.[23] Alfred's extreme eligibility made the Potters very conscious of how badly they behaved to the Cripps family earlier. Georgie wrote to Beatrice, with characteristic directness, that when planning this wedding they needed to remember that 'there is the whole Cripps family to be re-embraced . . . We must not make such a fist of it this time. They are worthy people, quite as good as we are.'[24] Mary echoed this view, noting that the wedding should be organized in the way most convenient to the Cripps family. They 'were not well treated at the last wedding with our family and ought to be well treated this time'.[25]

The enthusiasm about Theresa's engagement to Alfred Cripps, and the extent of family interest in her wedding arrangements, derives as much from Alfred's eligibility as from the family's interest in Theresa herself. She was, as Beatrice had earlier pointed out, acknowledged as the real family treasure—the greatest jewel offered by the Potters on the matrimonial market. She was an attractive member of the sisterhood, adding a very affectionate disposition and a gentle charm to the intelligence and practical capabilities which she shared with many of her sisters. She had shown unusual tact and skill in her years as house-keeper and in her dealings with a difficult family, amongst whom she was a general favourite. Blanche, by contrast, was a family problem. Although considered to be the greatest beauty amongst the sisters, she was physically frail and mentally unstable, combining strange artistic talents and periods of extreme religious exaltation with severe lapses of memory and a lack of practical sense and skills. It is not possible on the available evidence to diagnose her condition, but it is clear that she suffered in an extreme form from the various neuroses and fits of depression which were common to the Potter family. Her lack of practical skills is evident in the fact that she never took a turn as housekeeper, nor did she accompany Richard Potter on his travels. Beatrice, although many years younger than Blanche, wrote of her with unusual condescension, making it evident that during her adolescence she felt both superior to Blanche and that she was in some sense responsible for her. For Blanche, as later for Rosie, the other sisters would accept a man whom they would not countenance for a moment for themselves.

Although the marriages of two of the Potters to Cripps brothers in the late 1870s and early 1880s absorbed much of the family's time, theirs were not the only marriages in these years. Indeed it was in the years intervening between Blanche's marriage and that of Theresa that Maggie made the marriage which was 'the envy of all the mothers of daughters in the county of Gloucestershire'.[26] Whereas all the other sisters married men who were engaged either in professions or in business, Maggie moved one stage above this in the social hierarchy by marrying into the gentry. Mary Playne had some years earlier married a local squire, but he was a man much of whose income came from the mill which he inherited from his father. He was moreover a local man of a respectable but not particularly distinguished family. Maggie, by uniting herself with Henry Hobhouse, married into an older family with a larger estate and a national reputation. Henry was the nephew of Lord Hobhouse, a judge whose standing and repu-tation were warmly acknowledged by the Potters. Henry had inherited Hadspen House and the estate of two and a half thousand acres which surrounded it in 1862. His family had lived there for close on a century and had established themselves firmly within the county, playing in particular a major role in petty and quarter sessions. In 1880, the year he and Maggie were married, Henry was called to the bar and became a county magistrate, thus commencing his own quite distinguished career in politics and local government.[27]

The engagements and subsequent marriages of Maggie and Theresa were the last to occur during the lifetime of Lawrencina Potter. Her sudden death in 1882 brought to a close one substantial phase in the life of the family and ushered in a new one in which the sisters took more significant roles in the running of the home and in the organization of their lives. Indeed it is interesting that it was Lawrencina's death which precipitated Kate into taking the definitive step in establishing her engagement to Leonard Courtney. One wonders if she would have had the courage to do this during her mother's lifetime.

Kate had met Leonard Courtney in 1878. He was a friend of Canon Barnett, to whom Kate had become very close when she worked in Whitechapel for the Charity Organization Society, as well as knowing many of her other friends. Leonard was a Liberal Member of Parliament, already known for his independence of outlook and his uncompromising and unpragmatic political rectitude. Over the next three years he became one of Kate's most regular companions, visiting her rooms in Great College Street, meeting her often at dinners and parties and being included in the group of friends she took to Standish for Easter in 1881. In the course of that year she noted in her diary, 'I get to count more and more on my friend—without looking for any definite result from my friendship'.[28] By the end of that year, however, the relationship was causing her both anxiety and depression: 'sad time in London—my friend doesn't come and even seems to avoid natural opportunities for doing so'.[29] Kate tried to make herself stop thinking about Leonard, advising herself that she must 'localise the pain' and not let it invade her whole life. She met him at a dinner at the Barnetts and afterwards summed up the situation. 'I feel that he likes me but also feel that there are difficulties in his own mind—and I recognize that my feelings are so much engaged that the only thing is to wait patiently for the solution which time may bring.'[30]

In April 1882, Lawrencina was suddenly and severely taken ill and Kate was called home to her mother's deathbed. She returned to London feeling miserable and very lonely. In this state she wrote to Leonard Courtney asking him to call. 'When one has gone through some great event which creates in one a whole world of new thought and feelings, one seems to want one's friends more than ever to help one solve the problems and put things in the right place and proportion.'[31] Leonard replied that he would come the next evening. He had been 'much distressed at the end of the Easter week to read of the great blow that had fallen upon you. I could not help thinking of the same time last year when we had spent such happy days at Standish in the house that had become a house of mourning.'[32]

Leonard duly came to call and Kate, under the sway of all the various emotions of her previous few months, confessed the full extent of her affection for him. Leonard had to leave Kate in order to keep a previous dinner engagement, but he wrote to her as soon as he returned home. Throughout his evening he had experienced a 'vein of thought and feeling . . . A sense of great pleasure—of exquisite pleasure—has been mixed with some shame. I have been moved beyond words by the expression of regard for me, and I have been ashamed for not having been sufficiently master of myself.'[33] Leonard's sense of shame was increased by his belief that it was impossible for him to enter into any kind of formal engagement to Kate. He was at the time nearing 50 and had long accustomed himself to the thought that he would die a bachelor. His own habitual reticence, combined with his lack of an independent income, made him feel unable to undertake the responsibility of supporting a wife. He had recently been made Secretary to the Treasury, but his political future was still uncertain and he did not feel sufficiently secure financially to set up a family life.[34] Kate handled Leonard's shame and uncertainty with great composure. She explained to him that his 'outburst of feeling' had taken her by surprise, but she neither regretted it nor did she blame him for it. 'In sending for you to comfort me in my trouble about poor little mother I was bound to take the risk.'[35] It seems more than likely that Kate had deliberately engineered this risk, realizing that Leonard was too retiring and too modest and perhaps too set in his ways to take a step that would bring about a drastic alteration to his life and circumstances. She did not press him for an engagement: the 'special friendship' which was all he felt able to offer suited her very well. It provided the closeness and emotional dependence which she wanted while not upsetting the routine of life which she had established for herself. It was her family who found this unacceptable and pressed for them to formalize their relationship through an engagement.

Kate's marriage to Leonard Courtney in 1883 left Beatrice and Rosie, the two youngest sisters, as the only two who were single. Rosie was still at school and so the family's attention focused on Beatrice. She was already nearing her mid-twenties by this stage and had noted the way in which, one after another, her sisters had left their family of origin to establish new homes and families. She was in a state of chronic indecision about her own future in this regard, feeling a strong desire to make her mark through a career, while at the same time being very conscious of her own need for marriage and her desire for a home of her own. Beatrice's diary during these years shows the torment she suffered in trying to reconcile her emotional and sexual needs with her personal ambition and her desire for public recognition. This conflict was embodied in her relationship with Joseph Chamberlain.[36]

Beatrice met Chamberlain in 1883, when he had recently made the transition from Mayor of Birmingham to Liberal Member of Parliament. He was a man of considerable wealth and influence who was attempting at this stage to radicalize the Liberal Party programme by increasing its commitment to social welfare and, at the same time, strengthening its commitment to imperialism.[37] A man of charismatic public appeal almost at the height of his political career, with immense appeal to women, Chamberlain was an obvious choice for Beatrice if she was going to make the 'brilliant marriage' which her family sought for her. Beatrice was powerfully attracted to Chamberlain, who combined a handsome face and commanding physique with his political and financial attributes. Her own growing interest in politics and in the ways in which political power was wielded increased Beatrice's fascination with Chamberlain; moreover, he had a strength of will which was unmatched in her experience, except perhaps by her own. As for Chamberlain, although he was clearly interested in Beatrice, he refused to woo her. The difference between his lover-like wooing of his mass of followers and his casual treatment of her both piqued Beatrice and increased her interest in him. Beatrice had been wooed often before and this was the first time in which her interest was coolly met. Chamberlain was the first man with whom she was seriously involved and his casual approach to their relationship increased her desire and made her take the initiative. She was well aware of the basis of Chamberlain's attraction, and provided a minute analysis of it in her diary:

All the small 'affaires de coeurs' of past years I have left unmentioned, simply because they have not interested me. The commonplaces of love have always bored me. But Joseph Chamberlain with his gloom and seriousness, with absence of any gallantry or faculty for saying pretty nothings, the simple way in which he assumes, almost asserts that you stand on a level far beneath him and that all that concerns you is trivial; that you yourself are without importance in the world except in so far as you might be related to him! This sort of courtship (if it is to be called courtship) fascinates at least my imagination.[38]

It was precisely this imaginative element which was the key to Beatrice's relationship with Chamberlain. The whole relationship existed far more acutely and extensively in her imagination than it did in reality. Their meetings were few and uncomfortable. But in the long intervals between them, Beatrice did little but think about Chamberlain. 'His personality absorbs all my thought and he occupies too prominent a position for me not to be continually reminded of him'.[39] Following in the footsteps of Kate, Beatrice invited Chamberlain to call and provoked the situations in which the feelings and expectations of each of them were articulated. The result, however, was less happy for Beatrice than it had been for Kate. Beatrice confessed her feelings on a number of occasions, but Chamberlain did not respond in kind. He made his requirements in regard to a wife very clear to her—while never actually proposing. He showed just enough interest to keep Beatrice at fever pitch, and to fuel her own fantasy. She could not have found a man who more clearly embodied the principle of absolute male dominance than did Chamberlain. Marriage to him would have precluded absolutely the independent career and the personal freedom that she was so ardently seeking when she met him; it would have denied her both intellectual independence and the continued pursuit of her intellectual and social interests. Her very involvement with him suggests an ambivalence about the desirability of this freedom, and a lingering desire to allow someone else to control and determine her life.

In her long periods of solitude, Beatrice speculated about a possible marriage with Chamberlain and acknowledged how disastrous such a union would be. Despite her passionate sexual attraction to him, she never lost sight of his personal or political shortcomings. She saw in him a brutal man, loving power and prepared to use it without scruple or consideration. She never accepted his political ideas and she questioned the sincerity with which he held his widely publicized views on social reform.

If the fates should unite us (against *my will*) all joy and light heartedness will go for me. I will be absorbed into the life of a man whose aims are not my aims; who will refuse me all freedom of thought in my intercourse with him; to whose career I shall have to subordinate all my life, mental and physical without believing in the usefulness of his career, whether it be inspired by earnest conviction or ambition . . . If I married him I should become a cynic as regards my own mental life. I should either destroy my own intellectual individuality and I can imagine doing that under the influence of strong feeling, or I should become a pure observer and throw up the ball of right and wrong in 'matters of opinion'. In the latter case I should separate even more than I do now in my intellect from my feeling. When feeling became strong, as it would do with me in marriage, it would mean the absolute subordination of reason to it, or eternal separation; and if life apart were impossible the 'pure intellect' would die. I should become par excellence the mother and the woman of the world intent only on fulfilling practical duties and gaining practical ends.[40]

The clarity of Beatrice's perception about Chamberlain did nothing to reduce the intensity of her involvement. She had met him in 1883 and their relationship lasted, in a desultory fashion, for the next few years. By the end of 1887 they had had a series of unsatisfactory confrontations and all was over. But her life continued to be dominated by thoughts and fantasies about Chamberlain for a number of years after this. Again Beatrice was aware of why this was so. 'My intimacy with the great man brought about a deadly fight between the intellectual and the sensual but the intellectual triumphed not by its own strength but by the force of circumstance, it has beaten the sensual and denied to it satisfaction.'[41]

The shadow of Chamberlain, and the sense of opportunities lost in regard to him, lay heavily over Beatrice in the late 1880s. The loss was felt all the more strongly because her own life was so dismal and depressing at this time. The active and exciting period of playing at hostess and companion for her father lasted only a couple of years. It came to an abrupt halt in 1885 when Richard Potter suffered a serious stroke. Thereafter, until his death in 1892, Beatrice remained with her father, but now she was supervising the care and the comfort of a bed-ridden invalid with declining mental powers. The only respite she received from this was the few months each year when her married sisters either came to stay or had their father come to stay with them. During this time, Beatrice continued her social investigation. It was in one such break that she began working with Charles Booth in his pioneering study of London Life and Labour. Her months at home caring for her father sharpened her sense of social inequality as she pondered the household she supervised. In it there were 'ten persons living on the fat of the land in order to minister to the supposed comfort of one imbecile old man—all this faculty expended to satisfy the fancied desires of a being well nigh bereft of desire.'[42] Beatrice had also to look after Rosie during this period and this added an enormous weight to her burden as she found it very difficult to get on with her younger sister. Beatrice had always felt that the relationship between Richard and Rosie was a dangerous one, bad for them both, and she seemed to believe that Rosie's demands and dependence on her father were in some measure responsible for his stroke.

Beatrice was too dutiful a daughter ever to complain about her onerous domestic task—and she was too fond of her father and too uncertain about her own future to articulate any desire to be freed from this burden by his death. But she felt no such affection towards Rosie. Besides, there was an obvious way to release herself from the burden of Rosie: marriage. As Rosie later recalled, Beatrice 'always encouraged me to invite young men to the house, and was constantly impressing upon me that I was a "sweet young thing eminently suited to be married" but incapable of leading an independent life'. Immediately after Richard Potter's stroke, the sisters had sent Rosie to Corsica with an old family doctor to look after her. On her return, she 'set about to find . . . a husband'.[43]

The view that Rosie needed to marry was shared by Beatrice and all the other sisters. Rosie accepted it too, although she looked to marriage as the solution to her physical rather than to her moral state.

My physical health at this time was very uncertain for although I had gained in strength and looked well I was continually worried by a troublesome irritation of my lips which at times became almost unbearable. Whenever I spoke, whenever I laughed my lips felt as though they would crack, and were constantly hot and inflamed, though there was little visible sign of the trouble. I was extremely anxious to marry as I felt instinctively that all this would disappear with marriage, as indeed it did.[44]

Some time in 1883 or 1884 Rosie had met a young barrister, Dyson Williams, at a party. They were immediately attracted to each other, although their friendship was interrupted by Richard Potter's stroke and Rosie's visit to Corsica. On her return, she invited Dyson to the Argoed where Beatrice and her father were staying. Subsequently Rosie went to London to take a course in cookery and she continued to see Dyson there.

She wanted Dyson to propose to her, but when he did could not make up her mind whether or not to accept. In due course she did accept, although she constantly vacillated about it, and was never altogether happy about her decision. Part of this was the result of her ignorance about sex and her fears about the physical side of marriage.

During the three months before our marriage I got to know my future husband better, and he stayed for weeks on end at the Argoed. I liked him in many ways but was not altogether happy about the marriage, from which I felt a physical shrinking . . . I had only a vague notion of what marriage meant until the eve of my wedding when my sister Margaret explained to me in very plain language the physical facts of sexual intercourse. Her description filled me with fear and disgust, which Beatrice somewhat diminished by telling me that all that side of marriage was unimportant; only companionship and mutual affection and respect mattered.[45]

But part of it was the realization, confirmed on her honeymoon, that she and Dyson had little if anything in common. Rosie loved the country and throughout her life found her greatest pleasure in the contemplation and the painting of natural scenery. Dyson, by contrast, was at ease only in London, caring nothing for natural beauty, but finding his enjoyment in social activities, political discussion, and many of the other activities and dissipations of young men about town.

Rosie herself maintained that her family 'were mildly against the match, as they considered it a poor one in terms of money, for Dyson had only £400 a year . . . and the scanty earnings he made at the Bar. My sisters had all married rich and successful men, and I was anxious my future husband should be thought well of by the family, for I was still a good deal under their sway.'[46] But her anxiety for familial approval was unavailing. Indeed from the letters of her sisters to each other, it seems clear that while Dyson Williams would not have been considered acceptable to any of them, they thought him quite good enough for Rosie. Far from trying to make her give him up, one gains the impression that they encouraged her to enter into the marriage, having already given up on her themselves, and wanting her off their hands. The letter which Beatrice wrote to Mary announcing the engagement is nothing if not frank about her views.

Rosie is engaged to Mr. Williams . . . She is still in a state of doubt as to whether the family will think him good enough. He is very much in love, and is a good respectable young man! God preserve him! I am glad of it. I think the risk of Rosie remaining unmarried or marrying some undesirable character was terrible to think of . . . It is of course not a brilliant affair; but knowing Rosie I think it is suitable. Her happiness will, of course, be doubtful, her nature is so thoroughly egotistical.[47]

That the sisters saw it as a poor match is made even more clear in Mary's letter to Lallie. Neither of them wished to see the engagement broken, although this suggestion had been made. Mary opposed this step:

Rosie is evidently happy in it, & after all he will probably make money at the Bar & the work will be good for both of them—& in any case there is enough to live upon. The disappointment & mortification of breaking the engagement might have been disastrous to a girl like Rosie & I do not at all see why this should not terminate quite happily & well. He will have plenty to put up with as a set off to his want of means & I sincerely hope her husband will be able to feel that, at any rate, she brings him some good things.[48]

Kate commented in her diary that this engagement 'was not a good match, but his family & character will probably suit her'.[49] So the engagement continued and Richard Potter was too weak and feeble even to comment upon it. The letters from Beatrice and Mary are in themselves somewhat chilling and become more so in hindsight as one watches them consigning Rosie's fate to a man who never made any money at the Bar, and who, far from being 'respectable', opened Rosie's eyes to a whole world of dissipation and sexual licence of which her sisters remained ignorant. Her marriage to Dyson was brief and bitterly unhappy. She spent a couple of years trying to make it work—and the remainder helping to nurse him through the terminal stages of syphilis.

Rosie's marriage to Dyson Williams in 1888 left Beatrice the last 'Miss Potter', dividing her time between work and care for her father. In this and the subsequent years she began to publish articles based on her social investigation and came to be regarded as something of an expert on East End living and working conditions, and especially on the 'sweated' trades. The preoccupation with social and economic questions which she developed as a result of the severe trade depression of the 1880s led to her looking at ways in which the alternating booms and troughs in capitalism might be avoided. She was interested also in looking at social and industrial organizations which might modify, if they did not avoid altogether, the social classes and the exploitation of labour which she saw as an inevitable result of late Victorian capitalism. In 1889 she turned her attention away from the sufferings of the most exploited workers and towards the trade unions and the co-operative societies, the organizations which seemed to offer some alternative to unbridled capitalism. In the course of this work Beatrice was introduced to Sidney Webb as a man who might help with her work. He was a young civil servant, who had just made a name for himself as the author of one of the *Fabian Essays*. His essay on the 'Historical Basis of Socialism' impressed Beatrice and enabled her to make the transition she was seeking from the capitalism and the conservatism of her youth to the non-revolutionary state socialism which seemed to offer some answer to the problems of poverty and exploitation.[50]

Beatrice found Sidney 'a remarkable little man with a huge head and a tiny body, a breadth of forehead quite sufficient to account for the encyclopaedic character of his knowledge'. She liked him on first meeting. 'There is a directness of speech, an open-mindedness, an imaginative warm-heartedness which will carry him far.'[51] But this liking was very different from her passionate infatuation with Joseph Chamberlain, or indeed from Sidney's immediate and strong attraction to Beatrice. For several months their relationship developed very slowly and painfully, as they shared ideas and interests in a way which deepened Sidney's love and involvement, while Beatrice was concerned only to establish clear limits. Eventually, Sidney's persistent affection, combined with his insistence that theirs would be a working partnership, rather than a mere marriage, carried the day. Beatrice finally accepted the devotion offered, never shirking from the honesty which caused Sidney so much pain in the early stages of their relationship. But Beatrice explained that although she had agreed to marry him, they would have to wait until after her father died before announcing their engagement. 'My regard for you is not strong enough to face the terrible questioning of the whole family.'[52] Hence she waited for the death of her father which she knew would reduce her contact with her sisters before even telling any of them about her relationship with Sidney Webb. As she expected, her sisters were rather shocked by the announcement. They took it in good part, however, and did their best to welcome Sidney into the family. The process was somewhat trying: the Potters were rather imperious, while in his interactions with them Sidney was both assertive and abrasive. Kate hoped that when he dined with her, he would refrain from treating Leonard as he had Alfred Cripps as 'something between a pupil and a fool'.[53] Sidney did establish cordial relations with his future in-laws, although there was never anything approaching intimacy. The wedding of Beatrice and Sidney was organized and hosted by the Holts, but it was followed by an instant diminution in the extent of contact Beatrice had with her sisters. Her marriage to Sidney set the seal on the changes she had undergone in outlook and values which took her further and further away from her sisters and from her family and her society of origin. Good manners won out in the end, however, and cordiality was established between Sidney and the Potter family.

In marrying Sidney, Beatrice moved outside her own social class and that of her brothers-in-law. Sidney was from a lower-middle-class London family and only his mother's determination to educate her sons enabled him to rise through his own abilities and exertions—and through the opportunities offered by Civil Service examinations—to the social level where he could actually meet Beatrice. Her marriage to Sidney put the final seal on the distance she had travelled from the values and the outlook of her family, not only on account of his social origin, but also because of their arrangement to have a partnership rather than a conventional marriage. In personal as in class terms Sidney was everything that Chamberlain was not: in his behaviour to Beatrice he was devoted, conciliatory, interested in her work and her ideas, prepared even to subordinate himself to her and to her work. At the same time, he lacked the charm and the physical appeal which were so evident in Chamberlain and to which she had been enslaved. Indeed Beatrice had to work hard to overcome an initial physical repugnance to Sidney before she could agree to marry him. Having done so, she found in him the exclusive and absolute affection which went some way to making up for the sense of loneliness and neglect she had carried with her since her unhappy childhood. Hers could not be a simple or uncomplicated marriage, or one of unalloyed happiness. But it was, as she finally came to see, a fair compromise.

VI

Married Life

I

FOR the Potter sisters, as for most other Victorian women, marriage was a momentous step. It brought not only a new and intimate relationship with a man little known before the actual wedding ceremony, but also a change of name, address, legal rights, and social and economic status. Marriage in Victorian England involved much more extensive changes for women than it did for men. This is not to suggest that men did not experience a fairly dramatic change as they entered into a new intimate domestic relationship, or assumed the financial, social, and familial responsibilities which marriage brought. But the changes for women were both more in number and much more far-reaching. The differences between the sexes in relation to marriage can be seen in terms of their legal status. A man's legal status did not change on marriage, although he assumed certain responsibilities for the maintenance of his wife and for her debts. For a woman, by contrast, marriage brought a complete change in legal status as she ceased being a feme sole and became instead a feme covert, unable to own property, enter into contracts, sue or be sued in a court of law or even, for some of the nineteenth century, commit a criminal act of her own volition.[1] The legal personality of a woman was completely absorbed into that of her husband on marriage.[2] Married women thus suffered very considerable legal disabilities until the end of the century. Paradoxically, marriage brought a rise in their social standing. Here again there are marked differences between women and men. Men experienced a rise in social status on marriage only if they married into a wealthy family or into one which was not only superior to their own, but able to offer patronage and privilege. For women, by contrast, the mere fact of being married conferred social precedence over unmarried women, regardless of the standing of the husband. A Mrs, regardless of her surname, always entered the dining room before a Miss, and sat closer to the head of the table.

In the long debate about marriage which raged amongst feminists and anti-feminists in the nineteenth century, both sides agreed that there were marriages of many different kinds and qualities.[3] A knowledge of only the legal situation of married women, or even of the social and economic framework of marriage, tells us little about the personal experiences of individuals. Legally a woman was, as J. S. Mill pointed out, the bondservant of her husband, bound to reside where he chose, to do as he bid, and to provide him with domestic and social services which he could, if he deemed necessary, extract through violence or imprisonment.[4] But it is clearly not the case that all Victorian marriages involved the brutal subjection of women to the will and the whim of their husbands.

Marriage for the Potters, as for all other women of their class, was followed by the assumption of domestic responsibilities and the care of a husband as primary duties, but these duties presented themselves in very different ways. They were onerous and unpleasant for Rosie, sometimes impossible for Blanche, and distasteful much of the time to Georgie. But for Lallie, Kate, Mary, Theresa, and Maggie, the care of husband and home was easily mastered and often enjoyable.

The Potter sisters provide an excellent illustration of part at least of the range of situations and of relationships possible within the legal and social framework of Victorian marriage. They do not cover the full range, omitting entirely some of the most extreme suffering evident amongst Victorian women. The marriage settlements drawn up by Richard Potter, assuring his daughters an income for their own use, meant that they were never entirely dependent on their husbands financially. Nor were they ever subjected to physical brutality. Some were neglected cruelly by their husbands, others were made pregnant more often than they wished. But none of them were ever physically ill-treated or deprived. The Potters thus show a range of more or less unhappy marriages alongside a couple of exemplary affectionate and companionate ones.

The range of marital experiences evident amongst the sisters enables one to see something of the way in which personality and personal compatibility interacted with the legal and social framework of marriage. Within this framework some were able to negotiate satisfactory relationships while others were bitterly unhappy. None of the sisters was able to bypass entirely the laws or the conventions which governed marriage. But they were affected by them in very different ways. Nowhere is this more evident than in the way in which the sisters coped with the first imperative of married life: the removal of a woman from the home of her family into that of her husband. In some cases this meant leaving the locality of one's family as well: Lallie

resided in Liverpool after her marriage; Blanche, Theresa, and
Maggie all settled in London and the last two subsequently moved to
their husband's country homes. Marriage could involve not only
moving to one's husband's home town, but even moving into the home
he shared with other members of his family. This was the case for
Lallie, Mary, and Rosie, all of whom lived with relatives of their
husband. Lallie's sociability and self-assurance along with her great
warmth and fund of kindness made this situation an easy one for her to
handle. She had established a close friendship with the mother and
sister of Robert Holt before she married, and she fitted very easily into
their home in the early months of her marriage. She had, as her sister-
in-law noted on her wedding day, 'twined herself very closely round
our hearts'.[5] Subsequently she and Robert moved to a home of their
own for a few years but, after the death of Robert's mother, they shared
their home again with Robert's sister and all three maintained a
harmonious and easy relationship. Mary also married a family, not
just a man. She looked after her father-in-law for many years and, in
addition to this, she and Arthur adopted a child of Arthur's brother
when the little girl was orphaned. Mary had some difficulties in
dealing with both of these relationships, but she managed them in the
end and had the satisfaction of having done her duty quite as well as
could be expected.[6]

The facility with which these two sisters adapted to and managed
their new surroundings was not shared by Rosie. When Rosie
married, Dyson Williams had neither a home of his own nor the
capital and income necessary to acquire one. He was often out of London attending the County Assizes, and while in London lived with his
wealthy aunt. After he and Rosie married, she too moved into the
home of Miss Williams. This was not a happy arrangement. Rosie did
not manage to integrate herself into the household. She was jealous of
the intimacy and the political interests which Dyson shared with his
aunt and from which she felt totally excluded. Miss Williams in turn
was hostile to Rosie and could not refrain from criticizing her or her
family to Dyson. This angered Dyson even more than it did Rosie and
he terminated the arrangement by storming out of the house one night
after an argument—leaving both women ignorant of his whereabouts.
Dyson sent for Rosie the next day and they then moved into a small
flat.[7] But the lack of mutual interest and the disharmony evident from
the start of their life together continued in their new surroundings.

The capacity of some of the sisters to deal with the domestic situations of their husbands was paralleled by their ability to become involved in the whole extended family into which they married. Lallie became a central figure for the entire Holt family, establishing particularly close bonds with a couple of her brothers-in-law and their wives. These new ties lasted throughout her life and became in time closer than her bond with her husband. Kate too established close ties with Leonard's sister and some of his relatives. Even in some of the most unhappy marriages, close ties were formed with in-laws. Thus Georgie had a friendly and affectionate relationship with Daniel's sisters, despite the fact that they were much older than she and, or so she said, a little horrified by her sense of humour.[8] Only Beatrice and Rosie proved quite unable to form such ties. Beatrice could just cope with Sidney's lower-middle-class origins, but she was quite unable to establish any intimacy with his family.

Although marriage involved a physical separation of the sisters from their own family and an involvement in a new and more intimate relationship, it did not necessarily mean a diminution of close contact with the family of origin. Lallie for example corresponded very frequently with her mother and often had her parents and sisters to stay after her marriage. She spent quite a lot of time at Standish, sometimes with Robert and then with her babies, sometimes alone. The sisters differed in the amount of contact they had with their family of origin once married: Mary, Georgie, Theresa, and Maggie kept up very close contact. Kate, Blanche, Rosie, and Beatrice were all in various ways more distant. The kind of relationship kept up by the Potter sisters with their own family depended both upon the earlier situation at home and the nature of their marital relationship. Georgie had been happy at home, and the unhappiness of her marriage increased the importance of earlier family ties and her dependence on them. Kate, by contrast, had left home with relief and was so wrapped up in her life with Leonard Courtney that although she welcomed visits from her sisters and their offspring, she was disinclined to leave Leonard to visit her family.

II

Beatrice Webb rarely visited her sisters without commenting at length on the nature and the current state of their marital and familial relationships. Her attitude towards them was a complex one, as she took a distinct pride in the wealth and standing of her brothers-in-law, while at the same time regarding most of them as men of mediocre talents and abilities.[9] She regretted their limitations, particularly as these affected their wives. She saw her sisters as women of ability and intelligence who, lacking proper schooling, would have benefited from close association with men of intellect and breadth of vision. As it was, only she and Kate actually achieved this. In her view, Lallie, Mary, Georgie, and Maggie all married men who were manifestly less intelligent or narrower in outlook than they, while Theresa, although married to an able man, found her spritual aspirations thwarted in marriage.[10] Blanche and Rosie did not count within this general framework as their own inherent limitations and emotional problems put them outside the pale in this regard. Overall, Beatrice was strongly of the opinion that the only really happy and successful marriages amongst the Potter sisters were her own and that of Kate and Leonard Courtney.[11]

Beatrice's comments on her sisters were often sharp and insightful. At the same time, one cannot accept her assessment of her sisters or their marriages absolutely or uncritically. Beatrice's own ideal of marriage is very much in evidence in this assessment, but it is not one that was shared by all her sisters. It is undoubtedly the case that she and Kate were the only two of the Potters who lived in relationships in which close intimacy and warm affection were combined with shared interests, activities, and values. But not all the sisters wanted relationships of this kind.

Indeed one might, on the basis of Beatrice's assessment, hazard the general proposition that the likelihood of a happy marriage was inversely proportional to a woman's fulfilment of her prescribed familial role. Both she and Kate had found husbands as a result of their departure from convention, and from the confines of family life. Both subsequently shared the political interests and activities of their husbands, taking up such activities for their own sake instead of becoming immersed in family life. Whereas several of their sisters were forced to accept long periods of separation from their husbands, while they stayed with or met the needs of their children, Beatrice and Kate had undivided loyalties and could focus all their attention on their marriages and on their own immediate interests. The kind of close companionate relationships they enjoyed were only possible for childless women able to follow closely the exigencies of their husbands' careers and to organize their lives around them. It is perhaps not accidental that the marriage which Beatrice ranked third in happiness, that of Mary and Arthur Playne, produced only one child—and by contrast the least happy, that of Georgina and Daniel Meinertzhagen, produced ten children.

For all this, childlessness was itself a source of some distress. Kate and Leonard wished to have children and in 1888 Kate underwent 'a slight operation in hopes of having a child', but in vain.[12] However, having once accepted that this was the case, the lack of children does not seem to have caused any tension or discord between the Courtneys. Kate, as some of her sisters commented ironically, continued to be 'blissfully worshipful' towards Leonard throughout their married life. They spent much time together, writing two or three times a day when they were separated. Kate enjoyed her own social life while Leonard was busy in Parliament, but waited up for his return each night. They shared the same liberal political views and Leonard initiated Kate into the movement in support of Women's Suffrage—and she became active on the Women's Liberal Federation. They stood together in their controversial opposition to the Boer War and their pacifism during the First World War. Indeed, theirs was a relationship almost unique in its affection and its closeness. Unlike Beatrice, Kate does not seem to have wanted to marry anyone else before she met Leonard—and the very active part she took in that relationship makes it evident that her feelings were totally involved. Of her wedding day, she wrote 'It was a blessed marriage day and will be forever a holy memory for me. What had I ever done to be surrounded by so much love and above all to have my poor failure of a life crowned with the great love of my husband.'[13] This modesty—and the slightly gushing tendency deplored by some of her sisters—remained with Kate always, as did her sense of the happiness of her marriage. She devoted herself almost entirely to Leonard, even turning her diary into a work in which his life and career were recorded. On his death, she ceased writing it. But his devotion to her was every bit as strong, and the sorrows and troubles of their married life arose from ill health (Leonard's sudden loss of his eyesight in the early 1890s) and from political battles rather than from any problems between them.

The Webb marriage was obviously far more complex than this. Beatrice always regarded her marriage to Sidney as a form of 'self-renunciation' rather than the 'self-gratification' which marriage to Chamberlain would have been. Once she and Sidney were married, the complexity continued. On the one hand it seems unquestionable that she rapidly developed a strong dependence on him, that she found periods of separation hard to bear, and that he became the centre of much of her life. At the same time, she continued to suffer from periods of acute depression and of prolonged spells of inactivity. She also continued to think and to fantasize about Chamberlain, at least for the first few years of her marriage.[14] Moreover the closeness of the partnership itself involved costs. Whereas Kate apparently relinquished her independent life without a qualm and never thought about it again, Beatrice acknowledged her loss of independence, and not just in losing her name, but also in losing her privacy and her sphere of autonomous action.[15] Thus the diary which, in her adolescence and early adult life, had assuaged the want of understanding and companionship which she suffered within her family, became when she married the one area where she could speak and be really alone. In a most revealing comment she once wrote that everywhere else they used Sidney's language: here the language she used was truly her own.[16]

Looking beyond the relationships of Beatrice and Kate, it is clear that there are other problems with Beatrice's assessment of the marriages of her other sisters. For one thing, there were very different assumptions and expectations concerning marriage amongst the Potter sisters. While several of them seemed to accept the Victorian idea that marriage should be based primarily on romantic love (always assuming that the loved one had the appropriate income, profession, and social background), others inclined rather to an eighteenth-century view that marriage should be based on rational considerations rather than mere sentiment. Theresa, Blanche, and Kate belong to the first group, Lallie, Mary, and Maggie to the second. This is not to say that the latter group were not fond of their husbands, but rather to recognize that they accepted the need to balance personal feeling against such prudential considerations as wealth and status. For some of the sisters other relationships—those with their parents, their sisters, their children, even in some cases their brothers—or sisters-in-law—provided the warmth and affection which they neither found nor sought in marriage. Others were so detached and self-contained as to reject any real intimacy.

These differences in outlook were recognized to some extent by the family. Thus Lallie, for example, was chided by her mother for the lack of romanticism which she exhibited even during her engagement. She replied with engaging candour.

I was very glad to have your long letter the other day. I could not help laughing at the idea of learning to be romantic like a lesson at 22. I am afraid it is a hopeless case and I am too matter of fact for any improvement. At any rate if it could not be done at Standish by your most romantic self and all those mooning sisters it is not likely to be done in Edge Lane by this anything but sentimental family.[17]

In a similar way, Mary Playne insisted to Beatrice that there was not much romance about herself or Arthur or about their affairs. Although she devoted herself to ensuring his comfort, and did not like to leave him for long periods, she had no hesitation in acknowledging his limitations or the ways in which her own life had to be modified to make the marriage work.[18] Maggie was the third member of this particular trio and although she took only two weeks to decide to marry Henry Hobhouse, it would seem likely that this was as much because he was the most eligible man to propose to her as because she was passionately attracted to him. Maggie was known throughout the family for her interest in prudent and proper marriages—and the young man's income and background always took precedence for her over any endearing personal qualities. In regard to her own marriage, it is clear that she was devoted to Henry Hobhouse and set out earnestly to become a dutiful wife to him. She wrote to her sisters extolling the virtues and acknowledging the excellence of 'my lord husband',[19] but saw no incompatibility between this and the statement she left her children concerning her feelings for her mother: 'I loved her more than I ever loved any other being, and her loss was the greatest sorrow I have had.'[20] Her eldest son, Stephen, subsequently wrote about the reserve and lack of intimacy evident in his own childhood. He ascribed this to the nature of his parents. 'In both my parents' families there was a tendency to a rather self-centred independence and reserve which (save in a few gifted individuals) prevented the emergence of that kind of love or friendship which is ready to unveil and surrender the whole of one's being to the beloved one.'[21] Lallie, Mary, and Maggie all seem to have been women who found great difficulty in expressing emotion and who neither expected nor sought an emotionally compelling relationship in marriage. All of them lacked Beatrice's passionate streak and sought relationships in which clearly established roles and duties were combined with enough affection to satisfy their needs. Hence, although these relationships were not to Beatrice's taste, her taste was not shared by all her sisters.

III

But for all this, it is still clear that many of the Potter marriages were desperately unhappy. Those of Georgie and Daniel Meinertzhagen, Rosie and Dyson Williams, and Blanche and Willie Cripps are particularly notable in this regard. Others seem to have worked for some years, but then to have deteriorated as children grew up, and as age and changing preoccupations brought estrangement. This was the case in regard to the Holts, who seem to have been quite content with each other for about twenty-five years. In the later part of the 1890s, however, when both Lallie and Robert were in their fifties, strains began to develop. Lallie became more and more preoccupied with religious and spiritual matters and hence moved away from Robert, who continued to pursue wealth and social standing as the major human values. Tension amongst their children caused additional unhappiness and increased the distance between them. Lallie was a large woman who grew quite stout in her middle years and Robert apparently began to find her physical appearance and presence distasteful.[22] As we will see, her last years were ones of intense misery and complete isolation. Maggie Hobhouse also found herself increasingly isolated as her children grew up, and as the beliefs of some of her sons came into conflict with those of their father and placed Maggie in an uncomfortable situation between them. In her last years she stayed alone in London, suffering the excruciating pain of lung cancer, while Henry lived in the country. He visited occasionally, but brought little comfort or support when he did so.

The intense misery of the last years of Lallie and Maggie does need to be balanced against the long period during which their marriages functioned adequately, allowing them the pleasures as well as the duties of motherhood, an active social life, and a kind of companionship which, while not perfect, clearly had much to offer. Their situation was very different from that of Georgie or Rosie, whose marriages were failures from the very beginning, or from Blanche whose strange and complex relationship with Willie was always poised between pleasure and pain, with pain coming to dominate more and more as the years wore on.

The most intense marital misery was largely a result of fundamental mistakes in the choice of partners. It is hard to think of a worse choice for the dashing, charming, and whimsical Georgie than Daniel Meinertzhagen, a conservative banker with the conventional tastes of the man about town. In a similar way, Dyson Williams, a dissolute man with a mordant sense of humour and a complete lack of any balance or practicality, was a disastrous choice for an immature young girl seeking someone to replace her father, as Rosie was. In both cases, tension and distress was evident from the first few months of marriage.

Richard Meinertzhagen maintains that the marriage of his parents foundered even during their honeymoon, spent partly in Paris and partly in the Black Forest. 'It was not altogether a happy one, for mother, in her puritan chastity, could not respond to father's exuberance. In Paris my father insisted on buying my mother most unsuitable hats.'[23] In his view it was always Georgie who was at fault, combining frigidity with a sense of humour which always caused Daniel pain. Letters from other members of the family, however, suggest a rather different interpretation. In the letters from the sisters, it is Daniel's disinclination to share holidays with his family—or to share a bedroom with his wife—which was both symptom and source of strain. Georgie herself wrote about this to Daniel in 1876, in a letter asking if he would come to Folkstone, where she was staying during her second pregnancy, to visit her.

I don't think you will do badly here dear, if you don't mind rather a small bedroom and bed shared with me. I will keep it as tidy as possible for you. I hope you will be able to take a few days here. Mind you do darling. I can't go very long without seeing you. I hope Johanna will give you a pleasant little dinner at her club. What a nice idea! I must be a member and then on Derby nights and sundry other nights I need not cry my eyes out at home.[24]

Throughout the 1870s, there are comments in family letters about Georgie and Dee getting on better, and about his showing a new disposition to spend his holidays with his family or to share a room with Georgie, but these were temporary respites in a relationship which lacked any real foundation.

Georgie loved life in the country and her life, of necessity, centred on the ten children whom she bore after painful and debilitating pregnancies. Daniel preferred life in town, centred on his club. He enjoyed country weekends, but only those spent hunting and fishing with men friends. He had what the other sisters referred to euphemistically as an 'old fashioned view of women', as wives and mothers, but not companions. He enjoyed the company of pretty women, and felt no compulsion to give up his taste for variety once married. Moreover Georgie's frequent pregnancies excluded her from this category for much of the time. Besides this the difference in outlook between Georgie, with her vaguely radical political beliefs, her interest in scientific and historical questions, and her strange pantheistic approach to the world of nature, and Daniel, with his extremely conservative political views and his interest mainly in money, sport, and Society life, meant that they had no basis for companionship. Richard Potter, while not having anything against these interests, which he shared, was disturbed by Daniel's disinclination to engage in family life.[25] Daniel had no desire or ability to help or support Georgie either during pregnancy or in any aspect of childcare. Their letters to each other point to this again and again, as Georgie lamented her loneliness, her sense of ugliness during pregnancy, her feelings of inadequacy. Daniel never commented on these, telling her instead of his many social engagements and of his business and sporting triumphs. Georgie's letters are enlivened by her sense of humour and by a constant vein of whimsy and of self-deprecating irony which struck no response: Daniel's slightly pompous business-like missives were all she ever got in reply. Georgie came to accept the situation; indeed, she had no alternative. She was almost apologetic when she and the children moved into their London home in 1878 after a long spell away from Daniel. 'I shall be glad to get settled with the children and to see you again dear. I hope you won't mind having us. I never feel quite sure that you are not better pleased to be free to go your own way without me.'[26]

Where Georgie suffered both from Daniel's absences and from her recognition that he had no interest in her or in what she did, Blanche faced a rather more complex situation with Willie Cripps. She lived in London with him, so she did not have the long periods of separation experienced by other women who were based in the country while their husbands spent much time in Town. At the same time, Willie's profession demanded a great deal of his time and Blanche was often alone. A few months after her wedding, she wrote a sad letter to Beatrice telling of her isolation.

I see very little of Willie now, as he goes away early and comes home late and often has to go to various medical meetings, hospital cases etc., besides occasional Sunday work. He now has to attend the Royal Free for 4 and 5 hours twice or three times a week besides having the organisations of the Women's School there. There is one great charm to his profession; he does so thoroughly enjoy all his work, so different from the majority of men's occupations which are dry and comparatively uninteresting.[27]

Blanche coped with this by keeping very busy. She and Willie had little money in their first years of marriage and so she did a certain amount of housework as well as sewing in preparation for her babies. In addition she did a lot of work for Willie, using her considerable artistic talents to provide the illustrations for books he wrote on cancer of the rectum and on abdominal surgery. Blanche enjoyed some of this work. She was devoted to her husband, and was intensely interested in his medical career. Her diaries provide a detailed record of Willie's surgical work and career, noting the precise conditions of patients, the surgical procedure used, and their ultimate fate. Blanche believed in medicine as a noble profession and wanted to do her bit to help Willie. He was very demanding in this regard. He required not only illustrations, but also the copying out of manuscripts in Blanche's neat hand. Hence while he was not often with her, he insisted that she devote most of her time to his work. He often complained about the time which she spent with her children rather than working for him. Blanche's illustrations for Willie's books were extraordinary. Those done for his book *Cancer of the Rectum* are particularly strange: they were black and white drawings, made from microscopic slides, but they contain no suggestion of diseased cells.[28] Rather they look like exotic underwater caverns, filled with strange marine life. Her coloured pictures of abdominal sections published in Willie's book on abdominal surgery are almost as singular. They have a slightly bizzare touch, contributed by the way the skin is drawn back as if it were a theatre curtain, delicately held by hands at the side to reveal the organs underneath.[29]

Willie's behaviour towards Blanche was very unlike that of Daniel Meinertzhagen towards Georgie. He was jealous, exacting, peremptory, and selfish. At the same time, he cared for Blanche tenderly during her illnesses or confinements, not only ensuring her proper attention, but staying with her and often looking after her himself. Blanche in turn must have been very difficult to live with. Not only was she forgetful, emotionally unstable, and prone to breaking down completely under stress, but she lacked any ordinary political or social interests. She was always spoken of as a shadowy figure by her sisters, and she appears no less shadowy in her own diaries. These books, which she wrote regularly for nearly thirty years, list many of her activities and those of her husband. But they contain few statements of opinion and give one no sense of a personality. It is clear, however, that Blanche adored Willie and devoted herself to him. Willie demanded much, but he also coped

with her for many years, and in a way that few other men would have
done. In Beatrice's view, he was almost as strange as Blanche herself,
combining an appearance of caddishness and vulgarity with real
kindness. He was in her view both a cynic and an idealist. 'For twenty
years he remained Blanche's romantic lover, worshipping her mad
beauty and putting up with her innumerable and most aggravating
mistakes. The day came, when a woman who combined intellect, great
artistic talent, and considerable physical charm, crossed his path, and
since that day he has been an erring husband.'[30]

While one might sympathize with Willie's attraction to the young
opera singer, Giulia Ravogli, and understand also how in his forties he
fell into a relationship with a young woman overflowing with gratitude
to him for the excellent surgery he had done on her sisters, his behaviour to Blanche when this happened was almost incredibly cruel.
From the time that Willie met Giulia, she became a close part of his
family circle. She was invited regularly to Sunday meals and he often
took Blanche to visit her. She was a frequent guest at the Cripps's
holiday home in the north of Scotland, with Willie often sending
Blanche on ahead and only arriving for the time that Giulia was there.
He devoted time and money to her career, making Blanche organize
large parties at their home where Giulia would sing. As if the humilia-
tion and distress of this was not enough, Blanche had also to watch the
extreme harshness and financial miserliness with which Willie
behaved to their children, while he lavished money on his mistress.
Blanche's distress was increased by the way in which Willie's interest
in his career declined at much the same time as he became involved in
this relationship. Although he became a well-known and quite
successful surgeon, Willie never rose to the top of his profession. As
he became established, he began investing money and developed an
increasing interest in some of the businesses in which he had put
money. He became particularly interested in the Metropolitan
Electric Light Company—indeed, in 1900 he was made Chairman. His
instinct for commercial dealings made him a very wealthy man, but
Blanche had little interest in money and hated the way in which Willie
became more and more obsessed with it.

Willie met Giulia Ravogli in 1896. For the next four years, Blanche's
diaries record increasingly frequent meetings between herself and
Giulia. For some of the time, Blanche apparently tried to ignore the
real character of this relationship. She continued to work for Willie
and to devote herself to him and to their children. But her suspicions

grew, and by 1900 she could no longer bear it. In July of that year she went to visit Giulia and told her of all her own suspicions. Giulia was 'much surprised and grieved and would not at first believe it'. She denied any involvement with Willie: Blanche recorded that 'all doubts [were] cleared away immediately. Thank God for it!'[31] In a symbolic act of reconciliation, Blanche and Giulia ate lettuce together and exchanged sprigs of jasmine. But of course the denials of Willie and of Giulia were false and, as Blanche's deepening depression testifies, she found her life becoming ever more intolerable. Finally in 1905, after furnishing and making comfortable a new holiday home and ensuring that the children were more or less comfortable, Blanche hanged herself over a bath-tub. In Beatrice's view, this was exactly the kind of weird noble gesture Blanche would make, to free Willie to live a new life in his new home with a new young wife.[32] Blanche's own diaries suggest rather that, with Willie's new attachment, the life had gone out of her and that she could simply not bear to go on any longer.

Blanche tended to be excluded from the bonds of most of the other sisters. Taking little part in the political or social interests which they shared with each other, she saw them from time to time, but was never really close to them. There was, however, a strong bond of sympathy between her and Rosie, the other sister who was excluded from the general network. Blanche saw much of Rosie and sympathized with her unhappiness at home and in the course of her marriage to Dyson Williams. Willie too was called in to help diagnose the mysterious ailment which attacked Dyson soon after his wedding. The 'respectable young man', on whom the older Potter sisters felt it was almost a shame to inflict their difficult young sister had, as Rosie soon discovered, another side to his life. On their wedding night, as Rosie trembled with fear at the thought of what 'marital duty' entailed, Dyson told her about his past.

He insisted on my drinking some glasses of champagne which added to the one I had drunk at the breakfast had considerable effect on me. Over dinner he told me about his past life—the many affairs he had with women of all classes both married and single. His latest was the wife of a well-known Member of Parliament, a friend of the Courtneys in which he had narrowly escaped being co-respondent in a divorce case which would have caused a great scandal and perhaps have prevented our marriage .... Dyson then begged my forgiveness for his past life and promised always to be faithful to me, a promise which he kept substantially during our short married life.[33]

This was perhaps easier than expected for one of Dyson's previous habits, as his active sexual life lasted only two or three years after his marriage. In the course of his amorous adventures Dyson had contracted syphilis; indeed, he must already have been almost in the third stage of the disease by the time he married, for within about eighteen months he began to suffer from the intense pain and nausea which indicated the onset of spinal ataxia, from which he was to die in 1896.

Rosie indicates no shock at Dyson's revelations and subsequently, when he succumbed to temptation and slept with a young prostitute, she insists that she did not mind either. Indeed, as she often noted, her sexual jealousy was confined to her father and then to her sons—it was never directed to either of her husbands.

But life for the Williamses was not easy. The few letters from Dyson to Rosie which survive point to a relationship of constant stress and tension in which emotional scenes alternated with absences, and no basic *modus vivendi* was ever established. Dyson's letters indicate that part of the disharmony was caused by Rosie, whose later talent for always saying the wrong thing seems already to have been established. But his letters suggest not only that he was himself moody and erratic, but also that he had a mordant streak and a sharply witty turn of phrase well calculated to wound her. A letter he wrote shortly after he had stormed out of his aunt's house shows all of this—alongside a sort of helpless affection. 'My dear sweet wife without you I am hardly a living being and yet with you I am as you say an intolerably cantankerous beast; You always say something which pains me—you did tonight—but it pains me—if you could only understand because I am learning day by day to love you more and more. Darling love come and end my solitude *at any cost* even an eighteen penny fare.'[34]

Although it is clear that Rosie was sometimes difficult, there are many other letters from Dyson referring almost apologetically to his instigation of scenes and his savage behaviour during them. It is not unlikely that the pain he suffered, and indeed the whole of his illness, increased his irascibility. Letters like the following certainly suggest that this was so.

Dearest,

I thought of you all through my journey, my thoughts in connection with you not being altogether flattering to myself. For instance I thought of you as I saw you in the broad walk yesterday looking the worse for my bullying; a thin and drawn little face with a little bonnet perched upon your little head and a little thin body under all. Poor old woman I fear I lead you a devil of a life but I can assure you that I suffer when I think of my dreadful temper more than you can do .... Altogether how good and sweet you are and how little I do to reward you. However you may be sure that I love you more and more although I seem to become crosser and crosser as time goes on.[35]

In December 1889 their only son, Noel, was born and shortly after that Dyson began to develop the first of his symptoms: terrible fits of pain in his legs, which only gave way to large doses of morphia. For a long time his illness was not diagnosed, but it made the pursuit of a career at the Bar impossible. Dyson was advised to seek a warmer climate, and decided to try Egypt. He had first to spend some time in France, studying French and French law. He and Rosie were separated for several months at this time, although she joined him when his condition deteriorated and he needed her aid. In 1890 they sailed for Egypt and spent some months there. Dyson was not able to practise: he had originally been told that he did not require Arabic in order to practice law, and on arrival found that in fact he did. Moreover he remained unwell and was often unable to move from his bed. He studied Arabic to while away the time, while Rosie sketched and went sight-seeing.[36] They remained in Egypt for a couple of years, living comfortably enough on Rosie's income from her marriage settlement and the £400 a year Miss Williams gave Dyson. While they were there Richard Potter died, leaving Rosie quite a wealthy woman.

Shortly after that, in mid 1892, they returned to England living first in Oxford and later in London. In these years there was no suggestion that Dyson should work. His illness had at last been diagnosed, although no treatment was available apart from the large doses of morphia on which he was increasingly dependent. From 1894 onwards Dyson was immobilized, remaining in bed or sometimes being wheeled from one room to another in a chair.

Rosie, fortunately, was able to afford nursing help, although even with this her own life was fairly wretched. Mrs Thompson, the woman who had nursed Richard Potter through his last years, went to help her. Beatrice maintained that Rosie did nothing to help, and rather thwarted Mrs Thompson as a result of her jealousy. Although Rosie herself says nothing about this, she was jealous of Noel's nanny and was very likely to have felt the same about this competent woman who attempted to manage her whole family. Beatrice's description of the situation was, despite its odd mixture of contempt and sympathy for Rosie, probably fairly accurate.

... sad scenes at the Williamses. Dyson becoming a hopeless morphia and chloroform drunkard, the little boy nervous and ailing, Rosie a slave to her husband trying to recoup herself by having her own way in the management of her child. Mrs. Thompson suited them as a nurse to both husband and child—Rosie learning to hate her out of jealousy—she indescribably uncomfortable and wretched; trying her best to keep the child in health and the man from a suicidal death. Poor little weak miserly Rosie—a pitiable spectacle struggling on bravely enough but with an utter lack of grip and capacity.[37]

Beatrice felt that Rosie saved all her devotion and generosity for her husband, but Rosie herself did not see things in this way. Dyson's illness meant that for their last three or four years they did not have a sexual relationship and this, combined with the strain of constant attendance on him, told on Rosie's health; 'from frequent bad nights, and possibly from the celibate life I had been leading for the last three or four years . . . I grew thin, my monthly periods ceased, and I became neurotic and restless, full of disillusion and gloom.'[38] She longed for his death, but for years afterwards, possibly for the rest of her life, reproached herself with not having cared adequately for him. In a fit of acute depression in the mid 1920s, when she was prey to insomnia and various other nervous disorders, Rosie thought that these might all be punishments for her numerous 'crimes.'

Did I not at the last desert poor Dyson longing for his death which I may possibly have accelerated by my mean and criminal neglect of his comfort. Once I sacrificed myself to him but later I grew weary and longed for his death and meanly economised with his food possibly the thought that he would die the sooner even occurred to me. So I am a murderess perchance. For a time after his death the thought occurred. How well do I remember that last piteous scene when he no longer able to articulate tried to pronounce my name and I too late repentant tried to assure him of my love. How far I am guilty who can say.[39]

Beatrice's reference to Dyson as a 'semi criminal lunatic' in the Diary passage dealing with the Williams's tragedy suggests that at least some members of the family had an idea of the nature of Dyson's illness. There is, however, no discussion of it in the remaining papers—nor is there any suggestion that the rest of the family felt either remorse or guilt at having allowed and even encouraged Rosie to marry him.

After Dyson's death Rosie collapsed, and was ordered one of the 'rest cures' so favoured amongst Victorian doctors as a way of treating

women who had become frantic and hysterical through lack of interest
or activity. She was ordered complete bed rest, isolation from all
friends and relatives, total deprivation of all stimulus—and five large
meals a day. Her only respite during this ghastly ordeal was to listen to
the tales of her life recounted by her nurse. This young woman's *risqúe*
stories were accompanied by advice to Rosie to remarry as soon as
posible, as the only means whereby she would regain her health and
balance.[40]

The possibility of remarriage was presented shortly after this when
Rosie met a fashionable doctor who took a liking for both her and her
son, Noel. He proposed to her, and she was tempted to accept, recog-
nizing how suitable a marriage it would be. However, the first time he
attempted to touch her she recoiled, feeling 'as if a reptile had touched
me' and she felt quite unable to marry a man who filled her with
physical repugnance. True to her habitual prevarication and indecision, Rosie came to regret her decision as soon as he became engaged
to someone else, she even rushed back from Europe vainly seeking to
renew the relationship. But it was too late.

This episode provided Rosie herself with a clear insight into the
differences between herself and her sisters. All of them, she insists,
were very keen on her marrying the wealthy and respectable doctor,
and did everything they could to promote the match. Beatrice urged
Rosie to marry him, echoing the sentiments of Rosie's nurse—and
adding a bit of social prudence. 'She said one day to me "You need
marriage, physically, morally and mentally and you will not easily find
a more suitable man or one who will make a better stepfather to
Noel."' Margaret Hobhouse, who had earlier taken it upon herself to
explain the 'facts of life' to Rosie before her marriage, also urged her to
accept. She was even more insistent than Beatrice on the merits of the
match—from a wordly point of view—and she had no sympathy for
Rosie's physical repugnance. 'When I told her that I did not like
Drewitt personally enough to marry him she said that after we were
married it would come right, and added—"One man is as good as
another in that respect". I felt instinctively that for me at any rate this
would not be the case.'[41]

When her relationship with Drewitt came to an end Rosie went on
an extended trip to Europe, drifting in a leisurely fashion through
France, Switzerland, and Italy. Soon afterwards she began to realize
that her need and desire for sexual relationships did not have to be
accompanied by marriage—and without delay she began to act on this

realization. For the next two years, Rosie alternated between European travel and spells in her London flat. Both modes of life offered
her introductions to a variety of men with many of whom she had
affairs. A couple of these were friends of her sisters. Others were
headmasters of prominent boys' schools—and pillars of the community. From her experiences she gathered a quite new sense of the
actual conduct of the world in which she lived, and of the discrepancies between this and its articulation of morality.

For all her hesitancy over whether or not to accept the men who
proposed to her, Rosie was neither hesitant nor backward in seeking
or establishing new relationships. In the course of her travels she
stayed for some time at Capri. On her arrival, she tipped the head
waiter and asked to be seated next to any nice-looking Englishmen
who were staying at the hotel. That evening she found herself next to
two pleasant-looking young Irishmen—with one of whom she rapidly
fell in love. George Dobbs felt much the same, and they spent a few
blissful weeks roaming the island and luxuriating in its natural beauty.
In the course of this they became lovers. But Dobbs was only on a
short holiday and soon returned to Ireland with the young man whom
he had been accompanying. Rosie received a telegram from one of her
other lovers who had wished to meet her in Europe.

That afternoon in a fit of repentance and rather hysterical emotion I confided
all to G.C.D. and told him the story of the past three years of my life, and so
forged a link between us that ultimately sealed our fate. He was evidently
shocked by my story for though he himself was my lover he did not know that I
had others, and though no puritan, he was a clean minded young man and had
strict Irish ideas about the purity of women.[42]

After Rosie had met Dobbs she met and had an affair with George
Gissing, to whom she was also strongly attracted. Gissing and Dobbs
represent the essential conflict which underlay Rosie's life at this stage
and subsequently—and which she never managed to resolve. She
always wanted to marry a man who would be comparable to her
brothers-in-law, and who would 'have some real and permanent
interest in life and be doing something in the world'. Moreover she
sought a mentor and intellectual guide:

Since my first great affection and intimacy with my father I have had a great
longing to understand and enter into the mind of some man who was my
intellectual superior and to make my mind as if it were a mirror of his. I have
little or no independent intellectual life or originality of my own, and am, in

fact a sort of mental parasite and when I have no one to cling to my mind sinks into a sort of stupor.[43]

Gissing represented precisely this idea of a superior mind—but he was still locked into his disastrous marriage to Edith Underwood and was seeking a companion who would live with him without marriage. Whether or not he seriously wished Rosie to do so is something one will never know—but in any event it was quite impossible for her to flout openly the conventions of her society. Rosie does not say anything about the sexual side of this relationship, but one gathers that it was not quite all she wished from her comments about George Dobbs. Unquestionably Dobbs was the great sexual passion of her life, and the only lover who provided her with real sexual pleasure. When they became lovers, 'for the first time in my life I gave myself with joy and experienced in his arms the ecstacy of physical love, when for a few brief moments all is forgotten and one becomes united in body and soul with the loved one. In such an experience there is no sense of sin or degradation which otherwise even in marriage may accompany the sexual act.'[44] But Dobbs was a man without a profession, wandering rather aimlessly around looking for one. He attracted Rosie both physically and morally—he was, as she said again and again, 'a pure man'. But they shared no interests. Although Rosie sought intellectual interests, the two things which really mattered to her were an appreciation of natural beauty and questions of a religious and spiritual nature. Dobbs, by contrast, read a little, but was happiest when engaged in sport or bridge. Their resulting relationship was a stormy and strange one in which ties of affection, based largely on physical need, were combined with complete opposition of temperament and outlook. Rosie was apparently a quite execrable housekeeper, whose total lack of capacity to establish order or harmony in a home was matched only by her capacity to turn out consistently inedible meals.[45] Dobbs, who liked harmony and order, found this intolerable. For some of their married life this problem was solved by George living in hotels in Switzerland and close to Rosie's villa. There he had both the comfort he liked and the constant social life and activity on which he depended. Rosie in turn had her familiar chaos—and the beautiful sunsets and sunrises which alone brought her a real sense of harmony and peace.

But the Dobbs's more or less peaceful life in Switzerland followed on from an incomparably stormy beginning. During this Rosie was again subjected to the outrage of her sisters—and indeed to the full force of their combined censure. Rosie took a long time to decide whether or not to marry George, and only agreed to do so when he issued an ultimatum: either they marry or the relationship would have to end. Rosie felt fearful and vulnerable about this: she had told George about her past and was terrified that he would tell her sisters. As it was, they had heard much gossip. They accepted her engagement to Dobbs, although he, like Dyson Williams, was a man that none of them would have contemplated for themselves. In both cases, their acceptance was made more enthusiastic than it would otherwise have been because of their relief at having Rosie temporarily taken off their hands. In the case of George this was especially so, as they had become aware of Rosie's behaviour and greatly feared the possibility of an open scandal. Their knowledge and their fears were expressed in a letter from Beatrice Webb to Mary Playne.

I am very sorry to hear your bad impression of Rosie. . . . I do not however think that she is going to have a baby; the matron told Kate that her Periods were regular and her figure is frequently out of order from indigestion. However I should not be in the least surprised if she were. I don't think that Rosie with her character and her physique is likely to keep 'straight' if she does not get married. I am not sure that *sanity and celibacy* are both within her capacity. Unfortunately I don't believe that her sisters have any power over her. I spoke to her very seriously the other day and told her that her family would drop her if she behaved improperly and that she would find life unendurable if she was cut by every respectable person; but she assured me that she was the best and purest of women and devoted to Noel . . . . of course if she got into actual trouble, we could unite together and insist on her having a guardian lady of our choosing with her or definitely refuse to see her again. But before we know that she has behaved improperly it is difficult to do anything.[46]

Beatrice also knew that Rosie and George had been lovers and hoped despite the contempt she felt for the lack of restraint that this showed, that the marriage would work out and ensure that Rosie settled down. But this was not to be, at least not immediately.

After they married, Rosie and George settled in London while George tried to find work. Rosie had broken with all her lovers prior to the wedding, but she continued to paint in the studio of an artist, identified by her only as Cyril, a man whom she admired and with whom she worked for some years. She had told Cyril about her affairs and, shortly after her marriage, he began to insist that she should have an affair with him—or cease coming to the studio. This relationship was one she clung to desperately as it was the only one which offered her genuine companionship. For all her passion for George, this was absent from their life together. So she succumbed to Cyril despite the fact that 'physically he repelled me in the same way that Drewitt had done'. George was miserable and suspicious throughout the early years of their marriage and, eventually, shortly after the birth of their first child, Rosie told him about her affair. George responded by bursting into tears and then, in a fit of fury, setting off for the studio to administer a horse-whipping to Cyril. He did not do so, for on his arrival Cyril took fright and promised to end the relationship. Not content with this, George went off to tell Maggie Hobhouse about Rosie's behaviour, a step as Rosie later wrote 'not calculated to improve our relationship'. Soon all the sisters knew and they responded by bringing the full weight of their disapproval—backed by the punitive authority of the medical profession—to bear on Rosie. She was hauled before a panel of medical specialists who, after an hour of interrogation, pronounced her to be on the verge of insanity. Her own sense that this was rather a criminal trial than anything therapeutic was reinforced by the letter she received the following day from Beatrice, 'saying that if I did not take care I should find myself in a lunatic asylum and that both my children, Noel and Pat, would be taken away from me'. Feeling understandably defenceless and vulnerable, Rosie could do nothing. A few weeks later she and George went away together to try and patch up their relationship.

We were neither of us happy for I constantly regretted my lover and friends and could not forget them whilst G.C.D. guessing my thoughts upbraided me with them. Violent scenes during the day alternated with reconciliations at night for we were still lovers. Then suddenly after one violent scene we both gave way he promising to forgive and forget and allowing the freedom I wanted to remain always physically faithful to him and to try to forget Cyril. And this promise we have both kept. He has not interfered with my friendships with men and I can say that from that day I have never allowed any man to make love to me though I have had friendships with several nor have I been tempted to do so for I have loved G.C.D. with all the personal love I am capable of. Besides as years went by and Noel grew up I turned more and more to him for companionship and sympathy.[47]

Besides, shortly after this Rosie had another child, and then three more, and much of her time was occupied in supervising them in her scatter-brained way. The extent of the trauma that this involved is evident in the feverish way Rosie wrote about it many years later. She felt profoundly guilty—and not a little resentful that George had brought her sisters into their affairs. However, they subsequently settled into a more or less satisfying life in Switzerland, so the family was seen only on visits when Rosie needed them to house her growing brood.

VII

Domesticity and Motherhood

MARRIAGE for the Potter sisters was the prelude to establishing a home and assuming domestic responsibility. For most of them, this was closely followed by motherhood. The experience of housekeeping which most of the sisters had received in their late adolescence enabled them to manage their own homes with ease. Some new responsibilities were added to those they had known at Standish; they had now to hire and dismiss domestic staff, manage the household budget, set up a nursery, and arrange for much of the extensive social life which they followed as young matrons. In addition to these tasks, which had earlier been undertaken by Lawrencina, there was a range of new activities and responsibilities which accompanied the transformation of domestic life brought by industrialization. The advent of gas, improvements in plumbing, and new technology like the sewing machine involved changing patterns of consumption and the acquisition of some knowledge and supervisory skills, to say nothing of the upheavals in each household caused by the introduction of new methods, new commodities, and new staff.

Domestic life did not usually involve actual physical labour for the Potters. Blanche was an exception, albeit a temporary one, as she had to undertake some domestic work for a short while. Rosie, too, was an exception as in her later years she spent much of her time cleaning the homes of her children in an attempt to expiate her own sense of inadequacy as a mother. But these were the only two brief departures from the norm according to which, as Beatrice said, her family gave orders rather than obeying the orders of others. At the same time, the domestic life of the Potter sisters, like that of other Victorian women, was directed towards the comfort of their husbands rather than themselves. Home was their place of work, even if that work was of the executive and managerial kind undertaken by their husbands rather than manual labour. The smooth running of that home was often a time-consuming and arduous task, especially when it was accompanied by the care of children and by the need to provide extensive hospitality to family and friends.

I

The exact size and scale of the homes run by the Potter sisters after marriage varied according to the income and resources of their husbands. Most of them, however, married within the approved framework of their class and hence began married life in a substantial and comfortable home. Lallie, for example, began married life in the home of her mother-in-law, but moved within a few months to a new house which Robert Holt had had built. It was a double-storeyed house with ample entertaining space and bedrooms for its owners and their guests. Lallie began with three servants and soon added to their number, as the arrival of children meant employing a nurse, a nanny, and then a governess. A cook, a waitress, and a maid were, in Lallie's view, the minimum requirements of civilized life and she was fortunately never forced to attempt life without them.[1] Mary Playne began her married life at Longfords, the gracious country home which her husband had inherited and which, from the very beginning of her married life, provided a comfortable rural retreat and convalescent home for any sister in need of such a place. Georgie and Theresa both began in rented homes, but this did not mean that they were in any discomfort. Indeed Theresa was thrilled with the small rented house she and Alfred took in Mayfair. When they moved in, they found that Mrs Jones, 'our Irish landlady, had ordered such lovely flowers and plants and made everything so pretty for us. She is really a most generous landlady and has left out all her plate and table linen for our use and the three servants are well disposed to us and the cook excellent.'[2] The Crippses, like the Hobhouses, had a country residence as well as a London one and this, while requiring some administrative skill from the young wives who had to run two establishments, was obviously an indication of both affluence and comfort. Kate and Beatrice both married men whose incomes were markedly smaller than those of the Holts, Playnes, Crippses, or Hobhouses, but none the less they began married life in substantial London homes. Leonard and Kate had the lease on a charming house in Cheyne Walk where they spent the rest of their lives. Beatrice and Sidney spent a short time in Hampstead before moving to the formidable establishment so well known to Fabian circles at 41 Grosvenor Road.

The affluence of the Potters, and the lavish life led at Standish, inevitably set a standard for the sisters which made their own homes seem smaller and humbler than they were. Beatrice, after all her years of housekeeping for her father, was particularly imbued with Standish values. Her cousin, Mary Booth, wrote in some amusement about the impoverishment which Beatrice saw as the necessary consequence of her marrying Sidney Webb.

The difficulty about marrying is that until uncle R dies, she thinks they will not have enough to live on. As she has £400 p.a. now, and he has enough to keep himself even if he leaves the Colonial Office, I don't see the difficulty. Beatrice talks a little comically about the extreme poverty of her marriage, her willingness to live in the humblest middle class style and her indifference to the probable disapproval of us grand folk—ignoring the fact that she and Mr Webb will have a much larger income than the greater number of people we know at all intimately,—larger than that of the Marshalls, Sidgwicks etc.[3]

Beatrice was spared this fate by postponing her marriage until after her father's death, when she inherited an income of more than £1,000 per annum.

The values of Standish and the expectation of affluence were very much evident in the response of the sisters to the domestic situation of Blanche and Willie. The Harrison Crippses were the only couple, apart from the Williamses, for whom marriage was not followed by the immediate establishment of a comfortable home. Blanche and Willie began their life together in a very small flat in Victoria Street, too small even to enable Blanche to invite her sisters to stay. Their household staff was correspondingly small and Blanche had only one servant. Hence during her first years of marriage, she found herself very much occupied in 'getting things straight, needlework and little household jobs'.[4] By the standards of most Victorians, Blanche and Willie lived in great comfort. But by Potter standards they lived in miserable poverty. It was not until November 1878, shortly after the birth of their second child, that Blanche and Willie moved into a home of their own. Their taking of a whole house was greeted with great rejoicing by the other sisters. 'You will be glad to hear', Maggie wrote to Beatrice, 'that the Cripps have taken no. 6 Stratford Place out of Oxford Street, large, rent £260, premium £100 for 3 years. At last the poor things will have where [*sic*] to lay their heads. I do trust that they will get on now.'[5] Their new home did not bring any immediate relief to Blanche. A year later, in 1879, Theresa wrote to Beatrice that Blanche was 'getting rather overdone what between nursing the baby entirely and walking the chicks out, doing the housekeeping and devoting every spare moment in the evening to Willie's microscope drawings and writing for him, that as she put it with a tragical look at dinner the other night, she feels more like "an overburdened ass" than a human being.'[6] But as Willie began to establish himself they moved into an even larger house, described as 'palatial' by Theresa, and employed a full-time housekeeper who took over all the household management and the supervision of the children, as well as being a companion to Blanche.

Although the domestic burden carried by the Potter sisters was less heavy than that of poorer women who toiled throughout the day, it was not always easy. Domestic supervision was sometimes onerous and things did not always work out as planned. Lallie, for example, found herself facing a confinement just at the time that her domestic staff was in a state of total disarray.

First I found that Grace had got the influenza and was fit only for bed and the doctor. That though troublesome was nothing in itself. But then Caroline made an announcement to the effect that my new waitress was going to be married as soon as I was all right again and was not in a condition to make it desirable to keep her and certainly would not look fit to open the door in another month's time. Funny such a thing in a person with an excellent character and from friends. ... Robert and I agreed that it would not be creditable to keep her or even quite safe as no one knew what may happen and it would not be pleasant to have her being laid up at the same time as me. So have been waitress hunting since Monday.[7]

On top of this, Lallie had just received a letter from the woman she had engaged to be her monthly nurse, saying that she had recently fallen down some stairs and injured herself and hence would not be able to come. 'I don't think I ever felt so inclined to sit down and cry in my life', she wrote to her mother, 'but I thought better of it and got into the brougham instead and went in search of two nurses I knew of so as to lose no time.' Fortunately one of these nurses, the one she liked more, was able to come to her aid and so the emergency passed.

II

Problems like those faced by Lallie during her first confinement were in part a result of the fact that pregnancy followed so closely after marriage, usually while the young couple was still in the process of settling into a first home. The Potter family as a whole was merciless in this regard, putting pressure on its members to produce children almost immediately after marriage. Lallie, the first to marry, was particularly subject to pressure on this point. A couple of months after her marriage, she wrote somewhat ruefully to her mother about the need for patience.

As for your hopes of multiplication you are nearly as bad as Margaret who suggests the arrival of ten cousins at once and Kate too puts in her word for the nephews and nieces. I asked Robert what he said to your idea of such a tribe as the Standish one and he said he would think nine rather many but better than none so you see Mama if it was only for wishing there would be no delay but wishing does not do many things and there is nothing for it but waiting patiently.[8]

Lallie's first baby was born just eleven months after she married, so the waiting was certainly not protracted. She went on to have eight children, just one short of the official Standish total. Hers was the second largest family amongst the sisters: Georgie outdid her by having ten children, Maggie came after her with seven, followed by Blanche with six, and by Theresa and Rosie each with five children.

The Potters tended to follow Lallie in what was a quite common Victorian practice: that of giving birth within the first year of marriage. After that, the spacing varied considerably.[9] Lallie had her second child one year after the first and then another two years later. Georgie had three children within four years in the early part of her marriage and then, after a break of two years, another two within a two year period. Maggie Hobhouse had her first four children all within a period of five and a half years. As one would expect, the spacing between babies increased as the sisters aged. Georgie's last four children, all of whom were born when she was in her thirties and early forties, were separated by at least two years each. Lallie's last three children were also more widely spaced, as were those of Blanche. In addition to those pregnancies which led to live births, several of the sisters had miscarriages. Georgie was particularly prone to this and as a result was forced to be very careful during all her pregnancies. The size of their families and the increasingly wide gaps between children in the later years meant that some of the sisters were involved in childbearing for a very long time. Lallie and Maggie both had childbearing periods of fourteen years, while Georgie and Rosie exceeded this by having periods of seventeen years.

Recently there has been much discussion of changing demographic patterns in the last quarter of the nineteenth century and of the probable use of contraception amongst professional and upper-middle-class families. Patricia Branca has argued that although the major decline in family size, as evidenced from figures for the gross national birth-rate, can be dated from the mid-1870s, middle-class women began to use contraception and limit family size at least two decades before that.[10] Her insistence on the role of women in initiating contraception was intended to counter the argument of J. A. Banks, who had earlier insisted that it was middle-class and professional men who began to limit the size of their families in the 1870s, as the depression of that decade, combined with rising prices, made family limitation imperative for those who did not choose to suffer a deterioration in their standard of living.[11] Interesting as both of these arguments are, the Potter sisters provide no support for either. Indeed the thing that seems most evident about them is that they exercised no control over their fertility—even though some of them regretted their many pregnancies. This is the more interesting in that if one looks at the sisters overall, there is a significant decline in fertility as compared with their mother. Lawrencina Potter gave birth to ten children. Her daughters bore on average 4.77 children. But this average is in one sense artificially low. Two of the sisters had no children: Kate because she was unable to and Beatrice because she chose not to. One other, Mary, had one child and then a 'serious operation' which brought an end to her childbearing. The remaining daughters then averaged 7 births—and here it must be remembered that some of them married at a considerably later age than was customary amongst their class and indeed at a much later age than did their mother. Theresa was nearly thirty when she married, and died just twelve years after that. Maggie and Blanche both married in their late twenties and hence were like Theresa in having shortened considerably their peak fertility period. As one would expect, the two largest families, those of Georgie and Lallie, were produced by the two sisters who married in their very early twenties. In Georgie's case, moreover, it is clear that her family was only limited to ten by the fact that several other pregnancies were terminated by miscarriage.

It does not really come as a surprise to see that the Potter sisters did not engage in deliberate attempts to limit their families. Despite recent assertions to the contrary, it is clear that birth-control information was not widely disseminated in the later part of the nineteenth century.[12] The few explicit tracts which dealt with it, those by Richard Carlile and James Knowlton in particular, were read by radical artisans and 'progressive' groups, rather than by the established and upper-middle-class circles to which the Potters belonged. Moreover, although they had a medical brother-in-law, it seems unlikely that Willie Cripps ever offered any advice on the subject, if indeed he used it himself.[13] He and Blanche had six children, and would have had more had she not been seriously ill as the result of an ectopic pregnancy. In view of her precarious mental state and her complete inability to look after some of the children, this seems a large number.

The Potter family as a whole seems to have accepted that the years of childbearing would be ones of relative financial hardship. Richard and Lawrencina did what they could to help but this hardship was accepted as a temporary fact of life rather than being seen as a reason for family limitation. It is also the case that for the older sisters the numbers of children they had did not in any way reduce their standard of living. The depression of the 1870s and the rising prices of subsequent decades were more than matched by the increase in income within the family. In some cases this was a result of rising in status within a profession. Both Cripps brothers, for example, increased their income quite rapidly during the 1880s and 1890s as Alfred became a leading QC and Willie a very successful surgeon. Daniel Meinertzhagen too rose in wealth and status as he became one of the two senior partners at Huth and Co. In a similar way Robert Holt's cotton-broking business continued to be a prosperous one and he extended his range somewhat by engaging in other forms of imports. Henry Hobhouse was the one potentially most vulnerable to the depression of the 1870s and 1880s because of his dependance on rents from his estate and his abandonment of a legal career. These rents declined drastically: from £2,350 in 1880 to £821 in 1894, the year in which the last Hobhouse child was born. However, this decline was more than made up for by the increase in income from the investments on which the Hobhouses' comfort depended. Here the figures are almost reversed as Hobhouse's income from investments increased from £1,203.7.0. in 1884 to £2,466 in 1894. In this case, as in all the others, the substantial increase in income which accrued to each daughter after the death of Richard Potter in 1892 provided a lavish boost to their standard of living. In 1894 Maggie's income from investments was £1,026—a healthy second income by almost any standards.[14]

Rather than experiencing constraints of the kind that have been seen to cause family limitation, the Potter sisters and their husbands were imbued with a sense of their responsibility to help populate the nation and the empire. Large families were, in their view, a part of the civic responsibility of people of their class. It is perhaps ironic that Beatrice, who felt this most strongly—as regards other women—was the one sister who decided against having children. Indeed although Beatrice and Sidney decided against having a family, on the grounds that it would impair their general usefulness, Beatrice was never quite at ease with the decision. She was hostile to birth control in a general way, regarding it as a dereliction of one's duty as a citizen, which included having children. She also saw it as part of a shift in morality which made 'irregular' sexual liaisons more possible, and she was never happy about this. Even though she was very much aware that companionate marriage was more possible without children, she was concerned about the self-indulgence this entailed. In 1896 she and Sidney spent a week with a group of intellectual friends which included Bertrand and Alys Russell. She enjoyed both the holiday and the companionship immensely—but saw it as flawed.

So far as I can see there is only one serious criticism on the lives of the six persons gathered together in a Surrey cottage on this lovely June day—*no children*—all too intellectual or strenuous to bear children! whether the omission is 'intentional' or 'inevitable' does not much matter from the community's point of view. There is obviously some flaw in these ideal marriages of pure companionship—can we afford that these rather picked individuals shall remain childless? Is less highly wrought material better to breed from? I, at least, can fall back with complacency on the 37 nephews and nieces who are carrying on the 'Potter' stock and so far unperturbed with ideas or enthusiasm.[15]

There is no hint as to what form of contraception Beatrice and Sidney used although one of Sidney's letters does suggest that it was Beatrice rather than he who had any technical knowledge of the subject.[16] But for them at least motherhood was an issue of choice. For the rest of the Potter sisters, it would seem that far from having any control over their fertility or reproduction, they were victims of their own childbearing capacities. This would seem to be so even for Rosie, particularly when she was married. Rosie avoided becoming pregnant in the years during which she was having her various affairs. It is possible, even probable, that she used some form of contraception then. But this ceased with her second marriage and she became pregnant early, indeed within the first year of marriage. This happened before she and George had sorted out their life together and during the time she was having her affair with 'Cyril'. The child was an additional cause of conflict and was rejected by both her and George, he on the grounds that he was not sure that Pat was actually his son. Rosie welcomed her later pregnancies, as she had the one from her marriage to Dyson. But this pregnancy she did not want and, or so it would seem, would have avoided had the possibility of doing so easily within marriage been available to her.

To use the term 'victim' of some of the Potter sisters is perhaps an overstatement since although they did nothing to limit the number of children they bore, they seem genuinely to have wanted and welcomed them. It is, however, an absolutely accurate description of Georgie. Motherhood may have been a woman's highest calling, but in her case both it and its prelude were periods of loneliness, isolation, and misery. During her first pregnancies, Georgie lived in a house Daniel had rented at Wallop while he remained in London, visiting her sometimes at weekends. The unmarried sisters were called into duty at this time and often went to stay with her. This arrangement was not entirely satisfactory as the isolation and tedium of life at Wallop told on them too. Even Maggie, who was supremely equipped to take advantage of whatever social life and interesting events there were, was defeated by it. After a couple of weeks she wrote to Beatrice that she was 'beginning to get homesick and should take the first train to Standish were it not for Georgie, who, poor girl, would be too terribly lonely here ... Its frightfully dull here.'[17]

Georgie soon began to travel around during her pregnancies. Sometimes this was in order to have help and care for herself of the kind she was only able to get from her parents or married sisters in comfortable homes of their own. She also spent some time at seaside resorts in pursuit of healthy air for herself and the growing number of children.

Although these visits and the company of her family alleviated her situation somewhat, they did not make her pregnancy or her sense of loneliness much easier to bear. Georgie was one of the most elegant of the Potter sisters and found the physical changes of pregnancy distasteful. When staying with her family, she did not engage much in social life. Despite their entreaties to go out, she 'steadily refused to adorn the common with my engaging figure'. She disliked the heaviness and the clumsiness of pregnancy, and felt awkward at her inability to keep up with her sisters on walks. Only other women in a like predicament brought her comfort, as she wrote to Daniel while she was pregnant with her second child.

I find Mrs. Martin is in my happy condition, and looks it too; which makes me feel particularly comfortable. There is nothing like 'birds of a feather' for mes pleasures [*sic*] in society, and I have at present a particular animosity towards slight cool looking young married ladies. I can't help thinking they hop about, run and play lawn tennis to spite me.[18]

She was one of the heaviest smokers amongst the sisters—and the effort to refrain from this during pregnancy was yet another trial.

Daniel offered no support to Georgie during either her pregnancies or her difficult periods of dealing with ailing small children. He organized both his work and his social life to suit himself and made no concessions to Georgie's condition. His fondness for the society of attractive women and his lack of interest in those who did not comply with his standards of elegance increased Georgie's misery and insecurity during pregnancy. On one occasion, when she thought she was pregnant with her third child, they had both been invited to spend a few days with some of his friends. She thought she would be unable to go, but there was no thought that this would in any way alter his plans. Her letter is particularly interesting because of its clear indication that she did not want this pregnancy, but did not choose to act in a way likely to lead to its abrupt termination.

I have not come any nearer to solving my difficulty, but I feel so seedy and backachy whenever I move that I very much fear I shan't be able to travel on Thursday. Your mother says it is not safe under the circumstances. I should not like to be laid up in London for a week alone in our empty house . . .

If I don't feel all right tomorrow, I shall write to tell Mrs. Goschen to expect you without me on Friday. It is very tiresome as I should like to go with you there so much. We don't often go together anywhere. I am quite certain *if* there is a baby in the question, it only requires a little extra exertion on my part to take its departure very shortly; and although I could have done without another just now I don't like parting with it in that way.[19]

Georgie's repeated pregnancies were a source of worry to her sisters as well as to herself. Kate was present during one of the miscarriages and was shocked at how bad Georgie looked. Mary Playne, who often ran Longfords as a kind of convalescent home for her family and friends, wrote to Beatrice in the mid 1880s, 'Georgie came on Saturday looking wretchedly ill, but seems better already taking care of herself. Will you have us all on Saturday week the 2nd October? . . . The Argoed will set her up for the winter, if she will avoid the chance of babies.'[20] But the babies continued until Georgie turned 40 and, despite the strain and her continual smoking, her health did stand up to it. In her later years some at least of her children were her closest companions and greatest consolation.

As Georgie's experiences make clear, the Potters were all heavily dependent upon each other and on their parents during pregnancy and confinement. Unmarried sisters went to stay with others when needed, and in some cases married sisters were prepared to leave their own homes to attend each other. When Blanche was facing her first confinement, both Theresa and Georgie were prepared to go and stay with her. The sisters all swapped information and advice, ranging from the names of good monthly nurses through patterns for baby clothes and recipes for breast ointments. They also offered to have young nephews and nieces to stay in order to reduce the load of responsibility faced by any sisters having to cope with new babies. Lawrencina and Richard Potter also played their part and during the 1870s, Standish frequently housed young Holts and Meinertzhagens as new ones made their way into the world.

This does not mean that husbands themselves played no part in the preparation for or reception of babies and small children. Some, like Daniel Meinertzhagen, absented themselves from the entire process of pregnancy and childbirth. But others were considerably more involved. Willie Cripps attended throughout the birth of his and Blanche's babies and helped nurse Blanche during her entire confinement. It seems likely that his medical training and his concern for Blanche's health were the main motivating forces in this, for in subsequent years he was not closely involved with the children. It is not clear whether other Potter husbands were present during childbirth. Robert Holt and Alfred Cripps were certainly at home when their children were born and had been involved in planning for the care of children. From the moment of birth, however, it was clear that the fundamental responsibility for the care of children was taken by their mothers.

III

Motherhood in the nineteenth century was subject to almost as many warnings, injunctions, and instructions as it is today. The social moralists, the clergy, educationalists, advocates of 'woman's mission', and increasingly the medical profession, all wrote at length about the duties which motherhood comprised and the ways in which these should be carried out. Then, as now, there was a considerable range of opinion concerning every aspect of mothering and childcare: how children should be fed, who should look after them and how this should be done, when education should begin and who should take charge of it. All of these questions were constantly debated as part of the general discussion about the exact role of mothers in the nursery and in the education of the young.

As one moves through the course of the century, there are distinct changes in general ideas about mothering. The role of mothers became more and more extensive from the middle of the century onwards. In the early years of the century, concern was focused on the moral welfare of children and, for the middle classes, on the question of whether servants were really fit to provide the moral guidance required by young children. There was much stress in educational literature, in sermons, and in the many works on the duties of women, on the need for mothers to spend time with children and to ensure adequate supervision of their daily life. In the later decades of the century, concern shifted rather more to the physical well-being of children, and mothers were constantly charged with the importance of feeding and bringing up their young in accordance with the current dictates of science. The health of the nation, the empire, and the race became matters of general concern in the later nineteenth century and instructions to mothers became the favoured method of ensuring a healthy population. Motherhood was thus regarded as immensely important, too important to be left to mere women. The late part of the century saw not only an immense flow of books to instruct women on how to mother properly, but also the start of centres for maternal education and childcare. Most of these were directed to working-class women, but the emphasis on proper and scientific mothering was towards middle-class women as well. Indeed every aspect of motherhood was subject to discussion and debate as motherhood came to be seen as the most important aspect of a woman's life.[21]

The complex interweaving of scientific, medical, and moral ideas about motherhood is evident not only in debates but also in the very process of childbirth itself. Thus many doctors opposed the introduction of chloroform and other anaesthetics during childbirth on the grounds that they were 'contrary to the sound principles of physiology and morality, "In sorrow shalt thou bring forth children" was an established law of nature—an ordinance of the Almighty. It was not right to abrogate that law.'[22]

The Potter sisters mostly seem to have given birth without the benefits of anaesthetic. They were fortunate in being able to have their babies at home, thus avoiding the very high risk of puerperal fever which was incurred by those forced to use hospitals. The sisters were all attended by a doctor and by a monthly nurse. In Blanche's case, concern about her somewhat precarious emotional state also made Willie engage the services of a retired doctor who moved into their house during some of her confinements. The Potters were on the whole a very healthy family and survived their many confinements remarkably well. Their babies did so too, which suggests that little medical intervention was required. The state of obstetric knowledge and the design of obstetric instruments in the later nineteenth century made any form of intervention in childbirth a hazardous matter.[23] Only one of the sisters was ever seriously ill during childbirth: Theresa had a difficult first labour and required surgical help. Her doctor operated badly and for some days she was feverish and very ill. The family feared that she would develop pyaemia, and the lack of antiseptic precautions in childbirth made this very likely. Willie Cripps came to the rescue, however, rushing to her bedside and nursing her through to health. The presence of Willie was a substantial benefit to the family. He was both a skilled surgeon and an ardent advocate of antisepsis. The fact that he was called in to assist with the obstetric problems of the sisters increased their chances of survival.[24]

Once babies were born, the first issue to be dealt with was that of feeding. Breast-feeding by the mother was unquestionably the best source of nourishment for a baby, particularly in the absence of any adequate or satisfactory alternative to breast milk. There was no readily available infant formula in the late nineteenth century, nor were there any easily used or sterilizable bottles. Hence breast-feeding it was, if that was possible. The sisters seem to have breast-fed if they were able to do so. Lallie, Blanche, Theresa, and Maggie all did this for all their children. But it was not always possible for a mother to breast-feed. Georgie, although she breast-fed some of her children, was unable to feed all of them. Rosie too had to have other assistance.

The main alternative to breast-feeding for upper-middle-class women was the employment of a resident wet-nurse. This practice was, however, coming into disrepute by the time the Potter sisters were having children. There was some discussion in the press and in literary works of the iniquity of wet-nursing on account of the sufferings it entailed for the nurse and for her own unfortunate baby—who was likely to be sent to a baby farmer and to die as a result of maternal neglect.[25] But this humanitarian concern was of less significance to the Potters and to most other upper-middle-class women than was the fear of the deleterious consequences for their children of imbibing the milk of a woman who was socially, physically, and morally inferior to themselves. The Potter sisters have left no records of the ways in which they chose wet-nurses, or of the fears which surrounded this choice. Their cousin Mary Booth, however, left a series of letters describing how she set about finding a wet-nurse for her second daughter whom she was unable to feed herself. The minute she needed a wet-nurse, all the lying-in hospitals which were reputed to have lists of women seeking such an appointment seemed to have closed or to have no one on their books. Moreover, she was beset on all sides with dire threats of the appalling fate to which her daughter would be consigned if fed by a wet-nurse. She sent her husband a list of the things which she had now heard of as the consequences of having a wet-nurse. She was threatening her child with '(1) scrofula in all its forms, (2) consumption, (3) dypsomania, (4) murderous propensity, (5) vice and (6) insanity. Poor dear little Meg!', she added ruefully, but the experience had quite unnerved her.[26] In the end she found a patient woman who hand-fed Meg with a bottle. The Potter sisters seem to have had happier experiences than this: Georgie found a wet-nurse for a couple of her children, as did Rosie for hers. But sometimes other expedients were used: one of Georgie's babies was fed on donkey's milk—and survived, although she seemed to thrive rather less than did Theresa's baby, who was being breast-fed at the same time.[27]

The Potter sisters proved remarkably successful at feeding and caring for their babies: not a single death occurred during this most tenuous stage of life. Indeed there was only one death amongst the children of any of the sisters during infancy: Maggie lost a daughter, through a sudden and severe attack of croup. The child, Esther, was 2 at the time and had been very well prior to this, so it came as a shock to all. For Maggie herself this was a terrible tragedy, made worse by the death of Theresa just a few weeks later. Looking back, however, one extraordinary feature of the Potter family was its capacity for survival at a time when epidemics and infantile diseases were responsible for the deaths of so many children.

Once babies were weaned and moved into the next stage of infancy, the Potter sisters faced a whole new series of questions and decisions about mothering. The crucial question here was how much involvement mothers had with their children and how much of the care of the children they actually undertook themselves. Right from the start, the care of their children was undertaken with the help of servants. All the babies had nannies or nurses to look after them. As they grew older their staff increased as it began to include a governess and perhaps tutors alongside nannies. But while the Potter sisters all had quite large household staffs, with particular people designated to look after the children, there was still a question concerning how much involvement they had with the children themselves and what kind of involvement this was.

Within the family, there were divergent views about this. Lallie, the first to have children, became the focal point for much familial criticism regarding her behaviour towards them. Relishing their new-found opportunity to criticize this dominant older sister, the others all reported their views as to her shortcomings as a mother. Lallie's errors were ones of commission, not omission: she was criticized for spending too much time with her children, for lavishing too much attention on them, and for failing to keep them in check. All the younger sisters felt that the Holt children were growing up with inadequate discipline. On a visit to Liverpool in 1873, Kate commented to Beatrice that the Holt children were 'charmingly dispositioned but decidedly spoilt little monkeys. It is most funny that Lallie with all her determination in most things should be so soft to her children.'[28] A little later Maggie echoed this view, as Beatrice continued to do throughout Lallie's life. Maggie, however, added an interesting rider to her criticism. In her view, Lallie concentrated on the wrong aspects of mothering, spending too much time being with and caring for the physical needs of her children. 'I really think that there are many things that could be done for her in that line and leave her more time to cultivate herself and make herself more useful to them in the end.'[29] Maggie was particularly concerned that Lallie lost her dignity when she was with the children, shouting at them rather than keeping the serenity which could best be managed if one was a little distant.

Lallie herself found the unruliness of her children rather difficult, and she became happier when they were old enough to settle into a regular routine of lessons which she could teach them. When Dick, her oldest son, was 4, she began teaching him his letters each morning and noted the beneficial effects of this: 'he is much better in spirit and temper since he has some regular occupation'.[30] She taught him for a few months, until he was old enough to have a regular governess.

This involvement in the education of young children was one which many of the sisters shared. Maggie was particularly assiduous in this regard, regularly commenting on the progress and the problems evident amongst her offspring in her 'Children's Book'. Her notes show a very detailed interest in the acquisition of motor skills, language, and social skills in her children. She mapped out their educational paths and noted both her own role and that of governesses and other staff in the education of the children. When the oldest son, Stephen, was 5, she recorded his current state as follows.

> Stephen—writes a good round hand,
> Reads ordinary stories, has to spell out the long words,
> Understands French, and can make himself understood,
> Does easy sums, knew his multiplication table in the spring,
> Can say three of La Fontaine's fables.
> In a year's time from now he should:
> read English correctly,
> Know French well,
> Improve in sums,
> Be able to write a letter alone,
> Recite well a piece of poetry in English or French,
> Know something of Geography.
> Mlle. Thibergien has returned to France. She has been a nice
> governess for him, very bright, perservering and affectionate.[31]

Rachel, the second child, had not improved in speech and Maggie noted 'I must take her Pronunciation in hand, when I return from Sicily at Christmas'.

The interest and involvement shown by Lallie and Maggie in the education of their children was shared by some, but not by all of their sisters. Mary and Theresa certainly had it, and devoted themselves happily to their young ones, but Blanche, Georgie, and Rosie did not. Blanche loved her children dearly, but was not always able to care for them adequately. This was already evident with her first child, Lawrence, in his early years. When he was only 2 or 3, Blanche found it impossible to control him without resorting to violence. She whipped him to make him do her bidding. The other sisters were very much aware of Blanche's instability and felt that day school, at the earliest possible time, would be beneficial for her children as they lacked a mother's guiding hand at home. This lack was made up when, shortly after the birth of their second child, the Harrison Crippses employed Fanny Hughes as a housekeeper. Fanny took over the daily care of the children—and persuaded Blanche to stop whipping them.[32] With Fanny's help, Blanche established close relationships with some of the children. But her role as a mother was very different from that of her sisters.

Whereas Blanche was unable to take a central or directing role in the education of her children, Georgie seems never to have wanted one. The constant succession of pregnancies, often unwanted and undergone in loneliness and misery, inevitably had their effect on the way she felt about her children. She was fond of many of them in their later years, and was often delightful and amusing, writing plays, entering into their games and social activities, and charming them with her wit and vivacity. But this was not until later. Unlike Lallie, Maggie, and Theresa, all of whom adored their babies and enjoyed nursing them, Georgie found the physical activity of caring for babies 'rather a bore'. Like Blanche, she was fortunate in finding a competent substitute and she readily turned the nursery over to Sarah Peacock. Sarah was nanny to all ten of the Meinertzhagen children and ruled the nursery as her own domain. According to the biographer of Georgie's son, Richard Meinertzhagen, Sarah refused to allow Georgie to interfere in the nursery. 'If Georgina made a sally into her fiefdom and there was a disagreement, Sarah would clap on an old bonnet and leave, only to return within minutes and declare "No, I shall not leave my children to the mercy of Mrs. Meinertzhagen." '[33] This comment needs to be seen in the context of the very close relationship which existed between Georgie and Sarah Peacock. When the children had grown up, Sarah remained with Georgie as her companion and shared with her all the joys and the tasks of grand-motherhood. After Georgie's death, Sarah went to live with one of the Meinertzhagen girls, having become by then a member of the family.[34]

In view of Georgie's strong tendency to favour some of her children and to neglect others, it is just as well that she, like her own mother, had someone else to look after the children. At the same time, her del-egation of authority meant that the children grew up in Sarah's world rather than in the much more intellectual and broad-ranging world of their mother. Georgie and the children spent most of their time in the country and there the children were entirely superintended by Sarah. As Bobo Mayor later wrote in a private recollection intended for some of her nieces and nephews,

This was why their children, especially we girls, grew up so uneducated and entirely under the influence of our beloved Sarah—totally unaware of the big world around us. Nothing about the big world was ever mentioned. Our friends were the villagers, especially some of the very poor ones, and the gardeners, the grooms and then our charming station master, and many others with whom Sarah so easily made friends.

And Sarah of course, though so very intelligent, was totally, unbelievably uneducated. She used to talk of the Myninsagins of Montisfont Habbey.[35]

IV

The attitudes and behaviour of the Potter sisters to their small children reflects differences in personality and in personal style amongst the sisters as much as it does differences in their beliefs about what good mothering entailed. Indeed these beliefs were themselves at least partly a function of personality difference. Maggie's criticism of Lallie's undignified behaviour in her home, for example, was largely a comment on Lallie's volubility and spontaneity, qualities which Maggie did not share. The dignity and detachment which Maggie thought that Lallie should develop were very much Maggie's own traits—and were in turn qualities which others found very difficult to cope with as they made intimacy almost impossible. In later years Maggie acknowledged this difference between herself and her oldest sister. When Mary Playne wrote to tell her of Lallie's death and of the family breakdown which had preceded it, Maggie wrote back to say how pleased she was that all Lallie's children had been with her at the very end. 'She so dearly loved them and was such a warm-hearted soul that she suffered much from isolation . . . I am afraid I am far colder metal and if my children behaved ill to me, I should pass it by and try to put them out of my mind and at the same time to set it right and live on a cool level as regards affection.'[36]

Maggie's comment points to her sense of the way in which Lallie's personality and behaviour caused Lallie herself pain of a kind which Maggie avoided. She was aware, as were all the other sisters, not only of the generosity and warmth that were so much a part of Lallie, but also of the tactlessness and occasional insensitivity which accompanied them and which played their part in destroying the domestic harmony for which Lallie worked so hard. Lallie was rather like Mary, one of the sisters to whom she was very close, in her tendency to 'manage', to dictate and to organize, and in her capacity to interfere and to get on the wrong sides of people by the tactlessness with which she tried to manage their affairs. In their familial relationships, both were self-sacrificing to an inordinate degree, devoting themselves to their children in a way which Beatrice thought misguided. Their great personal strength and competence as housekeepers, hostesses, and organizers did not prevent them from an almost slavish devotion to husbands and children which was guaranteed to lessen their value in the eyes of those very families whom they served. Both incurred constant criticism from Beatrice for their excessive devotion to families all of whom became spoilt and self-indulgent as a result, imbued by their mother's sacrifices with an exalted sense of their own importance.

Maggie, although a devoted mother, was never a slavish one. Her control was always evident in her relationships with her children, as was her own strong sense of herself and of her worth. In place of Lallie's volubility Maggie exhibited an almost chilling detachment from her children in her concern to use every occasion for its full educational benefit. When her sons went to boarding-school, she used their letters home as the basis for exercises in spelling, returning them to the writer duly corrected in red ink. A reply to a child's letter like the following hardly seems conducive to increasing the ease or informality of communication: 'Try and find out the rule as to doubling consonants ... Your style and spelling are much improved but the latter still very defective. Do notice words when you read. It is the only way to learn at your age.'[37]

Maggie shared with Lallie and Mary an almost obsessive concern with the achievements of her children, especially her sons. Their places in class, their proper use of the social opportunities of school, their development as socially successful young men and women seem to have been of greater importance than their happiness or their spiritual well-being. This worldly concern appeared greater than it was in all three cases because of the great difficulty these three sisters had in expressing emotion. Few of the Potter sisters exhibited any capacity for expressing warmth or affection. The lack of nurturant mothering which Mary Booth had noted as a characteristic of them all as girls was deeply ingrained and made them in their turn into women rarely capable of an easy flow of warmth towards their own children. Lallie and Mary expressed their concern through the way they managed other people's lives. Maggie expressed hers in the careful note she took of all the doings and developments of her children. They loved the children to whom they devoted themselves so assiduously, but few of them had the capacity to express that love. Theresa was almost alone amongst the sisters in this regard. She sought an emotional intimacy with both her husband and her children, and her letters to them are strikingly different from those of all the others. In the late 1880s Theresa spent some time at Standish, helping to care for Richard Potter. While there she wrote daily to her children. Her letters are somewhat gushing, but for this very reason show a strongly marked contrast to the letters written by Lallie, Mary, Maggie, or Georgie to their children.

This afternoon, if it is fine, I am going to take Len and baby to dear old Dada, my old nurse, who nursed me when I was a baby, and who loves Mother, and all Mother's sisters, and all the grandchildren just as though they all belonged to her. Even now Mother thinks there is nobody quite so good as Dada, or quite so kind and fond of her (except perhaps old F——), you know whom I mean, don't you? But don't tell him. Just kiss him for half an hour without stopping instead, and tell Ruth and Freddie to do the same, and if he has not and you have not time, just pack up three lots of kisses with his sandwiches, so that he can eat them up with his lunch.[38]

But Theresa's degree of affection and involvement with her sons brought its own hardship, as she had to relinquish the boys when they were still quite small in order for them to go to boarding-school. Alfred Cripps, in the Memoir of his wife which he wrote for his children, indicated the conflict she faced over this. Seddon, their oldest child, started school in 1891.

Mother would really have wished to keep her boys at home, providing for them a good tutor, or sending them to a good day school, but she recognized that the best education could not be obtained by either of these methods, and her sole desire was to give them every possible advantage in fitting them for their future duties and responsibilities.[39]

Her first letter to him describes her own sense of grief.

Mother cried herself to sleep last night and perhaps you did too; but we feel better this morning, and you will find so much to interest you in your school life, when you have got over the trial of leaving home . . . Whenever you are unhappy, or in trouble, remember Mother's plan. Tell me at what time you are in bed, and that is when I will always think of you, and you must think of Father and me . . . The eight o'clock bell has just rung, and you are just sitting down to breakfast, feeling strange and shy, but soon you will know what a good thing it is to be at school, to learn to be courageous, to bear difficult things, and to go bravely through trials which we all have to meet when we are grown up.[40]

In Theresa's case, the need to give her sons the boarding-school training considered appropriate to boys of their class came into conflict with her own nurturant, affectionate, and intimate approach to mothering. Most of her sisters found it much easier to cope with the dutiful part of mothering: the sending of boys to school, the correction of behavioural and other errors, the pointing out to them of the path of duty. But in turn, they seem not to have had the same conflicts as she, never having even attempted to establish such close relationships with their children.

The last of the sisters, Rosie, was perhaps the one who of all the sisters found motherhood the most difficult. As the baby of the family, Rosie had not ever really grown up sufficiently herself to be able to undertake the care of children. Her terrible first marriage and the peripatetic life she led afterwards meant that she never settled into any stable domestic situation. Hence both she and her children lacked the support which the others had through paid domestic staff and through their extended family network.

Rosie was not accepted as a fully responsible adult either by herself or by her sisters even when she had married and had a child of her own. When she and Dyson were preparing to go to Egypt to see if the warm climate improved his health, they had planned to take their one-year-old son, Noel. But 'about a week before we started, my eldest sister, Lally Holt, a clever, kindly, managing woman, swooped down upon me, and insisted on taking Noel and his nurse up to her large and comfortable house in Liverpool.'[41] Dyson was rather relieved that she did so, and Noel flourished in Liverpool. But Lallie's action was based on the belief which she shared with Robert Holt that the Williamses were quite incapable of caring even for themselves, let alone for a child.

And this perception was not without some truth. Rosie never did manage to cope with or to care adequately for her children any more than she learnt to run a house. She continued as an adult to throw tantrums, constantly threatening her husband and children with suicide. Indeed she so often plunged into the sea or into rivers that no one took any notice of it. Just as she had always been the baby in her family of origin so in a sense Rosie continued to be the baby amongst her own children. Her various neuroses, termed by her 'manias', such as her need to have an alarm clock by her bed to remind her to turn over, soon came to dominate the lives of her children.[42] Rosie could not get a replacement for her father, but she did the next best thing by ensuring that rather than her having to look after her children, they would look after her.

VIII

Family Life

MANAGING a family was the main preoccupation for most of the
Potter sisters throughout their married lives. The familial role of the
Potters, as of other women of their class, was an extensive one, as the
entire responsibility for running large and complex households and
for supervising children centred on them. But the situation of women
within the family was a somewhat ambiguous one. Family life offered
upper-middle-class women a range of activities, many of which were
not only enjoyable but also called for both administrative and social
skills. It also offered a considerable measure of power, influence, and
prestige. At the same time, the legal and economic situation of women
was such as to make their power rather more apparent than real.
Women carried most of the responsibility for caring for a family, but
the real power was held by men. A father was the sole legal guardian of
his children, with absolute power to determine their upbringing,
schooling, religious observances, and location. His powers over his
children were similar in kind to those which, as a husband, he exercised over his wife. Hence when women controlled family life, they
did so through what was essentially a delegation of power by their
husbands.[1] He could intervene in the process at any time and, if he
chose, could remove the children from his wife. Most men did not in
fact do this. But their legal and financial power none the less played a
very important role in the structure and functioning of family life. The
deference women were expected to pay to their husbands, for
example, did not increase the respect they gained from their children.
Boys in particular were often beyond the control of their mothers,
assuming early the masculine prerogatives of their fathers, and usually
accorded a great measure of pre-eminence by their mothers and
sisters.

The complexity of the situation is in part due to the fact that in
family life, as in marriage, legal and economic structures do not of
themselves determine actual experience. It is clear that amongst the
Potters, as in other families, the real power of wives and mothers
varied very greatly. The individual personalities of wives and
husbands, the nature of their relationship, the position of the family

financially, socially, and geographically all played their part in creating very different situations. Maggie, for example, was a powerful woman, who took an active part in determining her husband's career and directed her children not only through much of their childhood but also well into their adult years. She was notably more successful in this regard than Lallie, despite the formidable organizing powers exhibited by Lallie from her early childhood. Maggie was successful because she was a very controlled and self-contained woman possessing a measure of tact quite alien to her oldest sister. Not only could she get her way, but she was very careful to limit her emotional involvement even with husband and children in order to reduce her vulnerability. Lallie, as Maggie herself saw, remained particularly vulnerable through her warm-heartedness and passionate devotion to her family. In order to retain power and influence, women had to continue to be able to charm, sway, or persuade their families. Personality could mitigate a situation; it could not alter its basic structure.

Not only were women subject to their husbands within the family, but they were also harnessed to a very tight rein in regard to the education and supervision of their children. In upper-middle-class families boys went to public school, and thus had to leave home at an early age. A mother usually had little say even in what school her sons went to, as they followed the family tradition of their fathers. A tender-hearted mother like Theresa could only weep at being separated from the little boy she wanted to have under her own roof, indicating in this very act the similarity of her powerlessness to his. The education of girls offered perhaps a little more scope, but their social life was as rigidly prescribed by convention as was the education of their brothers. Women had to understand and adapt to all the changing patterns of the nineteenth century, but they could not choose to ignore them except at the risk of social ostracism.

The familial responsibilities of the Potter sisters began with domestic supervision, and as their broods began to increase, so did their domestic responsibilities. Although none of them had as many homes as did Richard and Lawrencina, most of them had two for the greater period of their married lives. There was usually a London or, in Lallie's case, a Liverpool home, as well as a country house. The existence of two homes meant that children, servants, and household goods had regularly to be transported from one place to another. Houses were constantly being opened or closed and prepared for the arrival or departure of varying numbers of people. There were regular moves determined by the London Season: at the advent of summer people moved to the country and at the start of the autumn many returned to London. At certain times, changes had to be made in the scale of life at one particular venue. The Hobhouses began married life in London, but Maggie moved to the family home at Hadspen when the children were small. For a while they relinquished their London address, preferring to have Henry lodge with either the Courtneys or the Crippses. During these years, Maggie devoted her attention and most of her own income to improving and expanding Hadspen House, turning it from a modest country home into a very imposing gentleman's residence with an elaborate garden. But as the children grew up, their social interests made it again desirable that the family should have a London house and Maggie divided her attention between the two. The Crippses and the Meinertzhagens always had both large country homes, which served as the base for family living, and London houses for the Season. The Harrison Crippses did the reverse, with the family based in London but moving to very large holiday homes in the north of Scotland for the shooting season.

Domestic and social arrangements became more and more complicated as children grew up. School terms had now to be prepared for and special vacation arrangements made. The Holts and the Hobhouses engaged special holiday governesses and tutors to supervise the activities of school-age children and to provide what they saw as the necessary stimulation and discussion for their sons. The considerable age range amongst their families meant that a variety of different arrangements had to be made, as adolescents often wanted to see Europe while youngsters needed holiday care and activity. The families of all the Potters moved around frequently, visiting each other in addition to their trips to London, to the country, or overseas. These movements were sometimes undertaken in large groups, but more often involved different pairs and trios going in many different directions. Many of their moves were large-scale operations. The Holts in particular moved in style. When Lallie went to their holiday home at the Dell of Abernathy in 1876 she took with her three friends, two nurses, and four children. Ten years later, when she and Robert set out for their shooting lodge, High Borrans, Robert commented a little ruefully on the size of their party. There were 'five small children, four servants and our two selves—eleven in all with luggage in proportion', all taking the 11.40 night train to Scotland.[2] The fact that Robert Holt found it necessary to comment on the size of the family travelling party on this occasion points to his unfamiliarity with all that was involved in moving his family from Liverpool to High Borrans. Usually Lallie did that without him and he travelled alone, or with a friend or relative, arriving only after the family was already established there.

II

A discussion of the family life of the Potter sisters is for the most part a discussion of the life shared by a woman with her children. The immersion in family life prescribed for women within Victorian domestic ideology was the necessary concomitant of a situation in which men were increasingly absorbed in their professional, business, or political activities, and also chose to spend much of their leisure time with other men, seeing their families only infrequently. The husbands of the sisters exhibited a wide range of differing views and practices concerning the involvement of men in family life and in child care. But the typical situation for them, as for most other families of their class, was one in which family life centred on women, with men playing only an occasional part.

The ready acceptance that family life did not require much male participation—or indeed even regular male presence—was clearly evident in those families in which men spent most of their time in London, while their wives and children lived in the country. This pattern was established for the Meinertzhagens almost immediately after they married. But the Hobhouses too lived for many years in this way, as Henry's parliamentary career kept him in London while Maggie and the children stayed at Hadspen House in Somersetshire. In their case, unlike that of the Meinertzhagens, this separation was not a sign of personal incompatibility. Maggie often visited Henry in London, while he in turn spent a lot of time at Hadspen. This situation differed from that of the Meinertzhagens in another particular as well: whereas Georgie spent her time away from Daniel mainly because he wished to be unencumbered by her and the family, it was Maggie who bore much of the responsibility for her separation from Henry.

When Maggie and Henry first met, he was a young man vaguely contemplating a legal career—in the leisurely way made possible by the comfortable income he already received from the rents on his estate and from a sizeable portfolio of shares. Maggie did not approve of this approach, and did her best to persuade him to give up this dilettante's life and to stop approaching the law in a 'shilly-shallying kind of way'. In her view, a man needed a definite occupation. 'I should prefer (if one lived only for the present) to settle down with you in your sweet home, with all one's country pursuits and now and then a charming travel—living and studying from morning till night, but I think that in a few years such a life would pall upon *you*, and your country duties would not be in any way sufficient for your abilities.'[3] Other members of the family agreed: Alfred Cripps, who was already a successful barrister, offered Henry a room in his Chambers which was duly accepted. Henry worked at law until 1885, when he entered Parliament. He remained an MP until 1906, establishing a distinguished reputation for committee work and for drafting legislation. He and his family were separated for much of this time. Maggie missed him badly, especially when the children were small and she lacked any adult company. But she was a tough and stoical woman, accepting her duty, and consoling herself with the knowledge that 'my darling is earning his spurs'.[4]

The existence of two separate homes did not always mean that men kept aloof from their wives and children. Alfred Cripps, for example, was a devoted family man despite the fact that his legal career kept him in London while his family was based at Parmoor. He spent as much time as he could at Parmoor and, in their turn, Theresa and the children often went to be with him in London. Indeed Alfred Cripps had established so close a relationship with his children that when Theresa died suddenly in 1893, leaving him with five children under the age of eleven, he was rapidly able to take over her familial role, supervising the education of the children and becoming himself the pivot of a close-knit family group.

Just as a man could keep up close ties with his family though sometimes separated from it, so sharing the same residence did not necessarily mean that men were closely involved with their families. Willie Harrison Cripps is a case in point here, and an interesting contrast to his brother. Willie lived under the same roof as his children for most of the time. But this did not mean that he was closely involved with them. On the contrary, he even complained of the time which Blanche spent with the older children, seeing this as time which she could have devoted to writing out his books or doing illustrations for him.[5] Willie's extreme harshness and severity towards his older children continued throughout their childhood and adolescence and contrasted sharply with the interest and affection he showed his youngest daughter. Willie was extraordinarily harsh to his children, imposing hardships on them and depriving them of both comfort and familial companionship for no reason other than the pursuit of his will. This was most evident when, during 1898, the Harrison Crippses had temporarily to vacate their home to allow it to be renovated. The construction of the Bond Street Underground Station and of the train lines leading to it had undermined their home in Stratford Place. Huge cracks developed in the stairwell and in many of the rooms and, after much negotiation, the Harrison Crippses took the Electric Railway Company to court and were awarded £2,900 in damages.[6] The family split up for a while as Blanche and Willie, along with their daughter Julia, moved to the Langham Hotel. The boys were sent away to lodgings. They were very unhappy there, both Lawrence and Standish complaining of the meanness of their accommodation and of their forced separation from their family. Blanche tried to assuage their feelings by giving them money and by arranging for them to eat with her and Willie at the Langham Hotel. Sometimes Willie refused to allow this, on one occasion actually sending his son Standish away even though Blanche had specifically invited him to dine.[7] This extreme stinginess towards his sons was made harder for them and for Blanche to bear by the stark contrast provided by Willie's inordinate generosity to Giulia Ravogli and her family. Nothing was too much for him to offer his mistress. Three weeks after Willie had refused to allow Standish to share his meal at the Langham, he hosted a dinner for twenty-six at the hotel, followed by a concert for fifty people at which Giulia sang.[8] The fact that Willie also made his sons undertake training and careers which they did not like did not serve to endear him to them any further. Indeed, throughout the last years of Blanche's life, her continual efforts to mediate between her husband and her two oldest sons was one of her major tasks—as indeed the constant sense of strain and dislike between them was a major source of grief.[9] After Blanche's death, the feelings between Willie and his sons deteriorated further. They never forgave him for his treatment of their mother, whom they adored. Added to the anger and resentment they felt already, this created a bitterness which lasted throughout their lives, and expressed itself in a refusal ever to accept his new wife, whom they referred to contemptuously as 'the signora'.[10]

Willie's behaviour was not typical of those fathers who lived with their children. Robert Holt, although very different from Alfred

Cripps, also provides a marked contrast. Holt was always very involved with and affectionate towards his children. His diaries contain regular entries about them, noting their educational progress, their development, and their activities. When the children were away at school, he often went to visit them and evidently enjoyed their company when they were home. He was a somewhat querulous man, with a strong sense of his own importance and entitlements and, as the children grew up, he was often grieved at their lack of deference and devotion. He was, moreover, powerfully inclined to favour some of his children at the expense of others, and his influence on his family was not always healthy. But his constant interest and concern was always evident.

The role of fathers in matters such as discipline varies as much as does their overall involvement in family life. Here again Daniel Meinertzhagen illustrates one extreme, taking no role whatever in disciplining or controlling his large number of children. The Meinertzhagens were a charming but somewhat wild and unruly group, and the sisters often commented on the fact that they exhausted Georgie and were more than she could cope with. In regard to her sons there were particular problems, as she found them increasingly difficult to handle. Her second son Richard was, as we will see, a particular trial to her and she found his behaviour quite intolerable. Daniel ignored this problem as he did all others regarding his family. He behaved, as many members of the family noted, like a benevolent uncle, occasionally having one or two children to stay at his bachelor quarters, taking them abroad, dispensing treats and largesse, but refusing to be drawn into any of the details of their daily life.[11] At the opposite extreme from Daniel was an authoritarian father, like Arthur Playne, who enforced his will over his son by the use of corporal punishment. Within the extended family, Arthur was known as something of a martinet, though one whose severity was not reflected in obedience, seriousness of purpose, or self-discipline in his son.[12]

None of the Potter sisters, except Theresa, married men who were as integral to the lives of their children as Richard Potter had been for them. In those families where men did intervene, especially in the Playne and Harrison Cripps families, the women had constantly to mediate that intervention and to work hard themselves to ensure that their children could follow their own inclinations or their own best interests. In the Holt family, the involvement of both parents with their children reduced rather than increased family harmony, as the parents seem to have worked against each other rather than in any kind of unity.

III

Despite the differences among the Potter sisters and their husbands in the extent of their involvement with their children and in terms of their ideas about family life, the overall tenor of their approach to childhood was very similar. This was largely the result of the institutional framework which defined the proper rearing and education of children for their class. The boys all spent their childhood being taught by a governess and followed this by some years spent either with tutors or at a prep school before going to one of the major public schools. The girls, like their mothers before them, were educated mainly at home, sometimes going to a private finishing school for a year or two before they 'came out'.

As this suggests, there were very considerable differences in the upbringing of boys as compared with girls. The girls spent far more time at home than did the boys, and by this very fact were initiated early into the female sphere of domestic supervision and nurture. The general pattern which Carol Dyhouse has recently delineated, whereby girls in late Victorian England received their 'first lessons in femininity' at home, is very clearly illustrated within the families of the Potter sisters.[13] The girls not only learnt that home was the female sphere, while their fathers worked away from it, but they also learnt very clearly their own subordinate place and their role and duties in so far as providing nurture and domestic comforts for the family men was concerned. This was something which they learnt both by observation and by quite explicit instruction and direction. When Theresa was away from home for a few weeks, helping to nurse Richard Potter, she wrote to her daughter Ruth—then aged 6—as follows: 'Take care of dear Father when he is with you, and if he feels at all ill, or has a headache, put him to bed and light his fire, and see that he has nothing but broth and milk, and is kept warm. Ruthie is old enough now to take care of Father when Mother is away.'[14]

From an even earlier age, one can see that the assessment provided by the sisters of their children's characters and personalities incorporate a very clear idea of the appropriate developments and behaviour for each sex. Thus in an entry in her 'Children's Book' for October 1884, Margaret Hobhouse made the following observations about her two eldest children, Stephen and Rachel, then aged respectively 3 and 2.

Stephen has made a great advance. He is quite a boy now and only waiting his suits to look one. His activity is unceasing, running, romping, playing—much stronger. He is still difficult to manage and wilful. One of his worst mental qualities is a want of continuous application, and a rooted dislike to doing useful things which to him become irksome so soon as they cease to be new. Rachel, on the contrary, is quite the housewife and delights in nothing so much as tidying her things away, fetching and carrying. She seldom forgets to bring me the footstool when I nurse baby. Stephen seems sometimes to embody unsatisfied human nature.[15]

When Rachel turned 4, her mother summarized her as follows: 'she is pretty, graceful, bright, not very clever, timid, easily hurt and mortified, a cosy loving little thing, living in peace with everyone, very anxious to please and to look pretty, quite obedient, hardly ever punished, dreadfully upset by a reprimand.'[16]

Rachel was clearly learning very early about her place in the world as a woman whose future lay in marriage and whose life's work was the provision of home comforts and nurture for a husband and children. But lest the subtle influence of expectation and home education were not enough, Margaret Hobhouse spelled the message out to her quite clearly on her fifteenth birthday.

Many happy and happier returns on your birthday! May each year find you better, wiser, kinder, and stronger! You enter now upon your girlhood. As you employ these next few years, so will your future be useful and fortunate, or miserable and good for nothing. Remember that sweetness and unselfishness are the mainsprings in a successful woman's career. Without the latter she cannot fulfil her vocation and cannot be happy.[17]

Rachel's education followed the pattern one might expect from these comments. She learnt languages, music, and needlework at home from governesses, with frequent injunctions from her mother to practise the music and the needlework while Maggie was away. This was followed by two terms at an exclusive girls' school in London (where she was accompanied by her cousin Ruth Cripps) and then a year at a finishing school at Auteuil, near Paris. Maggie had been very hesitant about sending Rachel to school at all. She wrote to Mary Playne in 1899 expressing her dilemma: 'I find she [Rachel] rather wants to go to school for a year. I wonder whether it will be best to send her? What do you think? Brushing up against other girls is a good thing in some ways, it sharpens the wits and teaches a girl how to *live* with other people. Though I confess I don't like the school girl type.'[18]

As this letter makes clear, Maggie never contemplated providing Rachel with the kind of education she regarded as appropriate for her sons. Although by the 1890s there were a number of girls' schools which had established a curriculum of academic subjects, none of these entered into her scheme of things.[19] Nor of course did university Although by this time Oxford and Cambridge had both opened their doors—if not their degrees—to women, the idea that her daughters might take advantage of this, or that they might take up any kind of career, was entirely alien to Maggie, as it was to her sisters. She made it quite clear to Rachel that she was attending school to be 'finished'. 'I hope by the way, you are putting on some polish. It is not the forte of our family. We are rough diamonds without doubt. I look to you to redeem the character of the family.'[20]

Rachel's education was more expensive than that of some of her female cousins. Most of the Meinertzhagen girls received even less than she did. Georgie seems to have been less conscientious than was Maggie in ensuring reasonable governesses for her daughters, and they grew up apparently without much in the way of educational routine. Their days were spent roaming the countryside on horseback, visiting the villagers and the friends of Sarah Peacock, and indulging a propensity for wildness and adventurousness considered somewhat reprehensible by their rather staid aunts. Bobo Mayor later commented on the complete lack of intellectual culture amongst her sisters. 'The boys, of course, went to school and got their education there, but we girls depended on our German governesses who came and went, often staying only one term or less because we were so unteachable, so undisciplined. (After all, had not Bernard Shaw once described us as a lot of giggling hooligans?).'[21] Some of the Meinertzhagen girls did go to school. Betty, the youngest and Georgie's favourite, was sent for a couple of years to Miss Weisse's school in Surrey. She loathed it and counted the days until her holidays. Georgie commiserated with her. 'I knew you would miss home very much, for you have had a *very* happy home and more freedom than other girls get; in fact a very good time, and it stands to reason no school life can be the same. But I really think you will grow fond of school and certainly you will be pleased to have been there.'[22] Betty had, however, been sent to school for much the same reason as Beatrice Potter had been earlier: because her continued ill health and weakness was a cause for concern, and her mother hoped that an orderly routine, with less excitement than there was at home, would enable her to grow stronger.

This picture of her early life supplied by Bobo Mayor omits the one area of training which the Meinertzhagen children did receive, which was in music. Although the Potters were a remarkably unmusical family, the Meinertzhagen children apparently inherited both the musical talents and the musical interest evident in their father's family. Most of them played instruments sufficiently well to be in frequent demand at social gatherings. Various members of the family formed trios and quartets through their late adolescence, and throughout their adult lives many of them were engaged in daily practice and quite frequent performances. They also exhibited other talents—Bobo, like Georgie, writing, and Betty attempting to establish herself as an actress.

It is clear, however, that there was no thought in this branch of the family that the girls needed any kind of academic or formal training. It was the Meinertzhagens who had earlier been the least sympathetic towards Beatrice's intellectual and career aspirations, Georgie regarding her simply as a show-off, and Daniel making clear his lack of interest in intellectual women. It was ironic that they should have been the parents of one of the only two women in the next generation with aspirations towards scholarship. Barbara Meinertzhagen, better known by her married name as Barbara Drake, the author of several books on women workers and on women in trade unions and a prominent member of both the Fabian Research Department and of the London County Council, was perhaps a little more fortunate than Beatrice Webb.[23] There was at least her famous aunt ready and prepared to take her on as a disciple. But it seems to be the case that the only education which Barbara received outside her home was a stint in the cookery school which was founded by her aunt, Mary Playne. University, which she would have loved, was regarded only as a place of punishment for girls. The family apparently had a saying, 'If you're naughty, you'll have to go to Girton', but the leeway provided by Georgie was such that none of her daughters ever managed to be sufficiently bad to receive this most dire of punishments.[24]

The Holt family were slightly different in regard to the education of their daughters. All of the girls went to school, either at Miss Souvestre's school in Wimbledon or at Miss Laurence's (Roedean). Kitty, the eldest daughter, also sat the Cambridge locals and attended Newnham. She then married one of her tutors, Cecil Whetham, and with him wrote several books on eugenics, until a complete breakdown necessitated her removal to a mental hospital.[25] She was the only daughter of the Potter sisters to complete tertiary education.

The difference in attitude to the education of sons as compared with daughters could not be more marked. The schooling of sons was a matter of immense importance and every step was taken to ensure their adequate preparation for the entrance examination of the desired schools and colleges. In some cases, the boys simply followed in the steps of their fathers. Alfred Cripps's sons followed him to Winchester without difficulty. But for the others, attempting for the first time to gain entry to one of the great public schools, the matter required time and energy and involved calling on friends and relations who had some kind of influence. The Holts, for example, attempted to put Dick's name down at Winchester three or four years before he was ready to attend, but found there was no vacancy. They then had him prepared to enter the scholarship examination, at which he performed sufficiently well to be admitted as a foundationer.[26] Dick was followed to Winchester by his younger brothers and also by his cousin, Bill Playne. For Bill, too, there were great difficulties in gaining admission, and the Playnes attempted to have his name entered for both Winchester and Harrow in the hopes that he would be successful in one. The Holts offered them help, as did Alfred Cripps, and indeed the whole business was rather like a carefully planned and executed campaign, with Mary marshalling all her resources in the interests of her son. A letter she wrote to Lallie at the time indicates what some of this involved.

I have your two kind letters, the one from Winchester this morning and I am *most truly* obliged for the trouble you have taken with Mr Moreshead. I knew that 9 vacancies were absolutely at the disposal of the Headmaster, but Mr Fearon who is a true Scholar is sure to follow Dr Bidding's place of giving them to the 9 boys who do best at the Scholarship exam . . . as you say now, I must do all in my power with Alfred and Mr Fearon—I shall go to Alfred directly I get to London and put the matter before him and ask for his help. . . . It is *most* kind of you to take so much trouble to speak well for Bill . . . I am afraid you said more than is quite true, but it is just a case where a little exaggeration to obtain an object is admissable . . .

We had a nasty letter from Mr Watson this morning saying he cannot promise a vacancy at any time, but that our boy is more likely to get into his House if he goes in September in to a small House, but he says it is just possible after all he may take him in September, in fact I almost fancy he means to take him if we are polite and humble but firm.

It would be jolly nice to say Bill had a Headmaster's vacancy at Winchester and this we preferred even to his House at Harrow ... Please don't mention all this, as if Watson heard we were trying for Winchester he would not take Bill and we might be left in the lurch.[27]

Eventually Bill was successful in getting the coveted place at Winchester, although he lacked either the application or the social grace of Dick Holt and had continual trouble with his form and house masters.

Getting the boys into school was only the first step. After that, family correspondence shows an almost obsessional concern with their progress, their sporting prowess, and their establishment of the right kind of friends. The Holts, who seem always to have pushed Dick to do well in scholarly matters, were the most notable here: every letter Dick sent his parents mentioned his place in his class and his achievements for the week. The Hobhouses, as one would have expected from Maggie's preoccupation with social prestige and public advancement, were if anything more concerned about the social life than the academic prowess of their sons. They were instructed to write home saying who their friends were and were told quite explicitly about the importance of the friends made at school in later life.

School was followed by university for most of the boys in the Potter families—and university generally meant New College, Oxford. A few of them went either to other colleges at Oxford or to Cambridge, and the sons of Willie Cripps went to medical schools. But New College remained something of a family institution, particularly when Alfred Cripps was made a fellow of the college in 1904. None of the males of the next generation were particularly distinguished as scholars; indeed, as many members of the family pointed out, few members of that generation were distinguished in any way at all. Beatrice never tired of commenting on the declining fortunes and the lessening fame of her family, and others echoed these views. For Beatrice, only Stafford Cripps and Barbara Drake rated as interesting members of the next generation. Others added Richard Meinertzhagen and Dick Holt. Richard Meinertzhagen himself commented in his autobiography that in view of the 'deliberate selection' involved in the mating of the Potter sisters, 'it is remarkable that, of the 39 grandchildren who reached maturity, so few have become eminent'.[28]

The extensive formal education of the boys, as compared with the minimal education of the girls, obviously meant that there were quite different financial investments in the different sexes. The education of boys was extremely expensive, whereas that of girls required only a fraction of the cost. The precise differences can be seen in the Hobhouse family as Henry Hobhouse's account books for the late 1890s and the early years of the twentieth century include the amounts spent on the older children individually. From this it is clear not only that the boys' education involved a large expenditure over many years, but that every item of that expenditure was greater than was that for girls. In 1899 for example, Stephen, the eldest son, was at a private school which cost £132.00 per annum. Arthur, the second son, was at Eton and his expenses were £150.00. Rachel, although she was older than Arthur, was still being educated at home and her expenses are lumped in with those of the three younger children, all of them costing only £103.00. In 1901, when Rachel went to school, her education cost £126.00, still considerably less than Arthur's at £217.50 or that of Stephen's university fees which were £245.12. Rachel's expenses increased in the next couple of years. In 1903, the amount spent on her, which included her 'coming out trousseau', was £162.13. In 1905, the year of her marriage and of the birth of her first child, she received £209.50. But her expenses never matched those of her brothers. In these years, Arthur's university fees were £201.12.7 and £406.19.0 respectively, and when he finished university, there was a very expensive tour as well as the cost of solicitor's articles to be borne.[29]

The much greater expenditure on boys compared with that on girls, combined with the more extensive formal education which the boys received, had a number of implications for the situation of children within these families and for their relationship with their parents. On the one hand, the fact that the boys were away a great deal whereas girls remained at home often meant that the girls had an easier relationship with their parents, especially their mothers. Thus Maggie had an easy bond with Rachel, which depended greatly on shared domestic and social life. Similarly the Meinertzhagen girls were all very close to their mother when they grew up and again the bond of shared domestic, social, and familial life was a strong one. It was helped by the fact that girls were not subjected to the continual and nagging demands of parents to get on: to work at school and university; to take exams with due seriousness; to consider seriously their career opportunities and prospects; to think about marriage. As the chosen rather than the choosers, the girls simply amused themselves as best they could and waited for someone to come along. Frustrating

1. Photographs from Theresa Cripps's photograph album. (i) *Inscribed:* 'Our old Nurse Martha Jackson afterwards Mrs Mills. She came to my mother as maid in 1842 and stayed with us until 1879'. (ii) Richard and Lawrencina Potter and little Dickie, *c.* 1864. *Inscribed:* 'My Father and Mother and little brother (from portrait at Standish)'.

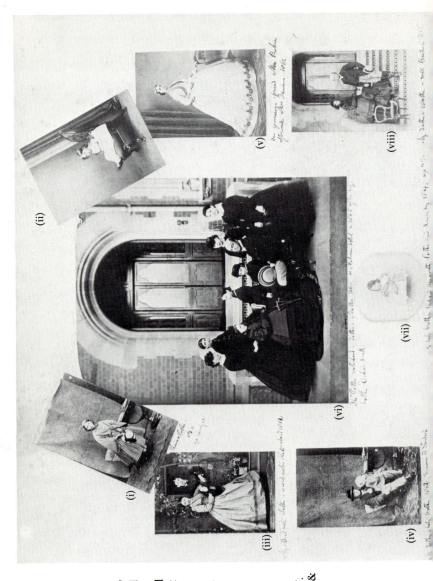

2. Page from Theresa Cripps's photograph album with inscriptions.

(i) 'Theresa Potter. 1862 age nearly 10.' (ii) Beatrice as a young child, c. 1862. (iii) 'My eldest sister Lallie & second sister Kate about 1862'. (iv) 'The "Potter" sisterhood & Father & Mother taken at Malvern Hotel in 1865 after my brother Dickie's death.' (v) 'Our governess & Friend Miss Baker afterwards Mrs James 1861.' (vi) 'My Father & baby brother 1863. Summer at Standish'. (vii) 'My baby brother Richard Heyworth Potter died Xmas day 1864, age 2½'. (viii) 'My Father & Mother & sister Beatrice 1865.'

3. (i) Kate Courtney outside Westminster, *c.* 1885. (ii) Mary Playne, 1883. (iii) Blanche Potter, 1876. (iv) Georgina Meinertzhagen, date unknown.

(i)

(ii)

(iii)

(iv)

4. (i) Theresa Cripps, mid-1880s. (ii) Maggie Hobhouse, *c.* 1916. (iii) Beatrice Potter, early 1880s. (iv) Rosie Potter, 1889.

5. Family group at Standish, 1883. *Left to right*: Arthur Playne, Willie Harrison Cripps, Blanche Harrison Cripps, Lawrencina Potter, Henry Hobhouse, Richard Potter, Theresa Cripps, Alfred Cripps.

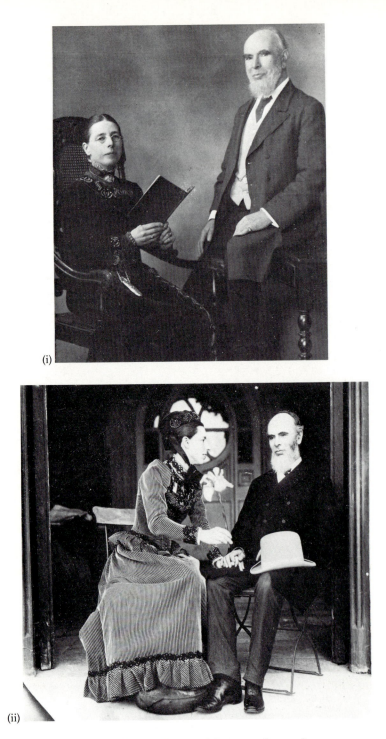

(i)

(ii)

6 (i) and (ii). Kate and Leonard Courtney, dates unknown.

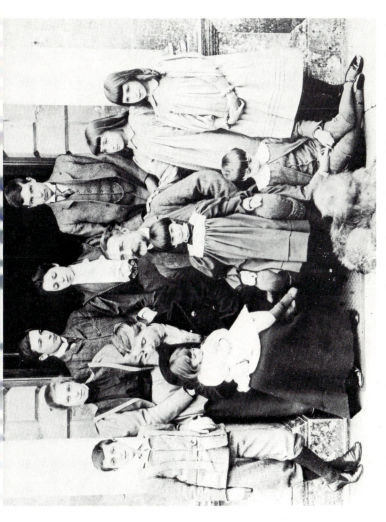

7. The Meinertzhagen Family, early 1890s. *Standing left to right*: Frederick (Fritz), Margaret, Daniel, Barbara, Richard, Lawrencina, Beatrice. *Seated left to right*: Georgina holding Betty, Daniel sen. holding Mary, Louis.

8. Blanche Harrison Cripps with Fanny Hughes, her housekeeper, companion, and children's nurse, and three of Blanche's children, *c.*1883. *Left to right*: Blanche holding Lawrence, Fanny Hughes holding Standish, and Julia.

9. The Harrison Cripps Family, 22 January 1895. *Standing left to right:* William Harrison, Richard Harrison, William Lawrence. *Seated left to right:* Alfred Standish, Blanche Julia, Rosa Beatrice, Blanche holding Henry Harrison.

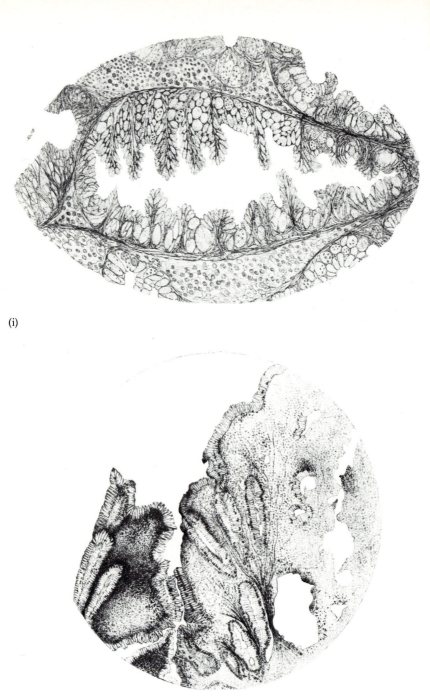

(i)

(ii)

10 (i) *and* (ii). Illustrations made by Blanche from microscopic slides for William Harrison Cripps, *Cancer of the Rectum: Its Pathology, Diagnosis and Treatment* (London, 1880).

11. The Cripps family, 1889. *Left to right*: Seddon, Alfred, Ruth, Frederick, Theresa holding Stafford, Leonard.

12. Margaret Hobhouse with Stephen and Rachel, *c.* 1883.

13. The Hobhouse family, *c.* 1892. *Standing at the rear, left to right:* Henry, Stephen. *Front row, left to right:* Arthur, Maggie, Eleanor, Rachel.

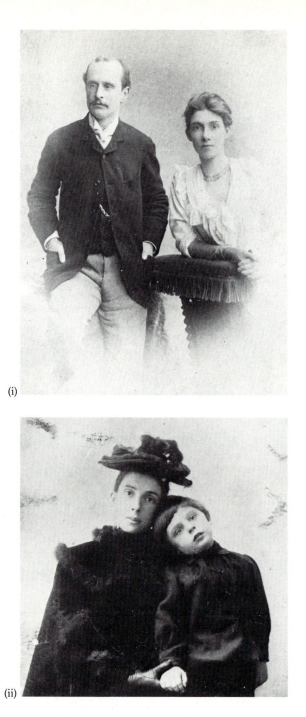

14. (i) *Inscribed*: 'A D Williams & R H Potter 1889'. (ii) Rosie and Noel Williams, *c.* 1896. Rosie is in mourning for Dyson.

(i)

(ii)

15. (i) Portrait of Rosalind Dobbs painted by Frank Carter and exhibited at the Royal Academy in 1903. (ii) George Dobbs exhibiting his prowess as a skier, a sport he was instrumental in introducing into Switzerland.

(i)

(ii)

16. (i) The last of the Potter sisters. Kate, Beatrice, and Rosie taking tea together in the mid-1920s. (ii) Rosie and George Dobbs, shortly before George's death in 1946.

and tedious this might have been, but it did not entail the same pressure or friction that some of the boys had to bear.

The reverse side was of course the fact that the girls were expected to assist their mothers in the provision of domestic services and to wait on and attend to the needs of their brothers. When Arthur Hobhouse was returning from a world tour in 1908, Maggie wrote to say that they would not be in London when he arrived, but Eleanor, his sister, would be sent to be his housekeeper. In a similar way, Rachel was constantly being written to by her mother to organize the house and the boys, see that things were packed properly, look after her father, and so on. The very fact of the close bond between mothers and daughters meant that daughters were expected to take over the maternal role and to exhibit the self-sacrifice and devotion to family which their mothers endorsed so strongly. It was all part of the preparation for marriage which the Potter sisters seem to have regarded as the only possible avenue open to their daughters.

It seems curious at first sight that the daughters of the Potter sisters were little more adventurous or independent than their mothers. Few were interested in careers. But their lack of outside activities is not really surprising. As Lee Holcombe has recently shown, the expansion in occupations for women which was a primary target of the nineteenth century women's movement, and which occurred in a quite marked way around the turn of the century, was largely an expansion in occupations for middle- and lower-middle-class women. There was also a slow expansion in professions for women, and in the range of options open to single women.[30] But their lack of formal education obviously put these outside the range of the Potter women. It is moreover evident that the nature of their family lives and the expectation of wealth and comfort in which they grew up could not possibly be sustained by the earning capacities of women. These could only be satisfied by marriage to wealthy business or professional men and this clearly was the path accepted by the Potter sisters as by their daughters.

The world of the upper-middle classes had changed very little from the time that the Potter sisters made their social débuts to the time when they were presenting their daughters. The Season became somewhat longer and included both larger numbers of people and a wider range of activities. But its purpose and its basic organization remained much the same as in their youth. The Potters were ambitious women and they took great pains to launch their daughters. For

Mary Playne, the establishment of her stepdaughter Polly in society was almost as large an endeavour as was that she had undertaken to ensure the entry of her son to Winchester. She was a shrewd, competent, and practical woman who saw clearly the competitiveness and the cut-throat nature of the society into which she wished to introduce her ward. Her description of Polly's coming-out ball shows clearly the extent to which this event was part of an expensive and carefully planned campaign.

Everything went off exactly as we wished—the right people came and the servants did splendidly and Polly's dress was perfect and she looked as aristocratic and chic as a girl could look and behaved, as Robert [Holt] would say, like a Vere de Vere. She was immensely admired by everyone and I cannot speak too highly of her charming simplicity and entire absence of vanity—and how she is so sweetly affectionate and grateful . . .

The house was so much admired and dressed in its gala costume, is really quite a sham, appearing more than many houses that are much finer and better furnished . . .

Preparing for the ball was a horrible bore and caused me some sleepless nights, for I was determined the child should have a real good coming out— but now it is over and so completely successful I think it worth more than all the trouble and expense. She was so completely queen of the evening and the smart people who give themselves airs nowhere. However they are all awfully gushing now.[31]

Unfortunately for the Playnes, Polly crowned her social success by becoming engaged to Erskine Pollock, a young barrister of good family and great pretensions who made extravagant demands in regard to a dowry and cast a rather bleak shadow over the Playnes' life for some years.

IV

All the Potter sisters were at least to some degree critical of their own mother and of the way in which she had run their family. Mary and Beatrice, the two who suffered most, were the most critical, but even Lallie found it necessary to admonish her mother about the inadequate care that was taken of Rosie during her adolescence. It was, however, inevitable that the sisters would replicate many features of the mothering and the familial organization of their mother. They had something of her imperiousness about them and much of her tactlessness. They found it difficult to express affection or emotion to their own children and were often somewhat aloof from them. They followed also, and in a very marked way, her pattern of favouring some children and rejecting others.

The favouring of one child as against another was much more readily accepted in Victorian England than it is today. It was a common feature of the life of many well-known families, especially ones in which there was a first-born son. Child psychology had not yet emerged as a science and hence no attention was paid to the psychological effects on a child of being unwanted or relatively unloved by its parents. It is interesting to see that it was only Rosie, the one sister who lived long enough to see the popularization of the ideas of Freud and the start of child psychology, who ever expressed either guilt or regret for the way in which she treated her favoured children as compared with the others.[32]

Favouritism was a feature of the parenting not only of all the Potter sisters but of most of their husbands as well. In its most extreme form, in the case of Georgie and Rosie, it involved the rejection of one or more children alongside the adulation of another. In other cases it was less extreme. Thus Maggie, while openly acknowledging that her youngest son Paul was her favourite and her special companion, does not seem to have disliked or neglected any of her children. Indeed she devoted herself to them in an extraordinary and courageous way, fighting hardest, as we will see, to protect and support Stephen, whose ideas and values she did not share but whom she none the less respected and cherished.

It seems almost inevitable that the Potter sisters, like their mother, would have selected sons for their special care and attention. While daughters were destined to share the same fate as their mothers, sons offered the possibility of living vicariously the active life of men. At the same time they provided some of that male affection and attention which was too often denied by husbands. Rosie was quite explicit about the way in which her oldest son, Noel, made up for the short-comings of her marriage. He offered her complete devotion and was an endless source of sympathy and compassion. His mind was better trained than hers, or than that of her husband George Dobbs, and it was akin to her own. She could talk with Noel about the spiritual problems which concerned her and he supplied ideas and information without ever making her feel inadequate or boring. She behaved to Noel as if he were her lover, going away from her home to spend days with him, and guarding him jealously from her second family.[33] He responded to her needs, and never evinced the interest in other women which would have aroused her jealousy.

Although Georgie did not write as revealingly about her feelings for her children as did Rosie, it was well known throughout the family that her eldest son, Daniel, was her great favourite. He too offered her something which went a little way to make up for the misery of her marriage. An intelligent boy with great charm, Dan was a general family favourite who appeared destined for great things. He was a talented ornithologist with a notable collection of birds when he died suddenly of peritonitis at the age of 23.

Dan's death in 1898 cut a great rift across the Meinertzhagen family life, from which it never recovered. Symbolically, they even moved house. Daniel senior and Georgie agreed to get rid of Mottisfont Abbey, the immense twelfth-century Abbey in Hampshire which had been their country home for many years, as Georgie could not bear the constant reminder of Dan which that house brought. He had not only lived in it but had also carried out his bird-watching and bird-catching there, arranging for the construction of large cages in which to keep his prey. After his death, Georgie collected and published some of his writings on birds. She talked constantly about him—to the chagrin of her next son Richard, who had also been very devoted to his oldest brother, but who felt keenly the difference between his mother's adoration of Dan and her cold neglect of himself.[34] Georgie's feeling for Dan never faded, and when she died her ashes were scattered over his grave in accordance with her wishes.[35]

Georgie's feelings and behaviour towards Dan were in striking contrast to those in regard to her third child and second son Richard. He was, as he later wrote, the 'black sheep' of the family, rejected by his mother and a source of suspicion and dislike for his aunts and cousins. He suffered severely as a child and never got over his feelings of anger and resentment at the differences he perceived in the way his mother treated him as compared with the way she treated his older brother. In his last years, Richard, now Colonel Richard Meinertz-hagen, wrote an autobiography, much of which deals with the horrors of his childhood, chronicling them with an intensity which suggests that the writing of this book was an attempt to lay to rest ghosts that had haunted him throughout his life.

Richard's story is quite appalling and it does seem that several years of his childhood were spent in the most extreme and acute misery. From his earliest infancy, he felt that his mother had neither interest in nor affection for him and attributed this to the fact that he was born at a time when the relationship between his parents was at a particularly low ebb. Georgie had spent a lonely pregnancy at Wallop, feeling miserable and insecure, and believing that Daniel was being unfaithful to her. She did not want this third pregnancy and, when the baby was born, was unable to feed him herself. Richard could not overcome his own revulsion at having been suckled by a common woman and an employee.[36] His childhood was unaffectionate but he was not desperately unhappy until he was 11. At that age he was sent to a boarding-school where he suffered from the most appalling cruelty and brutality. His account of this episode is quite devastating. His first experience of schooling was a happy one, shared with Dan, at Aysgarth in Yorkshire. But the harshness of the climate was bad for his health and he was sent instead to Fonthill in Sussex. Apparently his life there was an extended nightmare as the master in charge, Walter Radcliffe, was a brutal sadist who not only bullied Richard during the day, but pursued him to his bedroom at night. He was frequently bleeding and bruised from beatings and unable to participate in games from the severity of this treatment.[37] If Richard is to be believed, Georgie, on seeing the welts and bruises which remained when term was over, simply told him that he must have behaved badly. He was sent back to Fonthill to undergo more torment until one night, unable to bear it, he ran away and sought refuge in the home of a friend of his father's who, seeing the physical state of the boy, ensured that he was not sent back to Fonthill. Shortly afterwards Radcliffe was removed. This truly shocking story does ring true. At the same time, Richard accepts that his mother did not in fact receive many of the letters which he had written her complaining of his treatment and indeed did not know all about it until years later.[38] It is interesting, moreover, that the whole story is told as a means of illustrating the cruelty he suffered at the hands of his mother, and he never even suggests that his father might have some responsibility for it. Indeed, he accepts absolutely the notion that all the care of the children and all decisions concerning their education were taken by Georgie and that Daniel had no interest in these matters.[39] Yet while he comments on his love for his father and his admiration for him, and while he apparently wrote during these years to an uncle asking him to adopt him and take him away from home, Richard does not seem ever to have contemplated appealing to Daniel who was, after all, his legal guardian. Hence while Richard's story is convincing, the situation which gave rise to it is more complex than he will concede. None the less there is no question that the relationship between Georgie and this son was appalling, and that she may well have shown towards him something of the callous and unthinking neglect which Beatrice experienced at the hands of Lawrencina.

The other situation in which maternal favouritism on one hand and rejection on the other was a major issue was that of Rosie Dobbs. Rosie as we have seen, also adored her first-born son, Noel. But here too, the favouring of the eldest son was balanced against the rejection and dislike of the second. Pat, the first son of Rosie's second marriage, was born while she and George were in the throes of their earliest and most severe marital difficulties. She did not want a child then and was unable either to care for or to nurse him. Rosie was quite frank about this situation, to which she returned fairly often in her autobiographical writings.

He was a fine big child, but not an attractive baby, and from the first had a sullen and resentful look on his face, as if he owed a grudge to those who brought him into the world. Alas I felt little natural affection for this child, though materially I did all I could for him. I was not able to nurse him myself, cow's milk did not suit him, so on the doctor's advice I engaged a wet nurse for him, a young married woman whose husband had deserted her, whom I found at Queen Charlotte's lying-in-hospital. She proved a great success and was devoted to Pat, who returned her affection, but alas her own child whom she had put out to nurse died shortly after, a tragic occurrence indeed.[40]

George Dobbs did not care for Pat either, thinking then—as he and others continued to think—that Pat was possibly not his child, but rather the son of Cyril, with whom Rosie had been having an affair during the year prior to Pat's birth.

Rosie felt very guilty about her indifference to Pat and, having become somewhat interested in psychiatry, came to feel that many of the behavioural problems which he manifested, the worst of which was the kleptomania for which he was expelled from Marlborough School, were the result of her neglect and thus her fault.

How often have I tried to conquer my indifference to him, how often have I forced myself to kiss him, as I did my other children, and to show him the same affection, but generally I have failed to do so. So the poor little fellow grew up sullen and rebellious, for which we blamed him when really the fault was all mine. I think he embodied for me all those mental and physical characteristics which were antipathetic to me and he was the visible symbol of my loss of freedom in marriage.[41]

Her failings as regards Pat haunted Rosie for many years. In the late 1920s, when she was suffering from insomnia and depression as a result of the 'mania' which beset her from time to time, she contemplated suicide and wrote a 'Last Confession', in which she went over all her sins. Her neglect of Dyson in his last months was one of these, as was her behaviour towards Pat. One of her 'numerous crimes' was the fact that 'when Pat came and I could not love him . . . I allowed myself to treat him cruelly always showing preference for the younger ones and putting him on one side. Sometimes I tried to fight my want of love for him and at times treated him better but not for long.'[42] Curiously, while Rosie tortured herself about Pat, she rarely reproached herself for her treatment of Bill, her youngest son, and the one who ranked next only just above Pat in her estimation. Bill was born when Rosie was 44, and she somehow felt that her age meant that he was the most inferior of her children. She took little interest in his upbringing or education and decided that he alone of all the sons did not warrant a university education.[43] Instead she arranged for him to go into the Holt cotton business and then all but washed her hands of him. Her children were all apparently very well aware of the position they occupied in her affections. Noel was followed by Richard and both of them were the preferred and cherished sons. Next came Kitty, followed by Leonard, Bill, and then Pat. The children apparently coped with this hierarchy, always knowing who should ask for things they wanted and who should intervene at what time.[44] Rosie herself accepted this, often commenting in her later years that Noel and Richard were the only two of her children to whom she behaved as she should have—towards all the rest, she was guilty of neglect.

It was a cruel and tragic irony that the three most favoured sons, Daniel Meinertzhagen, Paul Hobhouse, and Noel Dobbs, should all have died while they were still in their twenties. Dan died of peritonitis when he was visiting Bremen to learn about his father's banking connection in 1898. The other two were casualties of the First World War. Noel was killed in the very last week of the War, having just returned to the front after a couple of years in Military Intelligence. Paul was killed a year before this, but he was listed as missing for many months. Maggie had to endure a long period of anxiety, hoping that he had been taken prisoner, but finally getting news and confirmation of his death.

V

The Potter sisters faced a number of difficulties with their children, of a kind quite unlike those which their parents had had to face with them. In part this was because so many of them had sons, and some of the problems with which they had to deal were ones which were by their nature confined to boys. Stephen Hobhouse, for example, turned towards Tolstoyism and then Quakerism in his late adolescence. As a result of this, he turned his back on the life-style and expectations of his parents, refusing to participate in shooting expeditions and even rejecting his inheritance and position as eldest son. Maggie found all of this understandably hard to accept, offending as it did both her taste and her sense of class position. In 1907, she wrote to Arthur that

Stephen had a fine holiday at Scarborough among his middle class friends of the Christian Social Union. He finds them restful and entertaining. But I wish he would go more among his own class in culture and refinement. It is a mistake to associate too much with inferiors as they flatter without meaning to do so, and make one vain and self-opinionated.[45]

Yet for all this snobbery, Maggie eventually came to support Stephen in many of his actions, and indeed to demonstrate both an extraordinary sense of duty and a kind of heroism in the process. Stephen's religious beliefs led him to pacifism, and during the First World War he declared himself a conscientious objector. His pacifism was strongly supported by the Courtneys, who endorsed this position themselves. Maggie, however, was not a pacifist by conviction. She supported the war and had two other sons, one of them her favourite, fighting in the trenches. None the less, she not only respected Stephen's position, but assisted him in every way she could. Maggie came to understand a new world when Stephen's imprisonment introduced her to military tribunals, law courts, and prisons. She was appalled at the savagery with which the conscientious objectors were treated and by all aspects of prison administration and, as we will see, devoted much time to working and writing on the subject of prison reform. In other ways too she tried to assist Stephen. After he had rejected his inheritance and shown that he would not follow any kind of lucrative profession, she established a trust from her separate income to ensure that he received a small income throughout his life.[46]

Just as it was sons who were the centre of concern during wartime, so too it was they who were the cause of worry and distress in peacetime, this time in regard to their sexual behaviour. Here again the Hobhouses were involved. Arthur, their second son and an attractive young man of great charm, was unusual amongst the Potter men in going to Cambridge. Whilst there he became an Apostle and a close friend of Maynard Keynes and of others who subsequently formed the Bloomsbury Group. While at Cambridge he succcumbed to the charm of Duncan Grant and was involved in a homosexual circle for some years. This was a cause of acute distress to his parents. When he came down from Cambridge, he was sent on a long round-the-world trip, presumably to break these associations and to prepare him for the serious business of selecting a profession—and a marriage partner.[47] The Meinertzhagens also had to deal with irregular behaviour in one of their sons. Fritz, their third son, never settled to any acceptable way of life and had a penchant for women of a lower class with dubious reputations. He eventually married a 'girl from the theatre', despite threats from his father that he would be disinherited if he did so.[48] The family, especially his sisters, did their best to welcome his wife and to include her, albeit in a limited way, within their activities. Indeed theirs became quite the favourite house to visit amongst their nephews and nieces and the one where one always got the best tea![49] The final case, involving Rosie and her son Richard, is an interesting one. Richard, while a medical student, began to live with a woman fellow student. Not wanting them to have to live in shabby surroundings, Rosie offered to let them share her flat. George Dobbs was appalled by their behaviour—and Rosie ruminated on why it should be the case that he would have accepted Richard's resorting to a prostitute much more easily than he could accept this situation, which was in her view a perfectly reasonable way for a young couple to sort out whether or not they wanted to spend their lives together.[50] Indeed, as Beatrice commented in her diaries, Rosie, who had so shocked all of her family by her behaviour, was merely showing the way of the new century. Her sexual experimentation and her indulgence in sexual relations without marriage were to become the norm to which all the others would have to adapt. But it was Beatrice who intervened decisively in this situation, eventually persuading her nephew to marry his girlfriend.[51]

While sons had a greater range of ways in which to cause parental anguish, they were not the only ones to do so. Indeed it is clear from the experiences of the Potter sisters that middle-class family structures were becoming looser towards the end of the nineteenth century than they had been in the earlier part of it, and that daughters too could, if they chose, move away from the family and exert their independence in ways which their parents disliked.

The extent to which this was the case was made most evident in the Holt family. Lallie, although a devoted mother, was a somewhat difficult and overbearing one. She was, as one of her daughters later recalled, 'very generous and very kind, but she was quite tactless and never stopped to consider feelings when her mind was set on anything'.[52] Robert Holt was altogether a weaker man, and apparently one of a self-pitying and querulous disposition. Neither of them was able either to control the behaviour of their children or to influence that behaviour in ways they desired once the children were in their late adolescence and early adulthood. Many events within the Holt family were generally disruptive and distressing at this time, and family tensions mounted steadily towards the horrible climax in 1902.

The first event which caused distress and disruption was the wedding of Kitty, the oldest Holt daughter. Whereas Potter weddings had either been small affairs with no bridesmaids, or large ones in which all the unmarried sisters automatically took their part in the procession, weddings for the next generation did not follow this easy formula. Kitty Holt was to have the large and lavish wedding appropriate to the daughter of a Liverpool grandee, but she insisted on choosing her bridesmaids herself—and refused to have her sister Molly as one of them. Despite his attempt to gloss over family problems, Robert Holt was unable to omit this incident or its consequences from the account of the wedding in his diary.

All the arrangements were good. The only serious regrettable drawback from a perfectly joyous and pleasant wedding was Kitty's strange obstinacy in refusing to allow Molly to appear as her bridesmaid—very rough on the girl and has created much feeling in the family—this curious attitude appears to arise out of some idea on her part that it might offend her Newnham friends, Misses Chamberlain and Ellis—most absurd. However rather than have serious 'ructions' we have yielded and Betty acts alone—this has offended Betty and the Boys and the home atmosphere is heated—a thousand pities.[53]

The friction surrounding this event was known to the rest of the family and for Kate, at least, it meant that the wedding was 'not a happy one'.

The next source of disruption and distress came from the second daughter, Betty, who followed Kitty in insisting on asserting her independence against the family's wishes. In her case too, it was the way things were done rather than what she wanted for herself which caused distress. For Betty, although she did not seek tertiary education, did want to engage in paid work outside the home. But she neither consulted nor informed her parents about what she was doing, behaving for a number of years in a rude and off-hand manner. Her rudeness was extended beyond the immediate family to her sister-in-law, Eliza Holt. Eliza felt for some years unable to visit the Holt family home if Betty was there.[54] This was all the more difficult for her as Eliza was very close to Lallie, and was indeed the one who attempted to comfort and support Lallie through her various family crises. Betty's behaviour, like Kitty's before her, produced not only bad feelings between herself and her parents, but rather more widespread family tension and conflict. This was particularly the case when, in 1900, Betty accepted a job at Roedean school without informing Lallie. She did inform Robert when the final letter confirming her appointment arrived, but Lallie was away from home at this time and hence was not told. When she returned to find that all the rest of the family knew what was happening, she felt that Robert and Betty had entered into a secret agreement without her and the already deteriorating relationship between Lallie and Robert became even more strained.[55]

In neither Kitty's case nor Betty's do the Holt parents seem to have made, or even to have attempted to make, any serious remonstrance. They did not assert themselves in any effective way. The final family tragedy shows this incapacity to intervene, or even to indicate that certain behaviour was unacceptable, in an extreme and almost incredible form. In this final family quarrel Molly, the youngest and gentlest of the Holt daughters, was again the unwitting victim of a power battle among her siblings. It took place in 1902 and involved a struggle between the youngest son, Lawrence, and Betty, over Lawrence's dog. This animal, which had been trained in obedience to its master, one day had the temerity to refuse to respond to Lawrence's whistle, and to run instead to Betty (who whistled in competition with her brother). Lawrence decided to punish this act of disobedience by whipping the dog and was engaged in giving it a savage beating when Molly tried to intervene. Lawrence turned his full fury on her, beating her so savagely that she was unable to leave her bed for more than three weeks and could not use one arm for many months.[56]

This ghastly scene finally brought an end to any kind of family unity for the Holts. Lallie was understandably appalled by Lawrence's behaviour, and felt that he was the one at fault. Robert, however, sided rather with his son, and refused to utter any reprimand or criticism of him. Kitty and the other three sons sided with Robert and Lawrence, and indeed refused even to talk to their mother or their sisters. Only Dick and Eliza tried to work with all parties.[57] Robert and Lawrence departed for the Holts' holiday home at High Borrans for a time, and then Lallie and the two girls went on holiday too. An agreement was reached by the family that Betty and Molly would leave Liverpool, settling not less than twenty-five miles away from it and that they would 'refrain from doing or saying anything likely to cause annoyance' to their father. In return, Robert agreed to pay each of them £200 per annum to maintain an independent home.[58]

That the son who behaved so brutally should remain at home, receiving all the care and comfort his family could provide, while the daughter who was an innocent victim of that brutality should be effectively banished from home, provides a very clear illustration of male dominance and patriarchal power. For Lawrence was to go into the family businesses, which he did with marked success, and hence he could not be upset. Lallie was angry and embittered at the failure of Robert to say or do anything to Lawrence. This failure seems to have been the result of Robert's habitual weakness and indecisiveness. He, like his oldest son, was apparently 'very much afraid that Lawrence would do something desperate if home is made too wretched for him'.[59] So home was made as comfortable as it could be, although Robert subsequently did have occasion to bemoan the fact that Lawrence appeared entirely lacking in feeling, or in gratitude for the many kindnesses which were offered him in the following years.[60]

This whole episode shows not only a particularly acute form of family breakdown, but also the extent to which women within the family, whether wives, mothers, or daughters, were ultimately dependent on the male head of the family. For all her feelings about the matter, Lallie was unable to do anything about her son. She was not his guardian, nor did she have any legal power to refuse him access to the home in which they had both always lived. She could use her separate money to increase the comfort of her banished daughters, but she was unable to alter the fundamental situation. The strongest and most powerful of the Potter sisters was, in such a situation of family breakdown, held firmly in check by the lack of legal power or status of Victorian women.

Beatrice and Kate watched sadly as their sisters suffered the pains of family life where once they had experienced joys. Beatrice believed that their suffering was a direct result of the excessive self-sacrificing devotion the sisters had lavished on their young:

She [Lallie] said to Kate and me a year or two ago, 'I can't see where exactly I have gone very wrong, I have always loved them and worked day and night for their comfort.' This was a mild statement of her deserts from the standpoint of a self-devoted mother and wife. Alas! poor sister: where you erred was in doing too much for them, in being a passionately attached partisan ... you made your children regard life as one constant ministration to their physical comfort and self-complacency without the obligation of good manners towards others. And in the last five years they turned on you—the one person who was defenceless—the qualities you had bred in them by your partial unreasoning self-devotion.[61]

Lallie was not the only one of her sisters to have years of devotion met with callous neglect. Mary Playne too had to cope first with the rejection of her by her adopted daughter and then with the hostility of her son, Bill, and his wife. In Beatrice's view this, though tragic for Mary as was Lallie's situation for her, was a result of her own life. Indeed Beatrice's comment on Mary stands as a general summing up of her own rejection of all that was held dear to middle-class mothers in Victorian England—and all that her sisters saw as their duty.

Poor Mary, she brought up both her own and her adopted child to be world-lings and they have treated her accordingly. Parents seem to be more cruelly punished for bringing up their children to seek their own interest than for oppressing their children—out of selfishness.[62]

IX

Public Life

I

ALTHOUGH organizing a home and a family made the first call on the time and energies of the Potter sisters, these domestic duties did not occupy all of their time. It was quite unthinkable, apart from being financially unnecessary, for any of them to engage in an activity to earn an income. Many of them chose rather to devote some time and energy to the range of unpaid public work which was becoming available to middle- and upper-middle-class women in the second half of the nineteenth century.[1] Philanthropy provided an introduction to public life for them as for so many other women, and several of the sisters gave much of their time to dispensing charity or to working for philanthropic organizations.[2] Some of them moved from these activities to politics, finding some scope for themselves in local government and in the women's auxiliaries which were established by the national political parties in the 1880s. Public activity of this kind was an accepted, even an expected thing, for the Potters. All the sisters engaged in it once they were married, with the exception of Blanche and Rosie. Their failure to do so serves mainly to point yet again to their personality problems, and to their differences from the others.

It is important to note the change in regard to public life which was brought by marriage. Only two of the sisters, Kate and Beatrice, had been active in philanthropic work or in social research prior to marriage. In both cases, the decision to take up such work was made in the face of strong familial disapproval. This disapproval was largely a result of the way in which the work chosen interfered with familial and social life. Kate, as we have seen, chose full-time work for the Charity Organisation Society quite explicitly as a way of withdrawing from her home and from the London Season. Her decision was an unusual one. Philanthropic activity was not a normal part of the lives of single upper-middle-class women at this time. The very prominence of such women as Florence Nightingale, Mary Carpenter, or Louisa Twining shows why this was so. All of them were unmarried women who dedicated their lives to a chosen cause. This made them admirable, but pointed at the same time to the impossibility of integrating such activities with the social round and the successful marriage which made up the agenda of most upper-middle-class girls.[3]

For married women, by contrast, there was a considerable range of public activity, all of which could be carried on in the time not required for domestic and familial duties. Moreover, as several of the Potter sisters demonstrated, many philanthropic, local government, and political activities could be shared by husband and wife. This often served to strengthen marital bonds by increasing the range of shared interests. It also provided ways in which wives could support and assist their husbands' careers or favourite projects. Public life could and did produce marital and familial tensions of its own, but it was none the less often an integral part of married life.

The division between public and private life was not as sharp as some recent discussions of Victorian domestic ideology might suggest.[4] Hence although most of the Potter sisters only became actively engaged in philanthropic and political activity after they married, it was not the case that public life or the public gaze was entirely new to them. They experienced something of it by virtue simply of the class from which they came and the kinds of men they married. In girlhood they participated in London Society, which meant that their social life was undertaken under public gaze and involved large-scale entertainments at which they met and became known to prominent figures in the political, business, and professional worlds. Marriage made this an even more significant feature of their lives. Not only did most of the sisters marry men whose wealth and position meant that lavish and large-scale entertaining was part of their normal wifely role, but in many cases this entertainment was directed towards specific public goals or towards advancing the career prospects of their husbands.

Marriage opened up the public world for some of the Potter sisters by virtue of the specific men they had chosen. Lallie, Theresa, and Maggie all married men whose families had traditionally been active in philanthropic or community matters and who had pronounced interests in these areas. Robert Holt came from one of Liverpool's most prominent families and one which was known both for its financial success and for its role amongst the Unitarian philanthropic community. Robert was particularly active in the Unitarian church and in local government, crowning his achievements by becoming Liverpool's first Lord Mayor in 1892.[5] Lallie did not give her whole heart to philanthropy, any more than she adopted the Unitarian beliefs and practices of her husband and his family. But she did participate in some philanthropic work, particularly the extension of district nursing to the urban poor. She also became involved in politics, becoming a prominent member of the Women's Liberal Federation. In a similar way, when Maggie married Henry Hobhouse, she allied herself with a man who was very involved in philanthropic work in London and in philanthropic and educational work in his own county, Somerset.[6] She too did her small part to help, but remained less than fully engaged in Henry's activities.

Whereas marriage offered Lallie and Maggie a new public life which was not entirely welcome, Theresa found in her marriage the scope for all the philanthropic endeavours that she had previously wanted to take up, but for which as a single woman she lacked the independence and singleness of purpose. She had long wanted to follow Kate into the Charity Organisation Society, or to establish a celibate sisterhood of charitable workers. She found support in Alfred Cripps, a man with social and philanthropic interests similar to her own, while at the same time marriage provided her with the status and the base from which she could enter early into a whole range of activities. She took part in technical and domestic education in the county of Buckinghamshire and had just begun to take her place alongside her husband in political activity when she died in 1893.[7]

Although in these cases the public activity of the Potters resulted from their sharing the interests of their husbands or the range of activities considered appropriate in the families into which they married, this was not the only model which the family provides. In the case of Mary Playne, the situation was reversed. Her husband, Arthur, was a rather aimless young man who enjoyed his small estate, his adequate income, and his hunting and shooting. It was Mary who became interested in and concerned about the domestic conditions of the local poor, and who set herself to remedy these through establishing institutions for domestic and technical education. Subsequently she entered into local government and, under her influence, Arthur too became a 'concerned citizen', a magistrate and an active member of the County Council.[8] Marriage was important here too, but only because it was this which gave Mary the impetus and the social basis from which to work. It also provided her with a family name which was known in the area and a large home which was invaluable for entertaining, staging fund-raising events, holding Red Cross exhibitions, and generally as a focal point in the community.

Marriage brought as substantial a change for those who had previously been active in public life as it did for those who had not, albeit
change of a different kind. Kate and Beatrice had both to give up their
earlier activities on marriage, taking up new ones which gave them
more time for domestic life. For Kate the transition was a smooth one.
She had to cease her work as a rent collector and as an organizer of
boys' clubs for the Charity Organisation Society, although she
retained her interest in the Society and in a number of philanthropic
matters. But she turned her attention to Leonard's career and towards
the various political issues which were of interest and concern to them
both. She devoted most of her time to Leonard, campaigning and
entertaining for him and becoming very involved in all the women's
auxiliaries which were established to assist the major political parties.
She also worked actively as an opponent of the Boer War and as a
pacifist during the First World War, engaging independently in
causes which were dear to both her and Leonard.[9]

It is somewhat ironic that Beatrice, the one sister who achieved
public prominence before marriage, should have been the one for
whom marriage brought an almost total cessation of public life.
Beatrice had followed Kate into the Charity Organisation Society in
1883. Unlike Kate, she was not motivated by philanthropic concern,
but rather by a desire to understand the basis of poverty and of the
endemic social problems with which so many people were concerned
in the 1880s. Beatrice used the Charity Organisation Society as a
starting point for her broader social investigation which was pursued
first as part of Charles Booth's monumental study, *London Life and
Labour*, and later as a series of investigations into particular aspects of
working-class life and organization. She had published articles,
appeared before a Royal Commission, and delivered public lectures
before she married and was considered something of an expert on
various aspects of working-class life.

Although Sidney shared her view that their marriage should be
primarily a working partnership, in the early years he also engaged in a
great deal of work outside it. The Webbs began their voluminous
researches by investigating the history of trade unions, before turning
to look at the history of local government and of the Poor Law. But
while Beatrice's time was given primarily to research, Sidney
managed also to occupy significant public positions. He was a
member of the London County Council and for some years the
chairman of its Technical Education Committee. His work here and

in the Fabian Society occupied a large part of his day and, for at least the first thirteen years of their marriage, Beatrice had no counterpart to this. She never indicated a desire for public activity during these years. The fits of depression, the insomnia, and the periods of ill health which she suffered in the years after her marriage left her exhausted and with the strong feeling that she was only able to do a few hours work each day. Moreover, despite her own courting of public renown, she was profoundly ambivalent about the private and public roles which women should adopt and she felt some unease about women appearing in public.[10] One senses that she was using Sidney as an excuse as well as deferring to him when she declined an invitation from E. R. Pease to speak at a Fabian Society meeting. 'The hidden masculinity of Sidney's views of women is incurable in his decided objection to my figuring among the speakers. See how skin-deep are these professions of advanced opinion with regard to women, among your leaders of the forward party.'[11] When she actually wished to become prominent in the Fabian Society some years later, Sidney's views did not present any kind of obstacle.

It was not until 1905, when she was appointed to the Royal Commission on the Poor Law, that Beatrice Webb really emerged as a public figure. The sittings of that commission continued for three years during which Beatrice came to feel more and more strongly opposed to the chairman and the majority of the other commissioners. Where they were proposing merely to use voluntary charity to supplement the poor relief which had been available in the workhouses since 1834, she wanted rather to see the Poor Law ended, and to have the various different kinds of poverty traced to their causes and treated accordingly. This would involve a whole panoply of different forms of state and local intervention through age pensions, public health care, minimum wage rates, and so on. Beatrice, as Margaret Cole says, 'bullied and harried her fellow Commissioners', but she did not make them change their views. As a result she and the others who shared her ideas produced a minority report, which was actually written by Sidney, and which became the basis for the campaign to end the Poor Law which Beatrice led for the next few years. She thoroughly enjoyed this venture, as her diary entries show:

Since we took up this propaganda we have had a straightforward job, with no problems of conduct, but with a great variety of active work—organising office work, public speaking and personal persuasion of individuals, work which absorbs all one's time without any severe strain on one's nerves. I enjoy it because I have the gift of personal intercourse and it is a gift I have never, until now, made full use of. I genuinely *like* my fellow mortals whether as individuals or crowds—I like to interest them, and inspire them, and even to order them, in a motherly sort of way. Also I enjoy leadership. Everyone has been kind and appreciative; and money has come in when I have asked for it, and volunteers have flocked around us.[12]

Although this campaign was unsuccessful, it gave Beatrice a taste for public life. Afterwards she took a far more active role in the Fabian Society and especially in the Fabian Research Department. She also achieved the prominence which made her an obvious figure for future commissions and inquiries. In 1917, she became the only woman on the Reconstruction Committee set up to plan for the coming of peace.[13] Indeed by the early 1920s she was probably the most prominent woman in Britain—a fact which she deplored, especially when it meant that she was constantly being appealed to whenever a female presence was required.

II

In marrying men who were engaged in politics the Potter sisters were simply following a family tradition, for their family had a history of involvement in political and public causes. Their grandfathers on both sides had been radical Members of Parliament and public benefactors.[14] Although their father forsook both the radicalism of his forebears and the tradition of parliamentary activity, he was both interested and active in politics. As a wealthy patron, he took quite a large part in local Conservative Party elections, introducing his daughters to candidates and to electioneering procedures at a very early age. He constantly discussed politics with them, and corresponded about political matters until shortly before his death. Lawrencina Potter was even more influential in establishing the primacy of political life with her daughters. She venerated her father and saw his political and public activity as the archetype of the desirable life. In her novel, *Laura Gay*, the heroine seems to enunciate Lawrencina's beliefs when she asks, 'What career can be more noble than that of the legislator of a free and constitutional country?'[15] In her journal, Lawrencina wrote quite openly of her desire to have Richard take up a political career.

Having considered my husband's abilities and integrity, I have come to the conclusion that he would well serve his country in Parliament, and with a view to his doing so I purpose to live economically, avoiding all useless expense in the way of society living, or the indulgence of taste; and devoting my time to study, the education of my children, and to those duties we owe to our mutual relations and to the poor around us.[16]

The wily Richard, although he flirted with the idea from time to time, preferred the making of money to the provision of unpaid service to his country. But Lawrencina's enthusiasm appears to have been contagious: in later years, Maggie Hobhouse did actually manage to persuade Henry to give up the life of a *rentier* and country gentleman and to enter politics. Indeed, Lawrencina would probably have been delighted to see four of her daughters married to Members of Parliament.

In writing about her desire to have Richard enter Parliament Lawrencina described her own life in very limited and domestic terms. Although she had apparently participated in the work of the Anti-Corn Law League, she does not seem to have envisaged a substantial political role for herself, even in the event of Richard entering politics. For her daughters, by contrast, there was a wide range of public activities associated with being the wife of an MP. The daughters grew up and married in an era in which demands for an extension of the suffrage to women were constantly being made, and in which women were generally more vocal about legislation and about public issues than they had been in their mother's day. From the early 1880s onwards, women were drawn into electoral campaigning on an ever increasing scale, particularly after the passage of the Corrupt and Illegal Practices Act of 1883.[17] The Act was intended to reduce the inordinate amount of bribery and corruption which had been a scandalous and expensive feature of British elections throughout the nineteenth century. It outlawed the bribery, treating, assault, and abduction of electors, and imposed a fine for a variety of other practices, such as the provision of conveyances to voters. In lieu of these tried if not exactly true electioneering devices, the use of women as unpaid campaigners began to develop. More reliance was placed on wives and other family members and the various political parties began to establish women's auxiliaries which co-ordinated the efforts of female political supporters. The Women's Liberal Federation, the Women's Liberal Unionist Association, the Conservative and Unionist Women's Association, and the Primrose League were all established in the 1880s primarily for this purpose.

Several of the Potter sisters were active in these organizations, finding in them a satisfying focus for their own political interests and a way to assist husbands or relatives. Kate was one of the originators of the Women's Liberal Unionist Association, which held its first meeting at her Chelsea home on 11 May 1888.[18] She supported Leonard in his refusal to accept Gladstone's ideas on Irish Home Rule, and she saw the WLUA as a vehicle for publicizing the unionist case and extending its range of supporters. In June, a month after the association had been formed, she noted in her diary that 'the Women's Liberal Unionist Association takes up a great deal of time as the chief brunt falls on me—it is very interesting work'.[19] A month later, while noting the high calibre of some of the women who were active in the Association, especially Lady Stanley and the women's suffrage leader, Millicent Garrett Fawcett, Kate conceded that 'we have not spread at all rapidly'. None the less she continued to work for the association acting often as secretary, in the hope that the enthusiasm and the merits of its members would make up for their small numbers. She organized large numbers of meetings and even ventured into the realm of public speaking, moving around the countryside to address meetings in Devon and in the north of England.

Unlike Beatrice, who was interested mainly in the centres of power and in the motives and the behaviour of the men who wielded or who sought it, Kate found the general tenor of a women's auxiliary association very much to her taste. She clearly enjoyed the mixture of political discussion and social activity. This mixture became an issue within the WLUA in July 1889. The monthly committee meeting

ended with a sharp encounter between Lady Frances Balfour and Mrs. Gibson of Birmingham (an excellent women but horribly serious and wanting in humour) on the subject of mixing political meetings and discussions with music and other amusements. This subject proved very exciting and one after another members jumped up to give their opinions and experiences—one lady, Mrs. Goddard, saying if only we had a Unionist poet who would write them a Marseilleis—the Union would be safe.[20]

Kate's enthusiasm for the WLUA began to wane in the late 1890s. The electioneering work of that group, especially its support of conservative and unionist candidates whose views on most political and social matters were contrary to hers and Leonard's, was distasteful to her. Finally the support the Association gave to the Boer War, which she and Leonard both totally deplored, made her feel the connection was intolerable. Much to the apparent regret of the other members of the association, many of whom said 'a great many kind things about my being the heart and soul of the Association etc.', she resigned from the Committee on 24 October 1900.[21]

Kate's activities in London were more or less paralleled by Mary Playne in Gloucester. Although Mary did not leave a diary detailing her daily or weekly activities, her obituary in the Gloucester Chronicle indicates the nature of her role: 'She rendered valuable service to the conservative cause being one of the founders of the Mid-Gloucester Women's Unionist Association of which organization she was one of the most active members.'[22] Through this association and the political contacts which it enabled her to make, Mary was able to be of great assistance to her brother-in-law, Alfred Cripps, when he stood as the Conservative and Unionist candidate for the division of Stroud in 1892. She did not experience the same disillusionment with the Women Unionists as did Kate: her political views were conservative and she supported very strongly the imperialist views of the Conservatives and Unionists during the 1890s. She was also a staunch supporter of the British Government in the Boer War.

The other sister who was active in this general area was Lallie. Her political position differed from that of her sisters. She and Robert Holt had stood almost alone in the family in their support of Home Rule, so this issue did not raise any questions about their adherence to the Liberal Party in which Robert was very active. Lallie devoted her time and effort to the Women's Liberal Association, and though she does not seem to have been one of the founders of the Liverpool branch of this body, she was quite an active member of it. Robert Holt recorded that in May 1889 she went to London to attend the Conference of Women's Liberal Associations. He joined them there and found 'the women delegates were an amusing lot—badly dressed but of a strong determined type—meaning business. No duchesses but women evidently as strong in mind as most were in body.'[23] Lallie attended some meetings of the Association and entertained its members at home, but it was for her considerably less of an interest than it was for Mary or Kate. Political activity, like philanthropic and social activities, took second place for Lallie to her care for her large family.

The electioneering assistance of wives was not confined to participation in women's auxiliaries. As Kate recognized, her presence was an important part of Leonard's campaigning and she always went with him when he visited his electorate of Liskeard. Theresa Cripps too campaigned on behalf of Alfred in the very short period of his first election campaign prior to her death. Maggie, who had first persuaded Henry Hobhouse to enter politics, also did her part to assist him. She had no taste for women's political organizations any more than she had for female philanthropy or community work. Her individualism sought rather to find its own path. In her electioneering for Henry, one sees something of the spirit which Beatrice so often noted when talking about Maggie's overwhelming and sometimes unscrupulous energy. Indeed Maggie's efforts probably appalled the cautious and courteous Henry Hobhouse as much as they did some of his indignant neighbours. For Maggie apparently went to work not only distributing electoral tracts and pamphlets, but setting up stalls from which Henry's supporters could address the tenantry on the various estates which were in his electorate. On one occasion, as an angry neighbour wrote, having been refused permission to do this by the park-keeper on the grounds that the owner of the estate did not want to have the different candidates haranguing his tenants, 'she went straight to the principal tenant, Andrews, who ... is about leaving and with whom my relations are severely strained, and actually had the good taste to request that the booth should be set up on his land in direct opposition to my express wishes'.[24] Whether or not Maggie's efforts were decisive, Henry Hobhouse won this election by a convincing majority.

The intense interest in politics of the Potter sisters and their involvement in political organizations and particular political issues did not incline them towards women's suffrage. Like many other women from very wealthy and well-connected families, they either took little interest in, or even opposed, most aspects of the Women's Movement. In 1889 when Frederic Harris on organized Mrs Humphry Ward and others to write a public statement of opposition to Women's Suffrage—ostensibly written and signed by women—both Beatrice and Maggie were signatories.[25] Indeed, Harrison attempted to persuade Beatrice to take up the cudgels and to continue this attack when the first 'Appeal' received angry replies from leading suffragists. Beatrice, who was just at that time beginning to establish her reputation as a social investigator, declined, not wanting to become identified with any political group at the very moment when she was attempting to make a name as an impartial observer.[26] Moreover her stance on this question was, to say the least, somewhat inconsistent with her attempt to establish a career and a position of public prominence. Her family was rather shocked by 'her emancipated ways', as she travelled around the countryside, attended trade union and co-operative conferences, smoked cigarettes, and generally took relatively little notice of the limitations which society imposed on women. She recognized some of the problems of her position but had no inclination to enter into battle.

Marriage brought two of the Potter sisters into contact with the Women's Movement. When Kate married Leonard Courtney in 1883, he had been for some years the leading Parliamentary Spokesman for women's suffrage. He was very friendly with the Fawcetts, and Millicent Garrett Fawcett was then emerging as the leading force amongst the suffragists. Kate in turn became friendly with Millicent Fawcett who, in 1892, 'persuaded me to join the Women's Suffrage Appeal Committee composed of all parties and I think it will be interesting to meet the different active women—Liberal Federation; extreme temperance and Primrose League'.[27] Kate continued to follow the fortunes of various suffrage bills with interest, but the cause was not one which she really took to heart. Leonard's support for women's suffrage was moderate and Kate took up his tone. Both he and Kate continued to attend and address occasional women's suffrage meetings, but they became demoralized when the militant suffragettes came to the fore. Kate was appalled by the window-breaking and arson campaigns which began in 1911. The behaviour of the suffragettes was 'simply idiotic as far as I can see' and she grieved for 'poor Millicent Garrett Fawcett' whose 'life's work was ruined by them'.[28] Kate's major interest lay in other political issues: the fate of the Liberal Unionists; opposition to the Boer War; pacifism and support for the Women's International League for Peace and Freedom during the First World War. Women's suffrage did not make a strong moral appeal to her, as did these other causes, and nor was it an issue in which she could use her position in the world and her personal knowledge of influential people. It seems clear that for her, as for most of her sisters, the influence which they could wield personally through their husbands, their contacts, and their general social position was of greater importance than any increase in the political power of women generally.

Beatrice too was converted to support for women's suffrage only after marriage. Sidney Webb had long been quite a strong supporter of women's suffrage, and he always claimed the credit for making Beatrice change her mind, and turn from an opponent to a supporter of the Cause. It is clear that he disagreed with her signing of the

Ladies' Appeal against Women's Suffrage and he wrote to her very early in their relationship that he thought she would need to do something to retract that position. In due course Beatrice did just this. In 1906 she wrote a letter to Millicent Garrett Fawcett stating that she had now come to support the idea of women's suffrage and explaining the reasons for her change of mind.[29]

Beatrice and Kate, even after they had been brought to see the need for women's suffrage and to support it in a general way, refrained from becoming directly active in campaigns for women's rights. Kate was always acting as Mrs Leonard Courtney—lending her name and her influence to women's groups. Beatrice too offered rather the use of her name than any more direct effort. This was very much the case with her public retraction of her earlier opposition to women's suffrage. The comment she made about it in her diary leaves one in no doubt that she saw her public adherence to the Cause as likely to provide great benefit. 'Here is my formal recantation. For sometime I have felt the old prejudice evaporating. And as the Women Suffragists were being battered rather badly, and coarse-grained men were saying coarse-grained things, I thought I might as well give a friendly pull to get things out of the mud, even at the risk of getting a little spattered myself.'[30] With Beatrice's permission, Millicent Fawcett sent her letter to *The Times*, with an introductory note pointing to the satisfaction which all suffrage workers felt at now having the support of some of 'the ablest women who have hitherto opposed it'. Beatrice also gave some support to the Fabian Women's Group and helped to have the Fabian Basis, the general set of beliefs of the Fabian Society, amended to include a commitment to equal citizenship for men and women. She gave donations to the Fabian Women's Group and edited and provided introductions for two very interesting special supplements of the *New Statesman* dealing with women's rights and the situation of women in society and in employment. But she was really only offering the use of her name, for her major energies were devoted to the Fabian Society and to the National Committee for the Prevention of Destitution which had grown out of her opposition to the Poor Law. She did not feel strongly enough about the situation of women to devote much time to improving it. Moreover she clearly preferred to spend her lobbying, social, and political time with men who were prominent in the Labour Movement or in national politics.[31] The women's movement was of marginal interest to her—and, in her view, it was itself a marginal movement.

The only one of the Potter sisters to take a deeply felt interest in women's suffrage was Georgie, who spent the last few years of her life passionately engaged in it. Involvement in the suffrage movement was one aspect of the emergence of a new woman which followed on the death of her husband. Daniel Meinertzhagen died in 1910 and Georgie, although she had nursed him devotedly through the last stages of his illness, and deeply mourned his death, seems to have been given a new lease of life by her final release from this terrible marriage. She immediately became involved in the suffrage movement. She followed Millicent Fawcett and the moderate or constitutional suffragists, but seems to have had some sympathy for the more militant and dramatic tactics of the Pankhursts and the Women's Social and Political Union. This is not to say that she supported their campaign of arson, but she did send a telegram of support and condolence after the death of Emily Davidson, who had thrown herself in the way of one of the horses running at Ascot in 1912. Georgie attended suffrage meetings, marches, and demonstrations and constantly drew attention to the cause until her sudden death in 1914.[32] She was often accompanied by her daughters—and indeed seems to have been instrumental in turning their attention to this cause. The very fact and the nature of her involvement underlines the lack of commitment of Beatrice and Kate, for Georgie was passionately interested and enjoyed all the activities involved in the suffrage movement, finding there a focus for her energies and a way to compensate for the imprisonment of the previous years.

III

Although the Potter sisters on the whole showed little interest in the various campaigns to extend the rights of women, several of them took full advantage of the expanded public sphere towards which those campaigns had been directed. Moreover, with the exception of Beatrice, they saw their public role as a natural extension of their domestic and feminine duties. While Beatrice was quite intentionally moving into masculine territory, through her social investigation and her interest in male organizations like the Co-operative Movement and trade unions, her sisters remained firmly within the feminine part of the public sphere. Like many other prominent Victorian women, they wished not to question the role of women, but to extend their range of concern so that issues pertaining to the education, domestic life, and health of the poor were included within it. As Anne Summers has recently pointed out, the expanding role of women in philanthropy provided a means whereby middle-class women moved outside the home only in order to point out to working-class women the full range and importance of *their* domestic responsibilities.[33] There was nothing very emancipated about any of this: it was all centred around stressing and enlarging the area of women's duties.

Several of the Potter sisters were quite explicit about their own desires to raise the level of domestic skills of working-class women and hence, or so they hoped, the level of comfort within working-class homes. This aim provided the stimulus for Mary Playne's efforts to establish the Training College of Domestic Science. The official history of the school made this concern a part of the story.

Early in her married life, she [Mary Playne] had come to regard with horror the home conditions of the workers during the first period of the Industrial Revolution, and somewhere about 1873 she had started an eating place for work people. Not content with that, and desirous to help the women in her neighbourhood help themselves, she herself in her own words 'obtained a diploma for teaching cookery in elementary schools, and carried on classes in Minchinhampton School.'[34]

Following the lines common to Victorian philanthropists and reformers, she saw the problem of working-class living conditions as the result of ignorance rather than poverty. She attempted to set up a system of training which would result in many individual women being taught to 'help themselves'.

In the 1870s, when Mary was still engaged in the teaching of domestic science on a small scale, the broader question of the place of domestic subjects in elementary school was undergoing much discussion. The Education Act of 1870, the first legislation which attempted to ensure the provision of elementary education to all children in England, had precipitated much discussion as to what education was appropriate and how this differed between boys and girls. There was much sympathy amongst many of those elected to the School Boards which the Act brought into existence for the provision of a sound domestic training for working-class girls, to make up for the inadequate instruction and practice which they would receive at home.[35] Before domestic subjects could be taught, trained staff were needed. In 1874 the first training school for domestic subjects, the National School of Cookery, was established in London. Similar schools in Liverpool and other provincial centres followed. In 1890, Mary Playne was offered the services of one of the graduates from the Liverpool School of Cookery, along with the suggestion that 'Gloucester might be made a centre for the teaching of cookery in elementary schools throughout the country'.[36] This idea filled Mary with enthusiasm and she immediately set about establishing her own committee and gaining assistance and money from local individuals and local authorities to set up a school. In 1892 the Gloucester Training College of Domestic Science began to train teachers of domestic science. Mary continued to play a major role in supervising the school. In 1902, when County Councils became responsible for education in their areas, the supervision of the college was transferred to the Education Committee of the Gloucester County Council. Mary Playne was an active member of that committee, and chaired its Domestic Economy Subcommittee to which the special responsibility of the College was given. She remained chairman of this subcommittee until 1909 when, at the age of sixty, she resigned that office, although she continued to be a member of the committee until shortly before her death in 1923.[37]

The Gloucester Training College of Domestic Science had an extensive curriculum which differentiated carefully between the needs of those who would be teaching domestic subjects in elementary schools and those seeking the more advanced diploma or looking for work as skilled cooks or seamstresses. All the subjects were taught at various levels; thus students could take instruction in cookery, artisan cookery, or high-class cookery. Similarly they could choose to learn plain needlework, elementary dress-making, dress-making, advanced dress-making, and millinery. Laundry and housewifery were also taught. The records of the college indicate that students were marked and assessed for their practical work, demonstrations, children's teaching, theory of the subject, and theory of education.[38]

Mary Playne's enthusiasm extended beyond the College to other areas of technical education. She was a co-opted member of the first Education Committee of the Gloucester County Council in 1903 and continued to work on that Committee until the War. Her husband, Arthur, was also a member of the County Council and of the Education Committee for all that time, and the Playnes divided matters between themselves so that Arthur took a greater interest in secondary education while Mary concentrated on elementary, technical, and domestic education. For a number of years she was on the Elementary School Management Committee as well as on the Domestic Economy

Subcommittee of the Gloucester County Council Education Committee. Her standing within that committee was made clear by the fact
that she was the first of the Governors appointed by the County
Council as part of its scheme to regulate Secondary Schools and Institutions for Technical Education in 1909. In the same year she was also
selected by the Education Committee as one of its two trustees for the
scheme to regulate the Minchinhampton Education Foundation.[39]

Mary's efforts in the field of education gave her a rather stronger
bond with some of her brothers-in-law than with her sisters. Sidney
Webb was for some years the chairman of the Technical Education
Committee of the London County Council and Alfred Cripps chaired
that committee on the South Buckinghamshire County Council.
Theresa showed signs of following suit: shortly before she died she
had been engaged in a scheme for the technical education of women
and girls in South Buckinghamshire. But the other sisters had rather
less interest in this field. Lallie did apparently play a small part in the
Liverpool Cookery School, but this did not extend to any large
commitment, nor did it last very long. Beatrice also gave some thought
to the question of education, especially of women, but did nothing
about it. She did participate in the founding of the London School of
Economics, being an assiduous and effective fund raiser and taking a
close interest in the staff and the problems of the school. But the
scheme was originally Sidney's idea rather than hers and she did not
extend her interest to other areas of education. Neither Georgie nor
Maggie took any interest in this question either. Indeed Maggie held
herself rather aloof from Sunnyhill, the girls' grammar school which
the Hobhouses had helped to found and of which they remained
governors. Henry took a close interest in many aspects of the school,
but Maggie seems to have confined her activities to the selection of
gifts and prizes for the end-of-year prize-giving. The lack of interest in
their own education, and in that of their daughters, did not predispose
the Potter sisters to a sense that this was a field of very great
importance.

But the extent of Mary's involvement in technical and domestic
education was also one facet of her general concern with community
issues. Her greater interest and capacity for public involvement than
that of some of her sisters was also evident in another field: that of
district nursing. The nursing profession had been the focus of interest
and attention from the middle of the nineteenth century. The
prominent role of Florence Nightingale and her little band of nurses

in the Crimean War, the agitation for the proper care of the sick in workhouses, and the rising prestige of the medical profession had all focused attention on the need for properly trained nurses.[40] In the last decades of the century, attention turned from the provision of nurses in particular institutions to the question of nurses for the sick within the community. Florence Nightingale supported this scheme and it gained wide public approval.[41] The Queen Victoria Jubilee Institute was established in London in 1898 and large numbers of Queen Victoria District Nursing Associations were established in cities and rural areas throughout the country. In Liverpool, where district nursing had long been established through the Liverpool Training School, the Jubilee effort led to the separation of district nursing from the school, and the establishment of a Queen Victoria District Nursing Association to extend the range of nursing which had been done previously.[42] Elsewhere district nursing associations were set up with committees to supervise the selection and the work of the district nurses they employed.

The Potter sisters were not interested in becoming or in allowing their daughters to become nurses. Their role, as befitted women of their influence and affluence, was to work as unpaid committee members or supervisors of the various nursing districts. The role of women on these committees, however, varied considerably from place to place. Liverpool was a pioneering city in this activity, but its general social conservatism was expressed by the total monopoly men held of all public and philanthropic office. The Committee which ran the District Nursing Association, like that which ran the Liverpool Training School for nurses, was made up entirely of men. They employed a Lady Superintendent to run the nurses' home and work with the district nurses, but the policy-making was done by a group of prominent men. The role of women in this situation was a relatively small one: they were charged merely with supervision of the day to day routine.[43]

When Liverpool was divided up into districts in 1893, each of these had a 'Lady Superintendent' whose task was the raising of money to cover the cost of the nurse employed for that district and the presentation of a brief annual report containing details of the financial situation and the year's work in their district. It is clear that the whole system hinged on the use of wealthy women as 'Lady Supervisors' since they were often the ones who contributed the bulk of the funds. Lallie jointly supervised 'district number 5' with her sister-in-law,

Mrs Alfred Holt. The two of them generally paid £40.2.0 per annum, which was just under half of the amount needed to finance their district. The Treasurer usually raised another £40.0.0, and the patients who were seen by the nurse added £2.15.6. Mrs Rathbone, wife of the man who had organized the training of nurses, also acted as a Lady Supervisor for one district. She generally contributed £30.0.0 per annum.

The wives of many of Liverpool's distinguished citizens were active in this area, doing their small bit to complement the larger functions of their husbands. It was seen by the Holt family as Lallie's central philanthropic and public interest. After her death, the district which she had supervised was renamed 'the Mrs Robert Durning Holt Memorial District'. The memorial was endowed by Robert Holt and provided an annual dividend of around £30.0.0 per annum.[44]

But the complete male domination of public life in Liverpool was not evident elsewhere. In Gloucester, for example, women founded and controlled the Stroud District Nursing Association. There too the money to found this association was contributed by those wishing to subscribe. The first meeting to discuss the establishment of a nursing association was called by a prominent local woman, Mrs Clissold. Both men and women attended, and there was general agreement at the meeting that Mary Playne should become the first president of the committee of the Stroud and Nailsworth District Nursing Association. The executive committee which she chaired met fortnightly and dealt with all matters of policy and employment.[45] This committee was responsible for fund raising, and Mary frequently donated her house and the services of her secretary to arrange concerts and other entertainments to raise money. But it was concerned with other areas as well.

Mary Playne was clearly a formidable woman with a broad experience of committee work and a sound sense of her own worth and ability. One of the first things she did as president of the committee was to establish the areas of authority of her committee and that of the local doctor who worked with them. He attempted to veto the appointment of a nurse chosen by the committee on the grounds that he wanted a nurse who had three years' training while they had chosen one with only two. Mary Playne challenged him publicly on this matter, arguing that it was practically impossible to find such a nurse for the salary they were offering. She insisted that two years' training at a good hospital plus wide experience would be better than three years at an inferior hospital with little or no experience.[46] She won her point both in regard to the particular nurse in question and as a matter of general policy. Thereafter the committee, along with the matron at Stroud hospital, supervised the work of the district nurse.

IV

The range of philanthropic and political activities undertaken by the Potter sisters remained more or less constant until 1914. Several of the sisters had died by this time, and age brought a reduction in the level of activity which Mary in particular could undertake. But the nature of their activities did not alter until the outbreak of the First World War. For them, as for so many others, the war brought a new impetus to bear on public life. It added urgency to the political activities of the Courtneys, while offering a new range of activities to Maggie and Henry Hobhouse. In Maggie's case, it made public life and public activity a dominant interest for the first time.

When the war broke out in 1914, Henry Hobhouse was Chairman of the Somerset County Council and also of the County Council's Association. He immediately became involved in some of the organizations set up to put the country on to a war footing. He took a leading part in the War Agricultural Executive for Somerset and in the Food Production Council established by the Board of Agriculture to devise ways to increase the home-grown food supplies. He was strongly in favour of the war and helped the war effort with a will. Maggie too accepted the necessity of war and the rightness of the British intervention in it. She also wished to participate in the war effort and, after working to extend recruitment, turned her attention towards the financial burden of the war and the need for national and domestic economy. In 1915 she became one of the founders of the National Economy Movement, acting as honorary secretary and using her many social and political contacts to gain support for the movement from prominent individuals. She also organized both public and drawing-room meetings, and addressed groups of workers in canteens.[47]

Maggie's enthusiasm for the war was somewhat tempered by having her youngest son, Paul, volunteer immediately for active service. But it was directly challenged by her oldest son, Stephen, who had become a Quaker some years prior to the war and hence refused to have anything to do with it. When the war broke out, Stephen was living and working in the East End but he very soon became involved in assisting the 'innocent enemy aliens' who were trapped in England. In the first few days of the war, Stephen, along with Kate Courtney and several others, established the Emergency Committee for Germans, Austrians, and Hungarians, to aid and support these unfortunate victims of international aggression. Stephen chaired this body until the introduction of conscription in 1916. When that happened, he felt it necessary to protest against the war in a more direct way by refusing to enlist. As a result, he was required to appear before one of the tribunals set up to hear the cases of conscientious objectors. He refused to apply for any kind of exemption or to undertake any alternative war service and was sentenced to a year's imprisonment with hard labour. Stephen's actions were strongly supported by the Courtneys, both of whom opposed the war, and his uncle Alfred Cripps who endorsed some of his pacifist views and was appalled at the treatment meted out to conscientious objectors. Maggie, although she did not share any of Stephen's beliefs, felt a great respect for the strength of his conviction. She was shocked that people 'who teach and believe, or rather imagine they believe, the Christianity of Jesus Christ' could be so hostile to the position of the conscientious objectors and wrote to tell Stephen that 'I honour you for your motive and for your courage. Such a motive and such courage will bear its fruit as a testimony of higher attainable ideals, and of willingness to undergo shame and sorrow for them.'[48] Stephen's health had always been a cause of concern, and Maggie was very worried about his capacity to cope with the rigours of prison life. She began almost immediately to campaign for his release. But as she became more and more aware of the dreadful state of the prisons, she extended her work first to campaigning for the release of all conscientious objectors and then, when the war was over, for prison reform.

Beatrice Webb wrote a somewhat sardonic summary of the conduct of both Stephen and Maggie during this episode. She had attended several tribunals of conscientious objectors and had very mixed feelings about them, noting that many of the young men in the Labour Movement who declared themselves to be conscientious objectors were only too delighted to find some other and more acceptable reason for refusing to enlist. Stephen was quite the reverse of this. At his tribunal he

calmly awaited his fate as a c.o. though, as a well known Quaker, who would in any other denomination be regarded as a minister of religion, he could easily have got totally exempt, if he had chosen to plead. As a matter of fact he would have been medically exempt had he undergone a medical examination. But Stephen was determined to be a martyr and all the effort of the War Office to prevent the scandal of 'Hard Labour' for a saint, who happens also to be the son of an eminent country gentleman of conservative opinions, was of no avail. Then followed a year or more during which he was challenging ever severer punishment by a conscientious objection to obeying prison regulations, whilst his mother was working with all her energy and somewhat unscrupulous wit for his release—a duel of wills in which M.H. eventually won and Stephen was indefinitely released.[49]

Beatrice had mixed feelings about Stephen himself, respecting his commitment, but not greatly liking the Society of Friends. She saw him as a religious mystic and fanatic, and although this appealed to her own streak of unsatisfied religious yearning, she never quite trusted him. But she was fascinated to see Maggie so concerned about him and so absorbed in his beliefs and his activities. 'She is in perpetual revolt against his uncompromising virtue. [But] The rationalist materialist—the believer in pecuniary self-interest—is under the spell of the religious fanatic.'[50]

Whether under the spell of Stephen or not, throughout 1916 and 1917 Maggie became very concerned about the harsh and, in her view, unjust treatment meted out to COs and devoted the greater part of her time and energy to doing something to remedy this. In her customary way, she began by writing to many of the influential political and other public figures she knew, seeking their support and assistance. She also engaged in an extensive correspondence with newspapers, sending many letters expressing her views. In 1917 she published a long pamphlet with the dramatic title 'I Appeal unto Caesar'. The authorship of this pamphlet has recently been attributed to Bertrand Russell, but Maggie certainly got the credit.[51]

Maggie's capacity to see both sides of a question was an unusual quality within a family which tended to have strongly divergent views on most major political issues. In the First World War, as in the Boer War, the Potter family was deeply divided. The Playnes strongly supported the British war effort and threw themselves into recruitment, and Mary turned Longfords into a centre for the provision of 'comforts' for English soldiers. On the other hand, the Courtneys were ardent pacifists, attacking the war itself and England's part in it. Indeed, during this war Kate's work and efforts overshadowed Leonard's.

Prior to the war, Leonard had watched the mounting aggression and the alliance system which Britain entered with growing concern, speaking out about it from the House of Lords, which he had entered in 1905. Kate in her turn had joined several women's organizations, speaking there of her pacifist views. When the war broke out, she devoted most of this energy to the Women's International League for Peace and Freedom.

Kate tried to use all her influence to persuade the various Ministers she knew to allow the English contingent to attend the 1915 Women's Peace Conference at the Hague. She was a member of the WILPF executive and had planned to attend this international conference herself. However, a few days before the conference was due to begin, she noted the obstacles placed in their path by the Government in her diary.

Urgent summons to our committee to say that the Government have cancelled all permits—subsequent interview with the Home Sec—a bit relaxed and probably a few will be allowed to go—but how to choose from the one hundred and seventy-five who were going is a difficulty. Yesterday I went to see Lord Haldane on my own found him very friendly as usual but frankly saying at first we could do no good and might do harm—later on he said the conventional mind would take that view and finally said he would let us go and would talk to McKenna that evening about it. I am afraid the F.O. won't ... Finally Mr. McKenna agreed to 25 going. 5 officials and 20 whom he chose out of the 180 booked. Then came the closing of the North Sea—why we do not know—and none could go.[52]

Fortunately, as Kate noted subsequently, a couple of women had already left and so there were three representatives of the British contingent at the Hague. Although unable to attend, Kate did much to defend the Hague Conference when it was bitterly attacked in the press, and later helped organize the trip Jane Addams made to England to speak to members of the Government and to provide public information about the activities and resolutions of the conference.

V

The public lives of Victorian women were, as we have seen, an extension of their private ones, involving an extension to the world outside the home of the nurturant qualities women offered to their families. The lives of the Potter sisters indicate that it was an extension of their private role in a more immediate way than this. For most of the sisters, public activity provided a way of supporting and assisting husbands or children in their political or other activities. Ideally this brought husbands and wives or members of families closer together and for Kate, Mary, and Beatrice this was certainly so. But in other cases it was the public arena which showed the real disagreements and stresses in family life, and women could find themselves forced to choose between different members of their family. Maggie Hobhouse is an example of a women pulled in contrary directions by her need to support all the male members of her family at a time when their various views were entirely opposed to each other.

As we have seen, it was only the advent of the war which provided Maggie with a public interest. The ordinary range of palliative philanthropy, and the involvement in women's auxiliaries which her sisters so enjoyed, had never taken her fancy. It was only the combination of the national emergency which came with the war, her concern about Paul fighting in it, and Stephen's sufferings as a conscientious objector combined with a recognition of some of the horrors and injustices existing in English society and government, which provided an engrossing interest for Maggie. At the same time, her crusade on Stephen's behalf cut short her work for national economy—and made her strongly critical of the government and the judiciary which she had previously taken for granted. She became furious at the thought of judges who could sentence idealistic young men to the horrors of penal servitude, without themselves having any ideas of the conditions which they were thus imposing upon them. Hence her public interest served to make her critical of her society in a way in which she had never been before.[53] It is not surprising that it drew her somewhat closer to Beatrice than she had been during the previous twenty years, when her own strong belief in individualism and in forwarding the claims of one's family had clashed powerfully with Beatrice's 'collectivism' and her strong views on the importance of performing one's social duty and being a useful citizen. Maggie's discovery of a public object, while it was directly related to the fate of her son, drew her some distance away from the outlook and activities of her husband. As she had always recognized, Henry Hobhouse was far more conservative than she, and he lacked her capacity for seeing different sides of a question and ability to see the need for opponents to be able to express and live by their views. Although there is no direct evidence to indicate that her interests in COs and prison reform caused an estrangement between herself and her husband, such an estrangement did develop in the last years of their marriage. When, in 1920, Maggie's activities were halted by the onset of lung cancer, Henry spent as little time as he could with her, remaining in the country when she went to their London house to seek treatment and to wait for death. It seems not unlikely that her fairly radical shift of position and of interests had a part in this as, while she continued to take an interest in what he did, the main focus of her activity shifted towards working for one son and then seeking spiritual consolation for the death of another. The public role which she adopted, in so far as it was supportive of her family, pulled in contradictory directions and, ultimately she had to choose between supporting her husband and supporting her son.

Maggie was perhaps unfortunate in having to deal with such a conflict over so crucial and emotional an issue as the war. However, other sisters had had to face some semblance of this conflict before: Georgie, for example, had spent her whole married life with a man whose staunch conservatism in politics clashed totally with her vague radicalism. This difference was a constant and underlying source of unhappiness and restraint rather than an active problem. It surfaced once, however, in 1899 when Georgie, who had been outraged by the Dreyfus case, wrote to Captain Dreyfus inviting him to come and recuperate at her home. Daniel was not amused—and fortunately the invitation was declined.[54]

Despite the much greater prominence of her public role, even Beatrice Webb demonstrates the extent to which women were expected to provide public assistance and support for their husbands. Her activities and her comments about them illustrate both her general acceptance of this fact, and the conflicts which, as an ambitious and in some ways very independent woman, she felt about it. It is not true to say that all of Beatrice's public work and activity was subsidiary to that of Sidney's, or that it was all designed to help and assist him in achieving their joint objects. There were very significant occasions during which it was Beatrice who was the dominant one and Sidney took the subsidiary and supportive role. This was so during the Poor Law Commission and in the campaign to end the Poor Law. After that, when Beatrice decided to take a more serious interest in the Fabian Society, and to set up and mould the Fabian Research Department, she worked largely independently for a few years. But these two situations, important as they were, were atypical of the Webbs' married life and occupied less than one third of their long marriage.

For the rest of the time, it was mainly Sidney who was the active one, in the Fabian Society, the London County Council, the London School of Economics, the Labour Party, and the Labour Governments of the 1920s.

Beatrice had little time for women's organizations, whether they were auxiliaries of political parties or of any other kind, but she played a conventional role in working towards her and Sidney's various objectives. In regard to the London School of Economics, for example, she acted as a fund raiser and subsequently attempted to keep the relationship between themselves and the school on an easy footing by regularly entertaining the staff of the school and attending and sometimes organizing functions for its students. In a similar way, she played the role of hostess to many sections of the Labour Movement and to all the Labour MPs, as Labour began to gain a parliamentary foothold. The Webb household and its hospitality were somewhat notorious for Beatrice eschewed meat, alcohol, and rich foods on health grounds—and was disinclined to allow her guests to engage in the kinds of self-indulgence which she deplored both morally and on the grounds of health. At the same time, her carefully selected little parties seem to have been of great interest and often to have been enjoyable. Certainly the Webbs were never short of people seeking invitations.

Despite her disinclination to engage in women's activities, and indeed what some of her women friends regarded as her general dislike of women's company, Beatrice did make some attempts to establish an informal woman's organization within the Labour Movement. This was the Half-Circle Club which she began in 1920, as a club for the wives of newly elected Labour MPs. She felt profoundly concerned about the situation of these women who suddenly found themselves in London, facing situations and demands for which their earlier experience, as workers or as the wives of working men and union officials, had not really equipped them. Whereas Liberal and Conservative politicians drew their wives from the social classes in which women were trained from girlhood for their social and public duties, the women of the Labour Movement had never received this training. But it is a revealing aspect of Beatrice's own social assumptions, and of her snobbery, that she should believe absolutely that the only form of social intercourse, and the only way of dealing with being an MP's wife, was that which she had experienced herself in the wealthy and cultivated Society of her girlhood. It was clear to the women whom she intended to benefit that she felt they were 'dreadfully unpresentable' and was attempting to educate them in proper manners. After a few coffee sessions and a few 'interesting' talks, the Half-Circle Club became defunct.[55] The women of the Labour Movement were disinclined to allow Mrs Webb to groom them in the ways of political society.

Yet at the same time as Beatrice was conspicuously failing as an instructress in etiquette to some Labour women, she was establishing a firm hold on the women in Sidney's electorate of Seaham. From 1919 until 1928 Sidney was the Labour representative for the division of Seaham in Durham. Although Beatrice was not very enthusiastic about the thought of Sidney's becoming an MP, she did everything she could to assist him. She joined in the work of studying the history of the mining industry in Durham and of learning all about the various institutions and problems that obtained in that electorate. She accompanied him on electioneering trips and spoke and lectured herself. Indeed some of the male electors took great pride in the fact that 'our candidate's *wife* can answer questions better than the other man himself'.[56] But Beatrice took the role of candidate's wife much further than this. She wrote a monthly 'News Letter' to the women of Seaham and encouraged them to form groups which would read and discuss her letters. In these she very carefully detailed her own life and work—as the wife of an MP—and then provided information and discussions about particular political issues and problems. She attempted to combine an educational letter with a gossipy chat about what she did and how she looked after Sidney. This endeavour was apparently a successful one: Sidney retained his seat until he felt no longer able to withstand the rigours of campaigning, and Beatrice was always a welcome figure to the electorate. She did manage, moreover, to convey a sense of herself as primarily the wife of their MP, who simply happened to be in London and thus knew the political details which she passed on.[57] She made no attempt to groom these women for polite society, but rather accepted them in their own surroundings. Margaret Cole is probably correct in her suggestion that the miners' wives of Seaham were members of a homogeneous community, 'of the type she had learned to love long ago in Bacup and in the Co-operative Movement, and whose natural good manners she had always appreciated'.[58]

But Beatrice's support of Sidney had its limits. When in 1926 Sidney was raised to the peerage as Lord Passfield, Beatrice adamantly refused to accept the title for herself. She was no longer interested in engaging in Society, preferring to spend the time when she was not working with Sidney in preparing an autobiography. She was, if anything, relieved when the Court and the Prime Minister announced that if she would not take the title, she must refrain from any official social activity. This, as she said, left her quite free to entertain friends from the Labour movement and elsewhere and removed an onerous obligation.[59] Here then, Beatrice asserted in a very forthright way a claim to independence and to limit her supportive role. But it came when she was already seventy, and feeling less and less inclined to enter into social or any other kind of public life. Moreover Sidney had not been very keen on accepting the title, and had done so only under duress. Hence her gesture was a rather smaller one than it would have been earlier. At this stage Sidney did not need her help or support in his social activities and she was thus quite free to refuse it. Whenever it had been important, she used her name, her extraordinary skills and abilities as a speaker, an organizer, and a manipulator to assist him and to work for the partnership. Her own needs and interests, as well as her personal views, were in fact rarely made public, but remained within the privacy of her Diary.

X

Old Age and Death

THE history of old age is the least well-known aspect of the female life cycle, and the part of women's lives which has received least discussion.[1] In part this is a result of the fact that old age is a variable and subjective category. There is no single barrier to be passed before one is old, and there are no rituals preceding the entry into this final stage of life. Menopause was and is obviously a factor in making women feel and be seen as old, but this itself occurs at different ages and in different ways and is not always noted. Hence old age lacks clear dimensions. Within the nineteenth-century context, it is particularly notable that while every other aspect of a woman's life was subject to prescription, no role or duties were laid down for old women. The absence of a defined role suggests that there was none: when women were no longer able to perform their reproductive and familial functions, they had no social value or purpose. But it is possible that this very lack of prescription opened new possibilities for women, particularly for those who had some measure of financial independence. For the first time in their lives, they found themselves free beings, subject neither to parental authority nor to the imperatives of maternal duties. Age in these circumstances offered opportunities which had hitherto been unthinkable.

Here as elsewhere the Potter sisters show something of the range and variety of experiences possible for middle-class women. For some, their last years were ones of inordinate and indeed of insupportable misery, during which they faced rejection by husbands or the callous neglect of children. This was so in varying degrees for Lallie, Blanche, Mary, and Maggie. But theirs was not the only pattern amongst the sisters. Georgie had a few years of radiant widowhood, as she rediscovered herself and pursued independent interests surrounded by adoring children. Rosie in particular emerged in a new light in her later years, discovering the joys of cheap travel and indulging to the full her love of scenery and of painting. In the course of this she even won the admiration of Beatrice.

One of the first and most noticeable differences amongst the Potter sisters was the age at which they began to describe themselves as old—and at which they began to be seen as old by others. It is not surprising to find that those women who had borne large families and devoted themselves primarily to the care of husbands and children became old at an earlier age than did their childless sisters. The many comments that were made about the ways in which their family responsibilities exhausted Lallie, Georgie, and Blanche were finally borne out in the early age at which they became old women. For the mothers of large families, it would seem that age came during the woman's fifties. Lallie was an ailing, weak, and vulnerable old woman throughout her fifties. Although Maggie and Georgie were not as weak as their eldest sister and experienced new interests and surges of activity, they too saw themselves as old during their fifties. By contrast, Beatrice only emerged as a public figure in the course of the Royal Commission into the Poor Law when she was in her late forties. It was this which gave her her first taste of leadership and provided the impetus for her to involve herself more fully with the Fabian Society and with public life. She did not feel herself to be an old woman until she was sixty, and the same seems to be true of Kate and of Mary. All of these women continued to engage in new public activities and to keep up their old interests well into their sixties or even beyond.

The difference in age at which the various sisters became old was paralleled by different activities, relationships, and experiences once they were old. Indeed the Potter sisters seem to illustrate one of the many tragic ironies evident in the situation of women. Those sisters who fulfilled their own sense of duty and the socially approved role of women by marrying, bearing large families, and sacrificing their own interests and desire to those families, had to endure early, lonely, and painful old age. In the course of this, the divergence between their interests and outlook and those of their husbands became increasingly apparent and they faced estrangement and neglect from men to whom they had devoted themselves. By contrast, the sisters who were childless—or who had very small families—and who had fulfilled their lives with public interests and activities shared in their late years the same kind of closeness and companionship with their husbands that they had in their youth. The continuity of shared public interest provided a more enduring bond and a firmer relational basis than did shared family concerns. Kate and Leonard, Beatrice and Sidney, Mary and Arthur lived and worked together until death or infirmity made this impossible. They present a striking contrast to the despair of Blanche, the loneliness and isolation of Lallie in her last years, the sad and lonely death of Maggie.

Most of those sisters who had children did have the redeeming pleasure of grandchildren in their later years, and one should not underestimate the amount of pleasure that this brought. Like their own parents before them, the Potter sisters were very helpful to and supportive of their children during the years in which they were beginning married life and producing families. Lallie looked after the daughters of her oldest son, Dick, while he and his wife had holidays and settled into their home. Georgie provided a similar service for all of her grandchildren and seems to have found it easier and more enjoyable to be affectionate and demonstrative to them than to her own children. On one occasion, she was left with a small grandson while his parents went on an extensive tour of North and South America. When they returned, it was to find that their son regarded Georgie as his mother, was happy only in her arms, and treated them like a visiting uncle and aunt. Maggie too played hostess to the daughters of her daughter, Rachel Clay. Here, as elsewhere, it was the sons that mattered most, and she indicated an enthusiasm about the impending birth of Arthur's first child which she had never shown towards Rachel. Rosie too enjoyed her grandchildren although, unlike the other sisters, she seems to have had the same extreme enthusiasm for some and complete lack of interest in the others which she had shown with her own children. But while the joys of grandchildren were an additional bonus, they could not make up for a fundamentally lonely or miserable situation. Moreover they were usually an occasional presence: none of the sisters actually lived with their married children and hence grandchildren could not fill up empty days. They were not, as public and political activity were, a complete occupation.

I

Within the Potter family, the alternative to a life of public activity and political interest in old age was one of private misery or marital neglect. Several of the sisters had to face marital conflict and complete marital breakdown in their later years. Here they were very much the victims of cultural values and stereotyping, as they were left isolated old women while their husbands continued to be active in business and social life—and usually replaced their aged wives with younger women. Sexual attraction and sexual activity were assumed to end for women with menopause, but men suffered no such curtailment of their activity. Both Alfred and Willie Cripps and Henry Hobhouse all married again when they were in their sixties or beyond, while George Dobbs established close relationships with a number of women in his later years.

The situation of women within family life was shown at its most vulnerable when they were old, especially if age was accompanied by infirmity. At this time one could see most clearly the powerlessness of women, and the extent to which they depended for their comfort on charm and on the capacity to arouse strong affections in the hearts of their husbands and children. Unfortunately, as John Stuart Mill had suggested earlier, the self-sacrifice and devotion which women offered to their families tended only to make their menfolk selfish and arrogant.[2] It did nothing to enhance the value of these women, or to ensure that when they needed it their devotion would be returned.

It was Lallie whose situation was the most miserable in old age. In her younger days she had been the terror of her sisters, swooping down on them from time to time, and managing, or trying to manage, everything. In her last years she was a lonely and distraught woman, rejected and disliked by both husband and children. Lallie's powerful personality did not fit easily into the mould of wife and mother. She lacked tact and charm and was able only with difficulty to repress her force and her vitality. The many insights, the rapid flow of speech, the warmth and generosity which won her outside friends and interest from strangers would have been well suited to large public objects. But these qualities were disliked by her husband and undervalued by the children who followed his extremely conventional cast of mind. Beatrice despised Robert Holt, seeing him as a timid and vain man, jealous of Lallie's abilities and of the admiration which she excited. Her dislike of such a man is predictable: his wealth, his lack of concern about major political and social questions, his immersion in a social world which she had rejected would all have contributed to it.[3] But Kate, who was herself more moderate and more conventional, held a very similar view both of Lallie and of the inability of Robert to appreciate or deal with her.[4] After Lallie's death, Kate reflected sadly on the life and loss of the sister who had been closest to her in age, and of whom she had been fondest.

That sister of mine always knew what she liked and though she often saw with blinkers on she saw far and absolutely straight and clear and was one of the most genuine persons I came in contact with—and her large warm heart gave her numbers of outside friends of all sorts and conditions, who admired and loved her and have now lost something out of their lives—even casual acquaintances were struck by her personality . . . she had a great flow of talk— sometimes a little overwhelming and she was subject to the family habit of being possessed by a subject—then her words would tumble over each other in their eagerness . . . Unfortunately her husband's conventional cast of mind was very foreign to this hearty unrestrained and unmeasuring woman and her persistent affection for him did not smooth over difficulties as it surely should have done. She tried pathetically but not always successfully to supress herself but the natures of some of her family were not always compatible.[5]

Although Robert Holt seems not to have cared for anyone else, he was almost totally estranged from Lallie for the last eight or nine years of her life. Incompatibility between the two of them was exacerbated by broader family tension and the complete family breakdown of 1902, and eventually Robert hardly spoke to Lallie at all. She remained with him, wanting to ensure that he did not refuse their proper entitlement to any of the children. Without youth, energy, or independent financial control, Lallie was powerless and victimized within her family— and, as Beatrice said, her habit of self-sacrifice did not inculcate any consideration for her in her children.

To her warm expansive nature, passionately attached to husband and children—this cold methodic boycott was just torture. Naturally enough she takes to drugs—cocaine to make some hours less gloomy. As her physical habits deteriorate the distaste for her company—now amounting to a positive repulsion of her husband increases. And yet he wishes to retain his right to her constant attendance on him. Even her little pastime of playing 'patience' becomes a grievance—the 'click' of the cards becomes intolerable, though at the same time he refuses to permit the use of a separate sitting room, on the ground that two fires when one would suffice is extravagant. One extra fire grudged with an expenditure of £12,000 a year.[6]

In her last years Lallie was reduced to a state not dissimilar to that of Blanche as an impotent victim. Blanche, as we have seen, had not only to put up with her husband's neglect, but with his crude and blatant display of a new and younger woman. Both Beatrice and Rosie commented on the fact that Willie ceased showing any concern for Blanche the moment that he had ceased to find her sexually desirable and had transferred his sexual attentions elsewhere. Blanche was forced to visit Willie's mistress, Giulia Ravogli, at least once a week and to have her and her family frequently as guests both in London and at the Harrison Cripps's holiday home. She had to suffer almost as painful a loss as that of Willie's affection as she watched him become less and less interested in his medical profession and more and more interested in business and in the making of money. Blanche venerated Willie's scientific pursuits and had given much of her time and energy to helping him in writing the medical books which had made his reputation. In her later years, she lost not only her husband but the entire life to which she had devoted herself. She spent much time painting and translating Shakespeare into French to fill the hours,[7] but these activities did not help to make her life bearable. Blanche was strangely methodical at the end: she worked hard to furnish and decorate their new holiday home in Scotland and returned to London to see her children. She saw or spoke to all of them, attended a last social occasion at which Giulia Ravogli was present and then, having said goodbye to all her family, she simply hanged herself from the shower in her dressing room with one of Willie's bandages.[8] Although brought on by despair, her last act had, as Beatrice noted, something of a bizarre nobility and generosity about it. 'Did she think that now Willie had a grand new place he might be better with a new wife? And in her heroic way try to bring it about?'[9] Blanche did not have to cope with neglect by her children. They, especially her sons, were devoted to her. The bitterness and dislike evident between them and their father, however, served as an additional source of grief, and it was yet another aspect of her situation that she was powerless to change.

While Blanche and Lallie had to deal with extreme situations, others faced slightly milder ones. Maggie and Henry Hobhouse became estranged in the last years of Maggie's life. They remained in contact with each other, but Henry was rarely present by her sick-bed and showed little concern for her in her last and terrible illness. Subsequently Henry remarried—and although Beatrice resented this on Maggie's behalf, Maggie herself did not have to face it. Indeed, apart from her private discussions with Beatrice, she left no hint or suggestion that there had ever been fundamental problems and disagreements in her marital relations with Henry.

The other sister who had to face a new kind of marital relationship in her later years was Rosie. In the early years of her marriage to George Dobbs, it was she who had sought and enjoyed the company of other men. But in the later years this situation was reversed. During all the years they had spent in Switzerland, in most of which George lived in hotels while Rosie stayed in a villa close by, George had met a number of other women who became close personal friends. One in particular, Mrs Westby, was a widow to whom he became very devoted. The relationship was apparently a platonic one although George spent quite long periods of time staying with his new friend. Some of the time he and she and Rosie were all together. They visited Sicily together and, when George and Rosie settled in England during the Second World War, Mrs Westby came to stay with them and even accompanied them on a visit to the Webbs. Rosie had less difficulty dealing with this situation than one might have expected. Her own earlier experiences, her lack of sexual jealousy of her husband and her interest in her children, her sketching and travel, all stood her in good stead. As Beatrice said, when it came to questions of sexual behaviour, Rosie

has the last laugh on her prudish sisters. She shocked us with her free ways during her widowhood. Today her free ways are *a la mode*. From first to last she had maintained that there is no harm in free love. Towards her husband's warm friendship with a lady twenty years younger than his wife she shows friendly sympathy, remarking that 'George is so much happier and pleasanter when Mrs Westby is there'.[10]

The loneliness and the general neglect suffered by some of the sisters is particularly striking in view of the care and attention which they had lavished on aged relatives at earlier periods. All of the sisters—with the exception of Blanche, who was too unstable herself, and Rosie, who was too young—had been closely involved in the care of Richard Potter in his last years. Especially during the eight years between his first stroke in 1884 and his death in 1892, they had all taken their part in ensuring his comfort. Beatrice bore the major part of this burden, but Lallie and Mary had Richard to stay for long periods and Maggie, Theresa, Kate, and Georgie all took turns in coming to stay with him and to cheer him. He had a full-time nurse as well, and a diminished but still lavish household staff. Nothing that could have been done to increase his comfort was omitted.

Of course their immense wealth meant that the Potter sisters, although sometimes miserable and sad, never had to face the real physical want which was the lot of many old women during their lifetime. Indeed their wealth not only ensured the provision of physical comforts, but also provided the means whereby some aspects of the family situation and their isolation might be alleviated. Several of the sisters had paid secretaries or companions who provided them with help and company as well as assisting with some of their day-to-day problems in regard to families and households. In most cases there seems also to have been great affection between the wealthy older women and the dependent younger ones. Even for Lallie, whose lot was probably the most wretched, a paid companion was a great boon. For the last two years of her life, when she was bed-ridden and suffering from a weak heart, the family employed a young woman to care for her. Both Beatrice and Kate regarded Miss Parsons as bringing a new ray of light into Lallie's existence.[11] As happened in other cases as well, Miss Parsons became a very necessary person within the family, and after Lallie's death she remained with the Holts to care for Robert. Mary was carefully looked after by Beatrice Ross until her death. Miss Ross had come to Longfords in the 1890s and had been Mary's secretary for over twenty years. Their relationship was a close one, and it was apparently Bice (as Beatrice Ross was known within the family) who insisted that Mary's son Bill allow Mary the comfort which she considered her due.[12] It was not only that paid companions sometimes offered the Potter sisters care and attention which their own children refused, but also that some at least of the sisters were able to accept help from paid staff which they could not bring themselves to do from their children. Thus Maggie, who found it intolerable to receive help and sympathy, let alone personal care and attention from her children, was tended and cared for during some of her last illness by her secretary-companion. Ann Grant had previously assisted in the social duties Maggie had to perform as wife of the chairman of the Somerset County Council. Subsequently she assisted Maggie in her work for prison reform—as well as accompanying her to various spiritualists with whom Maggie sought sittings, and recording these sessions.[13] In this case, as in most others, the relationship between employer and employee seems to have been an affectionate one and to have spilled over into a more intimate nursing relationship as the situation demanded. Nor was it only in old age that the sisters had companions: Blanche had a companion for most of her married life. Fanny Hughes apparently ran the house, cared for the children, and coped with all the domestic responsibilities which Blanche's defective memory and general debility made her unable to do. In addition Fanny looked after Blanche and, as the children grew up, this occupied more and more of her time. She shared a bedroom with Blanche and was with her almost all the time until Blanche's death.

The growing up of the children as well as the ageing of the Potter sisters themselves could thus change the character of employment. Fanny Hughes was one case in point, Sarah Peacock was another. As we have seen, Sarah ran the Meinertzhagen nursery and was the nanny and chief support of most of the young Meinertzhagens. When they grew up she stayed on with the family as Georgie's companion. She and Georgie appear to have got on well together. Moreover she was greatly in demand, helping to care for Georgie's grandchildren when they came to stay and generally keeping things running smoothly.

The Potter sisters were unusual, as their own parents had been, in not keeping one daughter single to care for them in their old age. They filled in this gap by paying a poorer young woman to perform this service. The use of employment in this way was something they resorted to because they were women—and direct payment of salaries was the only way in which they could obtain the services of someone else. As we have seen, their husbands and brothers-in-law made use of a rather different means of obtaining care in their old age: marriage to a younger woman. After Blanche's death, Willie married Giulia Ravogli, with whom he stayed until his death in 1931. Alfred Cripps too, after having been widowed for nearly thirty years, married a younger woman in the early 1920s. But it is Henry Hobhouse who illustrates the full extent to which men could supplement an employment relationship by a familial one. After Maggie's death, he first adopted Anne Grant as his daughter and then married her—thus turning Maggie's paid companion into his second wife.

II

The difficult familial situations experienced by most of the Potter sisters in their later years meant that they turned more and more to each other for companionship and support. The reassertion of a close sisterly bond was one of the consolations afforded to them at this time. It was marriage which had first altered the close domestic relationship of the Potters, and marital breakdown and widowhood allowed the possibility of its resurrection in some form. When Daniel Meinertzhagen died in 1910, leaving Georgie a widow in dramatically reduced financial comfort, Maggie wrote to condole with her and to offer this consolation: 'Anyhow we old sisters can draw together again in our old age, close the bonds of family as they used to be in former times.'[14]

Even without the specific needs of some sisters and the willingness or ability to help shown by others, the Potter sisters found themselves drawing closer to each other as the years passed. One of the main reasons for this was the way in which their religious ideas began to converge. Although for much of their adult life there had been considerable differences between those sisters like Kate, who remained a devout and observing Anglican, and those like Lallie or Maggie who tended towards agnosticism, with increasing age all the sisters became preoccupied with religious and spiritual questions. The actual questions differed, as did the ways in which they sought solace. But the shared sense of religious and spiritual need acted as a new source of understanding and sympathy. At the same time this increasing interest in spiritual matters made some of the sisters feel distanced from husbands and children who did not share these concerns, and whose materialism and preoccupation with comfort and wealth came to be a matter of relative indifference to the Potters. It was to each other that the sisters turned, or to whom they confessed their predicaments and concerns. Thus Blanche, who had always had a special feeling for simple life, seeing a kind of purity and holiness in it, found it more and more intolerable to be surrounded by the lavish displays which followed from Willie's rise in his profession. 'I hate and disapprove the life', she said to Beatrice some years before her death, 'I could not have believed I should have to live this sort of life.'[15]

Few of the sisters had found in marriage a relationship in which their own religious beliefs and conflicts were shared. Kate was almost the only one whose husband shared and reinforced her own faith. Leonard Courtney was not only a devout practising Christian, but a man for whom religious faith was an integral part of everyday life. Indeed his ideas, as expressed in the *Diary of a Churchgoer* which he wrote in 1904, were of immense interest and importance to some of his sisters-in-law. Lallie in particular found solace in the way he articulated beliefs which she held, and which received no interest or sympathy in her own family.[16] Kate's situation was unusual and enviable within the sisterhood. Even those other sisters who married men whose religious observances they shared did not find in them real spiritual kinship. Thus although Mary Playne regularly attended the local parish church with Arthur and was active as a fund raiser within the congregation, this form of religious activity did not meet her real needs. In the early years of the twentieth century she became a Christian Scientist. It was this new belief, not shared with Arthur, which brought her a kind of peace and serenity which her sisters found noteworthy. Indeed it is interesting to note that Beatrice referred to the Playne household as an agnostic one despite its church attendance. It was only when Mary turned to the new life that Beatrice began to regard her as a religious woman.[17] Theresa too seems to have had religious and spiritual needs which were not met in her marriage to Alfred Cripps, despite their regular formal observances. Again it was Beatrice who was the one who commented on this most sharply. In her view, 'The marriage was absolutely happy—except that Alfred's companionship, able and warm-hearted man that he be, left unsatisfied the "spiritual" side of Theresa's nature . . . she seemed like a bird with its wings clipped—somewhat weary of the routine and longing to escape upwards.'[18] Theresa's spiritual side found expression in a book on the subject, as she believed in the possibility of spiritual communications with the dead—a subject to which Maggie was to turn many years later.

In the case of Theresa and Mary, the conventional religious observances of the society in which they lived were inadequate and inappropriate and they required something more immediate and intense. A similar situation obtained in Georgie's case. She often attended various churches, although her own beliefs were of a romantic, pantheistic kind. Her daughter, Bobo Mayor, once described how Georgie's children got an inkling of their mother's inner life and loneliness from her contagious and intoxicating enthusiasm for the stars on a particularly clear and beautiful summer evening.[19] Georgie's pantheism was as far removed from Daniel's conventional Anglicanism as were all her other enthusiasms and beliefs from his. Beatrice regarded the Meinertzhagen family as a purely materialistic one, with 'no religion and no philanthropy', and she demonstrated here, as she did in the case of the Playnes, her own strong sense that mere observance of church attendance had little to do with religion. Her picture of the 'positively comic' situation as regards religion which she observed at the Meinertzhagens when she visited them at Brockwood in 1906, goes a long way to justify her views.

Dee, who never goes to Church in London goes here for 'example's sake' to the Brandean Church—neither his parish church nor the one nearest Brockwood—because the walk to it lies through his own land which he likes to inspect. But as Georgie says, someone has to go with him, because as he does not attempt to listen to the service, and becomes wholly absorbed in business calculations, he forgets to stand up or sit down in the proper place. The girls, on the other hand, don't care to go at all and shirk when they can, but when they do go, they prefer the West Church because they have talk with 'the Hoares' and other neighbours before and after service. If Dick . . . is at home he refuses to go with either father or sisters and stalks off to the Parish church, four miles off, because he considers that attendance at the Parish Church is more respectful to the glorious institution of Church and State!—he being a staunch Tory. Exactly where religious feeling enters into these various practices, it is difficult to discover. Georgie, herself, who has a sort of vague mystical faith in prayer and aspiration, stays at home because she is not strong enough to sit through a long country service and sermon.[20]

The purely formal approach to religion of Daniel Meinertzhagen was not typical of all the Potter husbands and brothers-in-law. Indeed it is interesting to see that two of the sisters who married men who were very much involved in local church communities and activities declined to share in these—or any other—observances. Robert Holt was an active Unitarian who attended Church regularly and took a very large part in the philanthropic and religious activities of the Unitarian community in Liverpool. Lallie seems only to have attended Unitarian services when they were the ones at which her children were baptized. Apart from this, she seems not to have gone to church at all, and to have been pronounced agnostic until her last eight or ten years. Maggie Hobhouse followed suit. Henry was a churchwarden and a fairly devout man, but Maggie did not enter into this aspect of his life. She, like Lallie, was a rationalist and an agnostic—at least until her need to believe in some form of immortality turned her attention towards spiritualism. This regular church involvement in the case of both Robert and Henry went along with an easy acceptance of particular religious doctrines. Lallie and Maggie rejected these doctrines in youth, and found them unhelpful when age and loss and approaching death turned their attention to religion.

As they approached old age both Lallie and Maggie became very interested in and concerned about religion. Beatrice noted the change in Lallie when she and Sidney visited her in the mid-1890s.

Hers is a nature which improves with years—her character has softened and deepened and she has gained in intellectual interests. At present in the intervals of keeping a luxuriously comfortable house . . . she reads theology, trying to find a creed which combines rational thought with religious emotion. She has a strong mind but she has neither intellectual training nor experience, and it is pathetic to watch her struggling with wrinkled brow to reach conclusions which have been reached years ago by persons of her temperament.[21]

Lallie discussed her religious ideas with the Webbs and the Courtneys rather than her own immediate family, and found a responsive chord particularly in Leonard, about whose religious meditations she waxed quite lyrical.

Lallie's desire to find some firm basis for her religious faith was echoed many years later by Rosie. She too combined the Potter scepticism with a religious yearning and a desire for some satisfying faith. She had, like Georgie, a vaguely pantheistic approach, and found a sense of restfulness and of something beneficent, impersonal, and unifying in certain facets of nature. Sunrises in particular, which she loved to paint and for which she felt an enthusiasm unlike that evoked by anything else, provided Rosie with a sense of the beneficent external life force to which she could not attach a name.

The most incisive and detailed comments about the religious beliefs and activities of the Potter sisters come from the Diary of Beatrice. It is not surprising that this should be so for she, more than any other of the sisters, shared their mother's life-long religious pre-occupation. She also shared to the full the problem which Lawrencina had faced and which Beatrice later ascribed to Lallie. For her, as for them, the crucial problem was the impossibility of reconciling the intense need for and sense of religious faith with a critical and sceptical intellect and a rejection of Christianity.

Beatrice reiterated her sense of the importance of a living faith as a basis for life and action constantly throughout her life. The lack of such a faith was in her view one of the major problems, even the central one, for the twentieth century and she wrote often about gifted individuals like Virginia Woolf whose lives lacked purpose and direction because of their lack of such a faith.[22] Beatrice felt very intensely that religious faith was a source of morality and of solace. Throughout her life she frequently attended church services or entered a silent church for peaceful meditation. In moments of extreme distress, church was the only place where she sought comfort. She believed that Love, in its broadest sense, was the end of human life and that prayer was conducive to developing and extending the consciousness of 'communion with spiritual force outside oneself' which was an integral part of this love. But she could not accept Christianity as a religion for herself, or as the basis she believed to be necessary for society in the future.[23]

Beatrice's sense of the centrality of Love as a spiritual force was related to her ideas about the importance of social duty and self-sacrifice. She sought a religion which would be conducive to the kind of social transformation she and Sidney desired. She was in fact to find something that approximated to her ideal in the Soviet Union.

III

Just as a shared religious preoccupation drew the Potter sisters together, so too the deaths of some of the sisters acted as a binding force for the others. As we will see, Theresa's sudden death in 1893, when she was only in her early forties, resulted in re-evaluation of the sisterhood and various articulations of its importance. This death came to all the sisters, as it did to Alfred Cripps and his children, as a terrible blow. It was more unexpected, more shocking, and more devastating than were most of the subsequent deaths which came at a rather later age and, in many cases, after illnesses or suffering which provided some kind of preparation.

The Potter sisters were on the whole notable for their longevity and, after Theresa's death, there was a period of twelve years before the next two deaths, which followed quite closely on each other: Blanche in 1905 and Lallie in 1906. Blanche's death by suicide was also a sudden and unexpected one—neither preceded nor caused by illness. Blanche had contemplated death before. Her companion, Fanny Hughes, seems to have remained close to her in part at least as a result of this. Fanny reported to Beatrice a conversation in which Blanche had said, 'God only knows . . . how I am tempted to kill myself. I feel impelled by a spirit stronger than my own.'[24] Blanche's death struck an awful responsive chord in Beatrice, who was herself prey to suicidal thoughts and fantasies. It affected the other sisters rather less, however, as Blanche had always been something of a stranger to them. Kate noted the difference between her own sense of grief and loss when Theresa died, which left her feeling miserable and unable to resume normal social life, and the very brief period it took her to accept Blanche's death. 'Little more than three weeks have passed since our family tragedy but it already seems to have receded into the past. Not that one forgets it for long, but Blanche had not entered into my daily life for years or much into my life at all so that nothing one does or thinks is associated with her. She comes back to one rather as a character in a story.'[25]

About a year later came Lallie's death. She had a heart attack on 1 April 1906 from which she never recovered. She lingered on for seven weeks, but never managed to get out of bed. Her severe illness was in one sense fortunate: the family knew her death was approaching and made some attempts to make amends for the hideous years of neglect. Her three daughters took some part in nursing her and all the sons visited and made some expression of concern. Robert Holt's sanctimonious and conventional statement about Lallie's death in his diary goes far to show why Beatrice and Kate both disliked him, and Beatrice in particular regarded him as 'an honest little tradesman of narrow conventions', transformed by Lallie's ambition and abilities into 'a vainglorious egotist gloating on unearned social esteem'. After some five or six years during which he apparently hardly spoke to Lallie at all, and during which her sisters were filled with grief at the shabby treatment she received, his private record strikes something of a false note.

24 May 1906. *Lallie passed away about 1.45 this afternoon*, after much and rapidly increasing weakness of heart and circulation—though very feeble and drowsy yet I think she recognised us all within a short time of her decease. It was a happy circumstance having the three girls in the house and personally attending to mother. It is indeed a sad and irreparable loss—how we shall get on God only knows.[26]

Beatrice commented rather bitterly on how, at the funeral, Robert was eager to receive flattering condolences and to see a large congregation to 'do honour to *his wife*', while there was no grief or regret from him.[27] It was her many friends, her companion Miss Parsons, and her sisters who really grieved for Lallie, especially Kate, to whom Lallie had been 'my closest sister and constant companion for twenty years'. Despite her grief, Kate took pleasure in recording that Lallie's last weeks had been active despite her illness. She had had her children and Miss Parsons with her and had continued to read, to write letters, and to take an interest in current events. Nor had she lost her taste for organizing things.

She knew she was going and spoke of everything being nicely straightened out and gave Miss Parsons full directions about the service and the hymns and all the arrangements saying when this was done, 'now put that paper in your pocket and don't think about it till the time comes. It is as good an hours work as I have ever done and I feel much better already'. She directed that her body should be cremated and her ashes scattered.[28]

The deaths of Blanche and Lallie made a very considerable breach in the sisterhood. Rosie was then living in Switzerland. She had never really either felt herself or been felt by the others as an equal, and now the fact that she was still having children and in the full throes of family life while the others perceived themselves increasingly as older women, emphasized the gaps between them. For the others, the small-ness of the sisterhood and its fragility was becoming increasingly evident.

The years after 1906 were busy ones for the remaining sisters. Maggie and Georgie had much to do with the arrangement of the social life and the marriages of their offspring. Kate and Mary con-tinued their social lives and their various public activities, and Beatrice emerged as a prominent public figure with her spirited parti-cipation in the Royal Commission into the Poor Law. But these years were also ones in which the threat of death was imminent. Illness—mainly in the form of cancer—was a recurrent event and fear for the sisters. In 1907, Mary Playne wrote to tell Beatrice that she had a lump in the right breast, 'which Mr. Waddy thinks badly of—so it is to be removed at once and I suppose all the flesh on that side of my poor old body with it'.[29] How much flesh went in the mastectomy is not clear. But Kate, Georgie, Maggie, and Beatrice were all intensely distressed by the news, and by the threat to themselves as well as to Mary which this disease offered. Mary was operated on successfully, and although her wound took some months to heal, she was able to resume her nor-mal life.

But Mary's illness was the harbinger of things to come. Shortly after it, Maggie was sent to London for investigative surgery as her doctor thought she might have cervical cancer. This time the fear was without foundation, and she had some minor problem which was successfully treated. But again it was only a respite, for some years later Maggie developed lung cancer.

The next blow came in 1914, simultaneously with the outbreak of war. After four years of the vigorous political activity and enjoyable social and family life which Georgie enjoyed after Daniel's death, her own health became a source of concern. She suffered from severe abdominal pains and also from a weak heart. Investigative surgery, which her family hoped would reveal only gallstones, indicated cancer of the liver accelerated by gallstones and after a few weeks in hospital she died. Georgie's death was a source of immeasurable grief to her daughters. One of them chronicled her last days in a diary and commented that 'it is hard to imagine the future without her. She had a fine and courageous spirit to turn to in great times of trouble.'[30] The sisters grieved too, especially Maggie, who had become very close to Georgie, and Kate. Beatrice, who had never been close to Georgie, expressed the general fear which her death caused. 'Though Georgie's death leaves no gap in my life, it is yet another break with the past—a past which is rapidly becoming the greater part of my personal life. One wonders which one next?'[31]

IV

Four of the Potter sisters had died before the First World War. For the remaining five, the war provided the dominating experience of their later years. All of them, except Rosie, were involved in some aspects either of war work or of anti-war agitation. They were overwhelmed and aghast at the scale and magnitude of the carnage that the war involved—and the capacity people (including themselves) had for accepting the horrors of war. Beatrice regarded the war and the breakdown which she suffered during it as the turning-point between middle and old age. The war seemed to her, as to so many others, to signal the end of civilization as she had known it, and the beginning of a world which she could not understand. She was painfully aware of the inadequacy of her ideas and beliefs when confronted with the phenomenon of mass war. 'Such social philosophy as I possess does not provide any remedy for racial wars. Today I feel like the fly, not on but under the wheel.'[32] Beatrice's essentially abstract concern with the war was on the whole less intense than either Kate's vehement hostility to it, or Maggie, Mary, and Rosie's personal involvement which resulted from their having sons fighting on the Front.

As we have seen, Maggie's many-faceted involvement in the war resulted in her taking up various different kinds of public activities which utilized her energy and filled her time—even if they did not still her anxieties. From the very beginning these had been great, particularly in 1915 when Paul left Aldershot and was sent into combat. Maggie's feelings about Paul's departure were expressed in a letter to her oldest daughter, Rachel Clay.

We got up at six a.m. and Arthur motored Paul and me to Waterloo Station . . . it might be for the last time . . . He contemplates all possibilities without fear or even great concern, and if it is so decreed, will pass into the unknown with good courage. I can't tell you how cruel it is to me, and somehow it seems worse to lose him than anyone else. Yet when one thinks of the great national struggle, one's own sacrifice of the dearest is of small account.[33]

To Kate Courtney, she admitted that she was trying to

make a kind of magical safety for Paul in the fact that he is the seventh child of a seventh child, born on the seventh June, and if his twenty-first birthday (with three sevens) leaves him still safe, I shall imagine he carries a charmed life. Otherwise each telegram that comes fills me with evil apprehensions.[34]

Maggie had to endure several telegrams. Paul was seriously wounded twice, once in the head and neck and once in the leg. After each of these incidents he came home for a few months, but only to return to the trenches once he had recovered. He fought at Ypres and in France and every report of conditions and casualties filled Maggie with dreadful foreboding. Her other sons were also a source of anxiety, particularly Stephen, languishing in prison, and later Jack, who decided at the end of 1916 to resign from his protected occupation and to volunteer.

Throughout 1917 Maggie was taxed to the limit, agitating on behalf of Stephen, working for the COs, running Hadspen on rations, and for some months nursing Paul, who had been sent home wounded. The end of that year, as Stephen noted, brought 'the last comparatively happy Christmas of Margaret Hobhouse's life'. Paul and Jack were both home, Stephen out of prison and, although Arthur was still in France, he was engaged in Intelligence work and not in any serious danger. In March of the following year, however, came the dreaded telegram announcing that Captain Hobhouse was 'missing supposed killed'. Letters followed, some suggesting that Paul may have been taken prisoner, and for some months Maggie remained torn between despair and hope, able neither to accept her loss and to grieve, nor to have genuine hope that Paul might return. It was not until November that there was clear evidence regarding his death and then, as we have seen, Maggie had to face a loss for which there was no consolation.[35] Her other sons did not make up for Paul's death, nor did her daughters, who seemed to have ranked lower than the boys in her general affection.

The shared horrors of war brought Rosie temporarily within the ambit of shared sisterly concern. The war was a very testing time for her although in ways slightly different from her sisters. Rosie did not engage in any public activities during the war, and was indeed fully occupied with familial needs and problems. When the war began she was not in England but Montana, her Swiss home. All the children were with her, including Noel who was spending his summer vacation there. Rosie had no immediate intention of going anywhere, but within a few weeks supplies ran short and it became very difficult to get money from the banks. She first moved her family to a hotel, but that was not a permanent possibility and in September she and George decided to return to England. They settled in Folkstone while the younger children went to school—and Noel enlisted. For much of the war he was engaged in Intelligence work and Rosie, although missing him and very concerned about the conditions in the camps in which he lived, was not faced with the anxiety of having him in the trenches. This was just as well as another son, Richard, the one who ranked next to Noel in her affections, was taken ill with a serious kidney disease from which it appeared for some time that he would not recover. After Rosie and George had almost lost hope, Richard suddenly began to get better. Rosie took a flat for the two of them so that she could nurse him. During this time her other children were all at school. She decided, under the influence of Noel and one of his friends, to dispense with the single-sex grammar and public schools to which she had planned to send the boys and send the four youngest to the progressive coeducational school, Bedales. During all of this time, Rosie was forced to keep house with minimal help which was a great strain for her. She had, as Beatrice and others commented, a 'positive genius' for creating chaos and disorder and her housekeeping was dreadful. George got a job in England, helping to settle Belgian refugees, but Rosie never attempted to involve herself in the war effort. She looked after her home, husband, and various children as best she could.[36]

In 1916 and 1917 Noel remained in Intelligence work. The proficiency in languages which he seems always to have had, aided as it was by the lengthy period he spent in Switzerland, was of great help and he was sent to France to do Intelligence work in 1917. In June 1918, however, he resigned from the Intelligence Corps, feeling that it was his duty to return to his old battalion and take his share of the hardship of trench warfare. Rosie was appalled by this decision and lived in constant anxiety about him. He was sent home on leave in October 1918, and she had one of the happiest of her times with him. Just one week after he returned to the Front, however, on 24 October, she received the War Office telegram informing her that Noel was missing. Shortly after came a letter from his CO telling her that the body had been found. She later wrote about this episode.

And now the worst indeed had happened and the hideous horror of it had somehow to be borne. I do not know how I lived through those first few dreadful days. The horror and the pity of it seemed intolerable, and when, later, I heard more details as to the manner of his death and of how he was wounded in the leg and main artery severed and so bled to death, there being no doctor present, another stab was added to my grief, for with proper aid he might have been saved.[37]

She tried to console herself by being with her other children and then turned her attention to writing a memoir of Noel.[38]

Despite the devastating personal blow the war brought Rosie, for her as for Beatrice there was much of life left when it was over. By contrast for Kate, Mary, and Maggie the war brought or signalled the end of the world they had known and to which they belonged.

In the years immediately after the war, Maggie seemed to be continuing the furious rounds of activity in which she had been engaged during it. She was not one passively to mourn or to withdraw in her grief, but rather chose to defy the barrier imposed by death and try to contact Paul beyond the grave. Like thousands of other bereaved parents and wives, Maggie turned to spiritualism in her sorrow. She joined the Psychical Research Society and sought the help of its president, Sir Oliver Lodge, in obtaining sittings with mediums who knew nothing about her, and who might help her to contact Paul. She had a number of sittings, sometimes taking Rosie Dobbs or some of her nieces with her. In the course of these she did manage to obtain messages of an apparently coherent kind from Paul. Equally important for her was the fact that her sister Theresa was often brought up during sittings—and hence she could believe that Theresa was able to welcome and help Paul to accept his own death. Maggie continued her activities in this area beyond her immediate needs, contacting others who were seeking spiritual aid and assistance and following up many of the leads which came up during her sittings. Although the rest of her family was adamantly sceptical about this approach, it was one which seems to have brought her both peace and some satisfaction.[39]

At the same time, Maggie continued her work on prison reform, writing letters and pamphlets and encouraging Stephen in the major inquiry into prison conditions which he was undertaking with Fenner Brockway. This project was undertaken under the auspices of the Fabian Society, and was of great interest to Beatrice Webb. Hence she and Maggie found themselves finally working at and sympathizing with a public project after years of disagreement about political and social issues.

Maggie had for some time been subject to considerable difficulties in breathing and to painful coughing fits, and late in 1918 lung cancer was diagnosed. In February 1919 she had an operation in the hope that it would be possible to remove the cancerous tissue. This was unsuccessful and in July she had a second operation. This too failed, and in December of that year she told Beatrice that the radiograph showed her lungs covered with cancer spots and that the end could not be long delayed.[40] As has been said, Maggie was quite unable to show or to share her illness and her suffering with her own family. Although Henry Hobhouse knew about her illness, she did her best not even to inform her children that there was anything the matter with her. After her second operation it proved impossible to do this any longer, and she wrote to them explaining the situation—and her own reticence.

I made up my mind that if the second operation proved the existence of the disease I should tell my family, but if it was perfectly harmless I should not. I did not tell you before it took place, partly for that reason and partly because I find it easier to undergo painful experiences without other people knowing. Their sympathy is apt to take away the necessary courage for bearing the misfortune reasonably. I hope you will not consider that I acted either unkindly or wrongly in keeping the secret from you . . .

And I hope you will not think that, while thus keeping you in the dark, I had any doubt of your sympathy and affection.[41]

Maggie had little reason to doubt this. Two of her sons, Stephen and Jack, were obviously deeply concerned and attentive. Stephen and his wife Rosa spent a great deal of time with her. Her other son, Arthur, visited too and his wife, Konradin, was one of the few people with whom Maggie seems to have developed a spontaneously affectionate relationship. But while this relationship was a source of joy to Maggie, and Konradin's pregnancy was one of the few reasons why she wished to prolong her painful life into 1921, it served to emphasize Maggie's sense of the need for reserve. In one of her many affectionate letters to Konradin, she wrote how much she was looking forward to seeing her—but added this injunction: 'Dearest Konradin you must not make me cry when you come as then I cannot bear it. I must banish emotional things.'[42] Maggie's attitude and behaviour was itself a source of grief to some of her children, especially to her eldest daughter, Rachel Clay, who felt that her mother did not really wish to see her.[43] The others also worried at the thought of Maggie's being alone and in pain, but she limited the amount of time she would let them stay. Her refusal to be comforted extended also to her sisters and, as we will see, she refused to let her family tell Kate about her illness as she could not bear the thought of having to deal with Kate's distress or sentimentality. She did, however, tell Beatrice and the two sisters resumed something of their former closeness as Beatrice attended Maggie's sick bed. She visited every two or three days, and sat with Maggie as she struggled for breath and tried to overcome the pain caused both by her disease and by the copper injections where were suggested as treatment. Beatrice was moved and deeply distressed by Maggie's illness. 'The thought that she also will have gone in a few months—the seventh and best loved sister—the oldest of my living friends—is gloomy for the survivor.'[44] Beatrice did not indulge in the sentimentality that Maggie deplored, understanding her sister's reserve, but they talked a great deal. And Beatrice noted in her Diary:

I am the only person with whom she talks freely and whose companionship seems to comfort and interest her. I tell her all about my work; we talk of old days at Standish and Rusland; of her children and her relations to her husband, of the symptoms of her illness, the course of the copper innoculations . . . we weigh up the desirability of an overdose, if life becomes too painful and dreary—whether it is worthwhile to hasten the end; we hazard guesses as to how long I shall survive her. She suffers from breathlessness and painful fits of coughing and can only sleep under narcotics.[45]

Fortunately Maggie's suffering was not prolonged and she died in March 1921.

Beatrice was understandably distraught after Maggie's death. She commented on the fact that cancer was replacing tuberculosis as the 'fearsome thought' and the most prevalent disease and cause of death amongst those she knew. The prospect of this disease and the loss of Maggie brought the thought of her own death uncomfortably close.

The memory of my poor sister, heaped up in bed, livid and struggling for breath, completely absorbed in her physical sensations, still haunts me. She was not at peace with her fate, poor soul: she may be now; if not, she is at rest. I take up my work again sorrowing and with a strange fear of the ordeal through which I like all others must pass.[46]

Her loss was a deeply felt grief to Beatrice. It was followed by other illnesses and other deaths within the sisterhood, but neither Kate nor Mary had ever meant to her what Maggie had, and in neither case did she experience the distress which Maggie's death occasioned.

During the course of the war, Mary had a recurrence of the breast cancer for which she had had an operation in 1907. Further surgery was necessary in 1916, at which time she indicated to Beatrice that she was becoming somewhat weary of life. Beatrice agreed and hoped that Mary would not have to endure prolonged suffering. Mary was becoming senile by this time, although the loss of memory was accompanied by an increasing gentleness, and one which was very appealing to her sisters. Beatrice noted that she had been

lost in wonder at her saintliness—there is no other word for her attitude towards life. She has continuously grown in grace with advancing old age. The mechanism of her mind is failing—she has lost her memory and her power of understanding many things and she has a strange restlessness, due I suppose, to her weakness. If it were not for Arthur and for the loss of her gracious influence at Longfords, I should wish her not to live much longer—especially if she has to face pain and weariness.[47]

Two years later Rosie visited Longfords for a few days and commented on the changes evident there. These were particularly significant for her as she had always been in awe of Mary and intimidated both by her and by her house.

Mary and Arthur are old people now, and lead quite uneventful lives. What a change since the days I can remember when Mary's ever active vitality was the life and soul of the neighbourhood. How changed she is and how vanished her constant restless activity. This poor little white-haired lady who sits, and knits, and reads, plays patience and smokes alternately to pass the time. She goes for little walks, comes back, has her meals and the cigarette she loves afterwards, rests and retires early to bed. This is all that is left of that eager, scheming personality that once ruled supreme at Longfords and of whom as a girl I stood so much in awe.[48]

In the years after the war, this life continued with both Mary and Arthur being looked after by 'their handsome capable secretary Miss Ross'. They ceased to take part in many of the local activities which had filled so much of their lives, and carried on the domestic routine described by Rosie. Beatrice was particularly aware of Mary's extreme restlessness, which meant that she walked several miles each day and was never still. She was trying to be with as her defective memory meant that she repeated the same questions or comments or stories endlessly. Beatrice watched her closely, and commented on the fact that Mary was aware of, and sometimes felt humiliated by, her mental deficiency. She noted also that Mary never mentioned her son, indicating by her very silence recognition of his lack of care or concern for her. 'It is significant that her pleasantest memories—the ones she most often repeats—are memories of her public activities the starting of the School of Cookery, the Red Cross and the Golf Club.' Mary also continued to attend church—and to show a clear capacity to distinguish between good and bad sermons. Beatrice noted that Mary, like their father, retained her judgements of men and things, without being able to apprehend or remember the facts upon which the judgement was based.[49] But Mary was apparently not unhappy and she and Arthur remained companions until 1923, in which year they both died. He died quite suddenly in March and she followed in September.

Mary's death left only three of the Potter sisters—Kate, Beatrice, and Rosie. Beatrice even now, and despite the fact that she was closer in age to Rosie than she was to Kate, could not see her younger sister as an equal or even as a member of the sisterhood. Mary's death occasioned this comment from her: 'Kate and I are left alone in the world; the dear old lady [Kate] clings to me as loving and open-handed as ever; whilst poor neurotic Rosie and her neurotic children are a burden on us both. So dwindles out of sight the "R.P. Family".'[50] This sense of aloneness was accompanied by a rather different set of relationships between the sisters. Beatrice continued to feel responsible for Kate until the latter's death in 1929. But this responsibility was not accompanied by any feeling of closeness or kinship: it was the result simply of being the last available relative. She noted that although Kate regarded her as a natural confidante, she herself never thought to tell Kate anything. She never mentioned to her the work she was doing on *My Apprenticeship*, even though the early sections of that book dealt with a shared life and a shared set of familial experiences.[51] When Kate finally died after a very severe attack of influenza, Beatrice noted the differences in her response to this death as compared with her reactions to the deaths of Maggie and Mary. Kate was in her view 'the most beneficent of my sisters', a pious and kindly woman lacking any of that 'hardness or cynicism' which all the other sisters had and which were qualities quite repellent to Kate. But as a result of that, Beatrice felt that she and Kate had nothing even approaching intimacy—and hence that the loss of Kate did not affect her directly.

For Margaret I had a real affection and her death was a direct sorrow. For Mary too I had a tender heart. Kate's death—now that it has come—is also a sorrow—but the sorrow is more because I feel I ought to feel her loss more than I do, than because I *do* feel it. I sorrow because her beneficent presence meant so little in my life. All I can say in answer to the innumerable letters I get of fervent sympathy for the greatness of my loss is that it was a 'great shock' which is emphatically true. The insignificance of the physical act of death compared to the passing of a personality out into the void—to become a mere memory which in its turn will fade away—is a shock to one's consciousness of reality—one begins to wonder whether one is alive oneself![52]

V

The decade of the 1920s was a strange and painful one for Beatrice. It was one in which the close companionship of her marriage was interrupted by Sidney's political activities, and hence one in which the satisfying working routine which they had developed over thirty years had to be set aside. It was also a decade dominated by her family of origin, at the very time that that family was breaking up and leaving her alone. The illnesses and deaths of her three remaining older sisters, coinciding with the fact that she was working on her autobiography, meant that she was working through old feelings and old pains and dealing with present loss at the same time. The deaths of the sisters also affected her with a sense of isolation as she felt little connection with her many nieces and nephews, despite her quite keen interest in them and their doings. Not only was Beatrice occupied with analysing her past at this time, but she was also forced almost to relive parts of it. Thus shortly after writing about her extreme ambivalence about social life as a young girl, she was again forced to come to terms with the thraldom of social activity and social prominence by Sidney's position as a cabinet minister—and then by his elevation to the peerage. In 1931 with the fall of the second Labour Government, the Webbs returned to their old life of research. They embarked on a major new project: their visit to and then their book about the Soviet Union. In the thirties, then, Beatrice turned away from her family and her past and began to reach out for new problems and new solutions of a kind which took her further than ever away from the world of Richard Potter and his offspring.

It is this which in large part explains the extent of her enthusiasm about the Soviet Union. This enthusiasm meant that after a life-long search, Beatrice could spend her last years articulating and describing the new object of her faith. As Margaret Cole has pointed out, without this new enthusiasm, Beatrice would have been very like some of her sisters in having a miserable and lonely old age.[53] The First World War destroyed the civilization she knew and, as she said herself, posed

a set of problems with which she was unable to cope. Her own philo-
sophical and social beliefs did not help her to understand mass wars of
destruction. The end of the war left her feeling old and defeated,
without the enthusiasm to engage in the social and political questions
which she had previously felt. She turned her attention back to her
past, and the activities in which she engaged with most interest were
the rereading of her Diary and the production of her autobiographical
works from it. It was only the trip to the Soviet Union which she took
in 1932 which gave her a compelling interest in the present and the
future by showing a new civilization in which faith provided the basis
for a massive social transformation.

Beatrice developed other new interests and activities at much the
same time. In the enforced solitude which she had to cope with while
Sidney was in London and she remained at Passfield Corner, she took
to listening to the radio. Talks, and especially classical music, became
major sources of pleasure to her. On the eve of her seventy-second
birthday she gave a radio talk herself which proved to be the first of a
number of such talks and which she thoroughly enjoyed doing.[54] At
the same time, Beatrice continued her contacts with the Labour
Movement and some of the staff of the London School of Economics.
Her curiosity about people's lives, relationships, and situations
remained unabated, as did her interest in chronicling her own feelings
and ideas in the Diary.

Beatrice Webb was an exceptionally active and interested woman
during her seventies and early eighties, but she was certainly not
immune from the ills or the depression of age. From the time of the
First World War she commented frequently on how old she felt,
noticing at one point the discrepancy between her feelings about
herself and other people's perceptions of her. While waiting for
Sidney's retirement from politics in 1931, she commented on her
dislike of the noise and bustle of London and feared that she might
undergo yet another breakdown. 'I am beginning to feel the helpless-
ness of old age, which with me is masked by will power and physical
activity; to other people I seem in full possession of my faculties—but
in my own consciousness I am depressed and dazed—memory fails
me—and I worry about this thing and that.'[55] Her health, which was
never particularly good, gave her a great deal of trouble. To the
persistent digestive troubles of youth and middle age were added an
almost equally persistent cystitis. She had a bladder operation in 1931,
but pain and bleeding continued and made her often think that life

was all but intolerable. Indeed, for most of her adult life Beatrice had been interested in the question of euthanasia and the desirability of a voluntary withdrawal from life appealed to her more and more strongly. Throughout the thirties she commented frequently that, were it not for Sidney, she would not be inclined to continue.

As Beatrice felt herself to be ageing and weakening, she became more and more interested in and enthusiastic about her younger sister, Rosie. Her Diary, which had previously contained negative and critical comments about Rosie's weakness, egotism, immorality, and inability to organize or manage herself or her life now began to reflect a quite different tone and approach. The first of these comments was made on 5 October 1929–and here Beatrice acknowledged something of her changing attitude.

Rosie here for a week. Whether because we are the only sisters left or because she is particularly well and pleasant I have really enjoyed her stay, and the gossips mostly about her own family affairs. Her five children are all now settled in the world, two married with babies, and all rather impecunious. She has the disposal of £1,500 a year—certainly she does not spend it on herself—her husband makes his own small salary of £500 and keep in the Hotel—so she is free to subsidise her children's earnings. Hence she has a position of her own which they must acknowledge ... She is amazingly tolerant of their unconventional ways and lack of consideration. As her recreation she travels adventurously, far and wide, at an incredibly cheap rate ... She has decided artistic talent—but not enough to be a professional. Altogether at 65 years of age, Rosie Dobbs is a remarkable woman who has weathered well; she has outgrown her strange mental derangements—miserliness and hysteria.[56]

A couple of years later Rosie had a breakdown in which her old obsessions and her guilt about her past threatened to overwhelm her—and Beatrice felt that perhaps 'voluntary withdrawal' from life might be the answer. But Rosie recovered and throughout the 1930s she visited Beatrice quite frequently and her visits mostly occasioned favourable comments.

Beatrice's interest in Rosie and her expression of something akin to admiration for Rosie's capacity to continue travelling, sketching, supporting her family, and taking up new interests and new friends was perhaps intentionally a means of making up for her years of denigration and dislike of this youngest sister. Although she never so much as mentioned the problems between herself and Rosie, it seems clear that this was the most complex and the most devastating of all the sibling relationships in the Potter family. Beatrice was entirely displaced and overshadowed by Rosie during her childhood, when both parents turned their fullest affection toward their youngest daughter while neglecting almost totally her older sister. This was followed by a period during which Beatrice was virtually Rosie's guardian—and through much of which she still had to cope with the intense and exclusive affection which existed between Rosie and Richard Potter. Beatrice never acknowledged that she felt any jealousy of Rosie— although it seems likely that she did exact some vengeance. She felt, and made Rosie feel, that it was the strain imposed by his relationship with Rosie that was largely responsible for Richard Potter's stroke. She also had a role to play in Rosie's unfortunate first marriage. Beatrice was as much a victim of the relationship between herself and Rosie as was Rosie, and her lack of sympathy for her younger sister is scarcely surprising. The absence of any comment about her feelings concerning Rosie remains a major and interesting omission from the Diary. She did in later years acknowledge this and berated herself for her 'lack of charity' towards Rosie during the period of Rosie's widowhood and second marriage. But the inner workings of the relationship remain a mystery. This background to Beatrice's comments on Rosie is intriguing because it seems to be the case that Beatrice overemphasized the satisfactoriness of Rosie's later life, in a way very similar to her underestimation of Rosie prior to that. Thus while Beatrice was fascinated by Rosie's enthusiasm for travel, sketching, and her family, Rosie's own diaries and autobiography and the comments of her daughter and son-in-law point to a slightly different picture.[57]

The tenor of Rosie's activity in the years after the war was much as Beatrice described. She did spend a great deal of time travelling—to Southern and Northern Europe and the Middle East, to North and South America, to Asia. Occasionally Rosie was accompanied by George, but his work and his lack of interest made him a reluctant companion.[58] It would also seem to be the case that Rosie's preferred methods of travel, which showed to the full her mania for economy, made it uncomfortable for others to be with her. She travelled third class wherever possible, but more difficult than this was her tendency to eat only at those times when meals were included as part of a fare— and as far as possible to fast at other times. She apparently had a digestive system rather like that of a camel. But George, who was accustomed to living in hotels and eating the three good meals a day which were provided there, found this all but intolerable.[59] Rosie thus travelled alone, sometimes meeting people on the way. She quite enjoyed chance meetings, but was deeply lonely for the close companionship she had never known. Rosie's acceptance of George's relationship with Mrs Westby was an acknowledgement of the fact that she and George were not really compatible as companions for each other. She felt constantly the inadequacy of their relationship but remained tied to George, as indeed he was to her.

Her trips were interspersed with spells in England or with her children, but these too were not an unalloyed source of pleasure to any of them. The favouritism which had operated towards her children while they were young continued—and indeed was evident again in her attitude towards her grandchildren. This, and the possessiveness towards some of the grandchildren that went along with it, made for difficulties. Rosie did not get on with any of her daughters-in-law and a couple of her sons immersed themselves within matrimonial ties to the exclusion of their mother. Rosie felt a need and desire to help her children, with money and even by cleaning their homes. But her lack of domestic skills remained a problem and she was not a great boon to those looking after homes of their own. Indeed her visits to her children seem to have been difficult for all concerned.[60]

The great joy and solace of her life was art. Sketching and painting, especially when the subject was a sunrise, was an activity of which she never tired. It brought her peace and contentment of a kind unavailable elsewhere. To some extent this was because it was while watching and painting the sunrise that she experienced her own sense of a divine being.[61] Natural beauty was connected to her often inarticulate sense of divinity, and at these times, while engaged in this act, she stilled her concern and her doubts about religion and a future life.

Rosie's peripatetic life could thus be seen by Beatrice as following a life-long interest and sense of adventure—while at the same time her son-in-law, Malcolm Muggeridge, saw it as an illustration of the rootless, shiftless, purposeless existence which had always been hers.[62] Some at least of the constant movement was to avoid settling anywhere where she would have to pay income tax—thus she was in a sense perpetually exiled as a result of her own miserliness.[63] This is not to say that Rosie did not enjoy travelling: it is clear that she often did and that the varieties of scenic beauty and of custom intrigued her. But it still seems to be the case that travelling was as much an escape as it was a fulfilling pastime and that the individual trips she took were as often tedious and disappointing and lonely as they were exciting and inspiring.

This life ended for Rosie with the outbreak of war in 1939. She and George returned to England and purchased a small house in Watling. Again, as during the First World War, Rosie was forced to undertake the actual housekeeping herself and the chore of cleaning and cooking threatened to overwhelm her. Her inability to organize or manage a home, or to provide edible meals, remained a source of amazement to her sister and her children. The war was a time of strain too as George was with her, and his standards of domestic comfort remained those of a large and well-run hotel. Besides, the sharing of a house was an unusual situation for them both and meant that they were constant companions in a way to which both were unaccustomed. George missed the regular games of bridge and the range of people he met in hotels; Rosie felt restricted and unhappy. Overall their last few years together were not in any way happy ones for either of them.[64]

Just as the First World War brought an end to the Potter sisterhood, so the second brought the curtain down on the remaining stragglers. Beatrice had lived through the war in pain and anguish—at first as a result of the Nazi–Soviet pact, later as a response to the general horrors of war and 'Hitlerdom'. In 1941 Sidney had a stroke which left him largely incapacitated and meant that Beatrice was really on her own. She continued the Diary and continued to see friends, but death, when it came in 1943, was a long sought-after release. Rosie lasted through the war but in declining health, and in 1949 the last of the Potter sisters died.

XI

The Sisterhood

THE Potter sisters, despite the fact that all of them lost their surname as an inevitable consequence of marriage, never lost a sense of themselves as the 'R.P. family'.[1] So large a family of daughters was an unusual phenomenon, and the subject of frequent comment during their lifetime. The term 'monstrous regiment of women' was apparently applied to them quite often, especially by brothers-in-law. The fact that all the surviving Potters were girls unquestionably gave a particular cast to the sibling relationship amongst them. It also provided all of them with a strong sense of belonging to a sisterhood. For some, the sisterhood provided a basic network of friendships and an almost constant source of support; for others it was rather a source of opposition and of censure. But none of the sisters could ignore it, and it remained a central feature of their lives from childhood until death.

The shared sex of the Potters resulted in a number of common experiences in childhood and throughout the course of their lives. As girls, the Potters spent more time at home and in family-based activities than did boys of their class. Therefore, they had rather less contact with the outside world and much of that was undertaken in company with other sisters. Education for the Potters, as later for their daughters, was something which took place mainly at home in the company of sisters. Whereas boys' schools presented a whole new world of companions, with rules and routines all of their own, for girls education meant some hours spent in the family school-room alongside one's sisters. This served to reinforce particular sibling relationships. Similarly, the years after school, with their emphasis on social life and the prospect of marriage, were ones in which the sisters found themselves facing new situations in each others' company, and often depending on each other for amusement and support. Rivalries, jealousies, and tension were probably exacerbated by this, as they must have been by the obvious parental favouring of some daughters as against others, but constant companionship continued through this and was an inescapable facet of the Potters' early lives. Marriage, while it brought physical separation and sometimes a decline in intimacy, was none the less usually followed by the common experiences of womanhood: housekeeping, pregnancy, the exigencies of childcare, in all of which the sisters shared their experiences and tried to assist each other.

The fact that there was no surviving son added of course to the similarities of experience amongst the entire Potter family. Lawrencina was not able to vest her vicarious longings or ambitions in any of her daughters in the way she had already begun to do in the very brief life of little Dickie. In a practical sense too, the fact of all the children being girls resulted in an equality which would not have happened had there been sons. For a family of daughters, there was no such thing as primogeniture. All the girls inherited the same amount of Richard Potter's estate and, although there were some differences in the amount they received for education and as marriage portions, these variations were very small, and pale into insignificance as compared with the differences between eldest and younger sons in English upper- and upper-middle-class families. While Lallie was very conscious of her position as head of the family, as indeed were her younger sisters, she did not exercise her authority from the family home. Indeed the contrast between her inheritance of one ninth of the family estate and that of her oldest son, who inherited the Holt family home and business in addition to most of the property of his childless uncle, is an illustrative and instructive one.[2]

The large number of Potter sisters, combined with their great age range and the differences in interest, outlook, and place of residence, meant that during their adult years, the sisters all met together only infrequently. Such meetings were usually of a formal and ceremonial nature and occasioned by family milestones. Weddings and jubilee annniversaries provided the major source of celebration, while deaths and funerals provided the opposite pole of meetings in which shared grief added its weight to family bonds. There were a few other situations when the family met: Kate sometimes decided to have a large family dinner party in order to assemble the sisters and their husbands. In addition, some members of the family tended to stay with others over Christmas or over the Whitsuntide or August Bank Holiday long weekends. These smaller meetings, often involving three or four of the sisters and their husbands and children, were far more frequent than were gatherings of the entire family. Problems and crises could also result in meetings: when the older sisters found out about Rosie's marital delinquencies, they had a number of meetings in each other's homes to commiserate with one another and review the situation.[3]

The extensive reports in diaries and letters of formal meetings and ceremonial occasions provide an essential insight into the structure of the Potter sisterhood and into the way in which the family responded to the various crises they faced. They also provide a means of following in broad outline the lives and fortunes of all members of the family, for any important development was immediately reported to all the family. At the same time, the fact that these sources concentrate only on major events, and record only large-scale family gatherings, means that relationships between the sisters are presented only in their most formal light. None of the sisters seems to have kept a daily diary simply recording appointments and engagements—or at least none has survived. Both Beatrice and Kate were quite explicitly keeping diaries in which they noted and commented only upon significant and memorable experiences. The large dinner parties, complete with toasts and speeches, are there, but none of the informal teas or sisterly chats which were so much a part of the lives of some sisters. These were probably taken for granted, and not regarded as something which warranted particular mention. Lallie, for example, seems to have visited London three or four times a year in order to see her sisters. Robert Holt's diaries mention her departures and returns home, but Kate, with whom Lallie usually stayed, did not record the visits unless a particularly interesting outing or dinner party took place. In a similar way, Kate noted the fact that she had visited her sisters in London only when the visit had been unusual. She comments, for example, on going to dine with Georgie and finding her in bed having a miscarriage, in a way that suggests that informal visits were a frequent activity on her part.[4] But it took so worrying or dramatic an occurrence to warrant such visits being recorded. Some of Maggie's letters to her children, discussing the plans she and Georgie made for sharing their entertaining during the season, also seem to imply an informal relationship with frequent meetings. The familiarity of Maggie with Georgie's daughters later reinforces one's sense that meetings between these two sisters were part of their daily life in London,[5] but there are no explicit records of this.

Some of the sisters, particularly Kate and Mary, seem to have worked hard to retain regular contact with all or at least most of their sisters. But others were rather more casual about this: hence some of the sisters felt almost like strangers to others of their number. When

Lallie died, Maggie indicated the full extent of her distance from this sister in a letter to Mary.

Thank you so much for writing me an account of the events at Liverpool and of Lallie's last days. She was a kind and generous woman and, to those she liked and who liked her, a delightful companion. I unfortunately saw very little of her either as a child or later on. Perhaps we never did each other justice or understood each other's ways of thinking, although we often made valiant efforts to do so. I am glad her children gathered round her at the end.[6]

I

Maggie's reference to the fact that she did not see much of Lallie as a child, in explanation of their lack of intimacy or cordiality, is very important. For it does seem to be the case that relationships formed in infancy and strengthened in adolescence were the durable and intimate ones, and that closeness in infancy was the main determinant of the grouping of the Potter sisters in later life.

The Potter family falls into a number of different groups. The proximity of the births of the first six daughters contrasts noticeably with the much greater separation between the last three, and indeed almost makes it seem like two slightly separate families. Amongst the older sisters there seem to be two main groupings: Lallie and Kate, with Mary in a subsidiary position, make up the first; Theresa and Blanche, with Georgie as the third, make up the second group. After that came the three rather isolated sisters: Maggie, Beatrice, and Rosie. When Theresa, Blanche, and Georgie went to school together, Maggie was too young to go and hence, like Beatrice, had her education and schooling alone.

Birth order seems overall to have been of great importance for the Potter sisters, for it featured not only in the relationships of the sisters with each other, but also in their relations with parents and in the personality formation. There were a number of generally accepted beliefs in the later nineteenth century about the likely distribution of intelligence and other abilities amongst the children of a particular family depending on birth order. These beliefs were obviously incorporated into the treatment of children and hence became a part of their upbringing. The idea that the oldest child was likely to have exceptional intellectual abilities was powerfully reinforced in the 1850s by Francis Galton's study of prominent intellectuals. In his analysis of *English Men of Science*, Galton found that older sons appeared twice as often as younger ones, and concluded that being born first gave a child decided advantages. Galton's explanation was derived from a study of males, and some of its terms apply only to men, but some others obviously apply to females as well. Older sons, Galton argued, have great advantages of nurture over younger ones. 'They are more likely to become possessed of independent means, and are therefore able to follow the pursuits that have most attraction to their tastes; they are treated more as companions by their parents, and have earlier responsibilities, both of which would develop independence of character.'[7] Lallie lacked the advantages of inheritance, but it does seem to be the case that the other advantages described by Galton applied to her. She was given early responsibilities and thrived on them, and moreover she of all the sisters seems to have had the easiest and friendliest relationship with Lawrencina Potter. It was also the case that Lallie was assumed to be the cleverest of the sisters, and the one whose opinion was given most weight. The younger sisters all resented this, and insisted that her sway within the family was not a result of any real superiority, but rather the fact that she stated her opinion more forcibly than any of the others.[8]

Psychological discussions about birth order and about family systems seem to throw some light on the personalities and the relationships of the Potter sisters. Here too ideas about the role and the behaviour of the oldest sister appear particularly useful. Lallie, indeed, can be seen almost as a classical example of the oldest child, asserting her own predominance and her right to criticize all the younger ones. She combined the stance of the most critical of the sisters with a strong tendency to enforce conformity to what she considered to be the appropriate norms of conduct for her siblings. Accustomed to the exercise of power early in her own life, she exhibited to the full 'the understanding of power and the conservatism' which Alfred Adler regarded as characteristic of oldest children.[9] Although accustomed to the exercise of power within her family, Lallie never questioned the proper channels of that power, nor did she attempt to break away into new directions. In her own life, Lallie exhibits the interesting picture of a woman with ability and self-confidence quite voluntarily limiting her sway by immersing herself within a family life which in itself served to reduce her power and to turn it rather into the more ambiguous form of influence. In a similar way, she added her own formidable weight to the opposition faced by any of her sisters who chose unconventional paths in life. She joined

with her parents in undermining Kate when she decided to leave the
world of Society and to take up philanthropy. Later she was vehe-
mently opposed to the unconventional relationship which Kate and
Leonard Courtney proposed to enter. Kate wrote to tell Leonard of
Lallie's opposition in terms which show that she saw it as an integral
part of her older sister's nature and role. She had, she wrote, tried to
explain the nature of the relationship she and Leonard proposed to
Lallie but without success:

She is as kind and true-hearted as can be but one of those very practical
people who believe much more in the outward condition of life being
necessary to happiness than I do and it was perhaps likely she would not
understand.

I can only hope that she will some day see that I am not quite such a fool as she
now thinks me.

For some years she was opposed with equal vehemence to my leaving home
and working in London and she is now quite converted to that.

My younger sister Beatrice is much more sympathetic.[10]

Kate had the quiet persistence which she needed to survive with so
overbearing an older sister, and now as on other occasions she turned
to her younger sisters for support. Beatrice and Theresa in particular
offered it to her.

Although Kate felt Lallie's force strongly, she was not the only sister
who was subjected to it. Lallie, whose strength of mind was equalled
only by her lack of tact, caused difficulties for Theresa when she
attempted to intervene in order to alter both the terms of Theresa's
marriage settlement and the arrangements for Theresa's wedding.[11]
She subsequently antagonized Willie Cripps by writing to tell him
how she felt he should manage Blanche during her periods of illness.[12]
Throughout her life, Lallie periodically descended on the family in
London, carrying members of it off for dinners and other outings.
Kate, who loved her dearly, none the less referred to her as 'swooping
down' during these visits, which is the same term Rosie used to
describe the way Lallie entered her life just before she went to Egypt,
in the vain hope that the warmer climate would help Dyson recover
his health. 'A week before we started, my oldest sister, Lallie Holt, a
clever managing woman, swooped down upon me, and insisted on
taking Noel and his nurse to her large comfortable house in Liverpool,
for she said I had enough on my hands with an invalid husband.'[13]

It is no accident that it should have been Rosie, the youngest and the least independent or powerful of the sisters, whom Lallie should have chosen as the one in whose course of life she would intervene directly. She may have made comments about Beatrice or Maggie or Theresa, but she would not have engaged in such immediate intervention. But just as she was the oldest and the most powerful of the sisters, so Rosie as the youngest was the weakest and the least independent.[14] Rosie grew up very much the spoiled baby of the family, favoured by her parents, nurtured, taught, and looked after by some of her older sisters, but the very energy and interest that went into her upbringing proved enervating for her. She collapsed under the strain of Lawrencina's scholastic ambitions and, far from sitting the Cambridge entrance exams, was one of the least developed of the sisters intellectually. Indeed Rosie did not really manage to develop any autonomy or, or so it would seem, any real maturity. She was petted by parents and then ordered around by the sisters who found her wearisome and unrewarding. She accepted a first husband without loving him, and a second through fear of blackmail as much as through any real belief that he was her chosen mate. She engaged in illicit affairs, but was quite unable to contemplate the consequences of setting up house with a man to whom she was not married, even though she acknowledged that the man in question, George Gissing, was exactly the kind of mentor and father figure that she really sought. In relation to the children she bore through her second marriage, she appears to have acted out the jealousies and rages of a younger daughter rather than to have been able to offer care and nurture.[15]

The remaining sisters do not fall into patterns quite as readily as do Lallie and Rosie, although some do at least suggest themselves. The three youngest were separated from the group formed by the older six as well as from each other, and make up almost a second family, so far at least as their early experiences are concerned. Theresa, who was placed in the middle position, as the youngest of the first six and the next one for the remaining three, was the sister who best related to both groups. She mothered the youngest sisters, while remaining on easy terms with all the overbearing older ones. It was Theresa who helped to support Kate against Lallie while at the same time she looked after Rosie and helped her with lessons. She was the sister Rosie loved most and the first one whom Beatrice felt was really trying to understand the outlook and objectives of the Webbs. Her letters to Lallie in particular show both the extent to which a sensitive younger sister had to defend herself against the ferocity and scorn of a powerful and tactless older one, and also her abilities to negotiate her way within the family, without either engaging in confrontation or being totally overwhelmed.

The other sister apart from Beatrice for whom birth order seems to provide a helpful explanation of behaviour and personality is Maggie. She, like Lallie, combined exceptional abilities and talents with a strong conservatism and a disinclination to question the accepted social order or the norms of female behaviour. And in some ways she shared Lallie's position within the family. As the one who was still at home when Georgie, Blanche, and Theresa were at school, she established a companionship with her mother which was closer than that of many other sisters. She too was given and enjoyed extensive responsibilities within the family, having an extended period as housekeeper and taking over the organizing of the Potter social life almost as soon as she came out. At the same time, the lack of any close sibling bonds in childhood may go some way to explaining Maggie's extreme reserve and her inability to talk about emotions, or to allow herself to depend on others for comfort and support. As Beatrice has written, she and Maggie only developed a close relationship when Maggie was already well into her twenties. Maggie had an important role within the Potter family. Her organizing skills, her practical common sense, and her social ease were all acknowledged and depended upon by the others. She regarded herself as an authoritative figure in a way quite similar to Lallie: she did not hesitate to give her financial advice to her father or to her sisters. Her authority, however, does seem to have been acknowledged by others. It is interesting, for example, that George Dobbs should have chosen Maggie to tell about Rosie's infidelity, rather than Beatrice or Kate, the two sisters to whom Rosie felt closest. It may also be the case that the similarity of the roles played by Lallie and Maggie was one of the underlying causes of the lack of understanding between them to which Maggie later referred. A hierarchical family does not admit of two competing heads. In her adolescent and adult years, Maggie did establish close friendships with some of her sisters, but she did not have the closeness which was evident between Lallie and Kate or between Theresa and Blanche. In all she seems to have occupied a middle position between theirs and the very much more isolated ones occupied by Rosie and Beatrice.

In Beatrice's case, the isolation of childhood was followed by an adolescence and early adulthood in which her central position in the organization of the family was accompanied by a continuing isolation as she worked out ideas and plans for which her sisters showed no sympathy. Hence she combined an easy association with the sisters with a lack of any real sense of intimacy or companionship. She developed her closest association with Maggie, but lost that when Maggie married. Later she became fond of Theresa and then of Mary and finally of Lallie. But, despite the affection she felt for her sisters and her recognition of mutual need and dependence, she was always very conscious of the lack of deep understanding which existed between them. She recognized that this was largely her own choice: the independence she demanded was contrary to the values of her sisters and incompatible with a close and frank relationship. While she sought and cherished her independence, she was very aware of the high cost at which it had been achieved.

Beatrice's sense of her isolation within her family was quite often the subject of comment in her diary. One of the most significant of these comments was made when, shortly after her marriage, Theresa died. This first death amongst the sisters was the cause of both shock and grief to all. Maggie, Kate, and Georgie were particularly devastated by it. Kate was unable to do anything but sit at home and see her sisters or her close friends for a couple of months. She, like Georgie, saw the occasion as one which could and should serve to draw the remaining sisters closer. Georgie indeed was moved by this loss to write a poem, the opening line of which ran 'Close the ranks, oh sisters dear'. Beatrice experienced none of the unity in grief which her older sisters seemed to feel, but rather a powerful sense of her distance from Theresa and of her own loneliness. Her diary entry thus moves quickly from a summary of the tragedy, particularly for Alfred Cripps and his five children, to her own introspections:

Sometimes one thinks that the blood-tie, though it makes death more painful makes it more difficult to win back intimacy if it has been lost. There is the whole past between you—not only as a tie, but also as a wall, intercepting intercourse. Your past self is really the 'self' presented on either side in the old family life with its frictions and clashing interests and tempers. Specially so has it been in my case. I had to choose between a life of caution, reserve and self restraint and a career foiled and interfered with at every turn. No sister— of the nine—stands so friendless as I do—No sister so independent of the opinion and approval of her family. Again is proved that you cannot gain the advantages of all courses: I chose to live apart, so that while in the very centre of the family I might yet live my own life. My sisters no longer know me, they know only the shell with which I covered myself. To me this death is in some ways horribly tragic. Tomorrow after the funeral I shall come back to my husband and my work: looking back through the years I shall not be able to recall one single word of intimacy from me to her.[16]

A month later, when the sisters met again at Georgie's, Beatrice continued this theme, but looked at the other sisters in terms of how their response to Theresa's death reflected their immediate situation. Georgie was the saddest and the one most affected, but this in turn arose largely from the unhappiness within her marriage. Rosie too was depressed, but this Beatrice took to be caused by the state of her husband, whose ill health was now chronic. The others too went their way: 'Mary, Margaret, Kate, all happy women—Blanche too nobly mad and madly noble to be disturbed by death—all and each of us going our own way'.[17] They were in her view 'eight sisters—bound together yet not combining'. Georgie's poem, touching as it was, would not in Beatrice's view alter this.

III

While the question of particular friendships amongst the Potters is one important aspect of the sisterhood, there are also others which seem equally important, but about which it is very much harder to obtain any information. For sibling relationships are clearly complex ones in which conscious and unconscious elements both play a part.[18] In addition to the evident and easily articulatable forms of companionship, there was also a sense of affinity and of kinship which could be as productive of pleasure as of pain. Beatrice, while she constantly commented on the lack of intimacy she had with her sisters, and the lack of intimacy they had with each other, was perhaps ironically the sister who actually wrote most about this aspect of the sisterhood. It was based on a sense of common heredity and shared characteristics and centred on the underlying resemblances among the sisters. This sense of sisterly ties could be very bitter. In regard to Rosie, for example, Beatrice recognized the fact that neither she nor the older sisters could wash their hands of Rosie, much though her infidelity to George Dobbs made them want to do so. They felt little sympathy for her, 'and yet after all she is the child of our parents, and poor girl, she was doomed from birth by a defective character and an unhappy life—and she has had ill luck all through. And each one of us recognizes in her the family traits.' A little later in her diary, Beatrice again referred to her consciousness of kinship with that terrible sister, 'a caricature of the family characteristics'.[19]

Beatrice's sense of kinship with Rosie did not make her any more tolerant of Rosie's failings; indeed if anything they had the reverse effect. But her sense of affinity with the other sisters did make for particularly intense reactions in certain situations. This can be seen most clearly in relation to Blanche's death in 1905. Beatrice was far more shocked and traumatized by Blanche's death than she had been by Theresa's, although she had seen very little of either Blanche or Willie since her marriage. The horror seems to have been caused entirely by her sense of the similarities between herself and Blanche. Earlier she had written of her fellow-feeling for Blanche, 'For we understand each others melancholy madness'. Now this melancholy had driven Blanche to commit suicide, an action which Beatrice had contemplated and fantasized about intermittently throughout her life. Beatrice recorded in great detail the sequence of events which had preceded and followed Blanche's suicide, and for weeks after it she could not get it out of her mind. 'Always my mind reverted to that tragedy', she wrote three weeks after Blanche's death,

not of Blanche's death—though that was horrible—but of her life—the long struggle that off and on, I had witnessed, ever since I can remember. Of this noble tempestuous inconsequent nature striving to keep heart against its own hopeless incapacity to choose and apply the method that reached the end. Then my thoughts would wander to the family—those young men cursed with sleeplessness and melancholy ... the youngest boy and girl—the only sane ones; on whom it had fallen to try and revive this dead mother for a whole hour by artificial respiration ... Over and over again my mind rehearsed the scene till I got dizzy with disgust.[20]

Beatrice was prey to sleeplessness and to nightmares for a while after Blanche's death.

Subsequently, although less moved by the deaths of Lallie and Georgie, she felt very strongly the way each one cut away at the past and at her own sense of her life. Her strongest reaction was reserved for Maggie, the 'seventh and best-beloved sister' whose announcement that she had terminal lung cancer caused Beatrice not only acute distress, but also 'nervous exhaustion'. She rallied and was able to offer Maggie comfort and support, but the initial news almost caused Beatrice to have a complete breakdown.[21]

None of the other sisters left any record of this particular sense of family bond. It may have been an element in Maggie's feelings about Theresa, and most particularly in her sense that Theresa would understand her fears and griefs about the death of her son Paul, and would help him in the afterlife which Maggie, despite her agnosticism, believed to exist.

The other aspect of the relationship between the sisters which was doubtless important, but about which there is very little information, is the extent of the rivalries and jealousies which presumably existed in childhood and continued in adult life. Parental favouritism was very evident to the Potters and it is hard to believe that this did not result in tensions amongst the sisters. Beatrice certainly believed that it did. Shortly before Mary's death she wrote at some length about 'blood relationships' and their many complexities:

So much affection and helpfulness, so little sympathy and understanding. There is the bond of a long common past which has been imperfectly shared and has given rise to endless misunderstandings and small grudges. . . . There is perhaps even a subtler and subconscious jealousy—jealousy which disappears when misfortune or pain bears down on a beloved sister but which rises to the surface in calm weather when anyone speaks well of her.[22]

This 'slight distemper' was, she insisted, the only stain on the relationship between the sisters. But Beatrice's comment applies only to adult life. It omits the infantile jealousies which may well have had a life-long and marked effect on the sisters.

This omission is particularly interesting in view of the likelihood that Beatrice was herself involved in such a relationship in regard to Rosie, on whom were lavished all the attention, affection, and education which she wanted herself but was denied. The extreme harshness of her early comments on Rosie, her insistence that Rosie was hopeless and would survive only if married off quickly, seem to be part of this. In her later years, Beatrice chided herself for her earlier 'want of charity' towards this youngest sister, but she never acknowledged that she may have been too involved in the whole situation to accord Rosie dispassionate analysis.[23] Rosie in turn, although never able to be friends with Beatrice, seems to have erected her older sister into a model to be emulated.[24] A substantial amount of Rosie's autobiographical writing is given over to describing Beatrice; her activities, beliefs, and life-style are all noted in a way not followed for the other sisters. Rosie's own children saw her admiration and attempts at emulation of Beatrice as driving forces in her life. Typically they took the form of inappropriate quotes, loudly voiced to unknown listeners—thus, for example, Kitty Muggeridge has a strong recollection of Rosie sitting in the lounge of an expensive Swiss hotel and saying, 'My sister,

Mrs Webb, thinks the idle rich should be exterminated'. But at a more fundamental level, the search for a purpose, the desire for a husband who would excel intellectually rather than in terms of wealth, the constant search after 'interesting people', seem all to be ways in which Rosie attempted to model her life on that of an admired and aloof older sister. That such aims were not realized does not diminish the force which this sibling bond had throughout Rosie's life.

IV

The question of particular affiliations or friendships is, as we have seen, only one part of the sisterhood. In addition to this, there is the broader existence of a familial network, taken for granted quite often, and coming into play in certain circumstances of need. The Potter sisters did provide a network of support for each other but it was one that worked only within certain fairly strictly defined limits. It was, as we have seen, at its most evident and extensive during the exigencies of childbirth and during the early years of childhood. It was also evident during the social season, the years of courtship, and sometimes in the early years of marriage. The married sisters provided information and sympathy for others as they in turn became pregnant or mothers.

The general point that emerges is that while the sisters helped each other in maintaining the socially accepted roles for women of their class, they refused to condone or to assist with any questioning of these roles. Indeed one might well argue that it was often they who articulated these roles and who took upon themselves the role of exercising sanctions against anyone who refused to comply. They accepted the fact that marriage and motherhood could bring great sorrows and great trials, and they did their best to help those, like Georgie, whose lives were rendered miserable by domestic discord. But they did not recognize the virtue or validity of other avenues for women and did their utmost to prevent their sisters from following new paths, or from behaving in unacceptable ways.

The Potter sisters did not lose their habit of criticizing each other with maturity or motherhood. Indeed, as we have seen, some aspects of their mothering and their housekeeping simply became added to the list of things deserving of comment. Lallie continued to have her say on the conduct of others, but she in turn was subjected to criticism from Mary, the one sister who was able to criticize Lallie to her face.

Beatrice entered into the critical circle as she entered her twenties, not just through her diary either. It was she who confronted Maggie Hobhouse over what some of the others saw as Maggie's excessive preoccupation with worldly success. After much thought and some discussion with Mary Playne, Beatrice made her views known to Maggie.

I told her pretty plainly that I found everywhere an *impression* that she tried to get 25/- to the £1 and that this was especially resented now that it was known that she was well off. She practically admitted that for the last 20 years she had tried to stretch the family income to cover more than it would properly do. 'I said to myself—Henry and the family have to have these advantages—I am a clever woman & *it can be done*—I will do it. I have often been hot all over at the things I have done and have had to do, of course now it is unnecessary: but can I get out of the habit? . . .

That was as far as I could get her to go: she would not see that the action was in itself objectionable or that she had not fulfilled her highest duty in pursuing a policy of family selfishness. . . .

In her heart of hearts she believes that no one pursues any other plan than self interest or family self-interest except perhaps persons . . . who are deluded by superstition—or fanaticism—or those who are bordering on insanity. Other people *seem* sometimes to be disinterested but they are conscious or un-conscious hypocrites, or gratifying some other passion like delight in flattery or power—Kate was an unconscious hypocrite, Lallie bought flattery . . . I had excellent manners and was cleverer than she was: Georgie was lazy.[25]

It is not quite clear what effect Beatrice's talk had. Maggie did become interested in questions other than those affecting only her family in later years, but only under the influence of war and her concern for her son.

Although there are isolated situations like this in which the sisters sat down to tell each other what they thought, the full weight of concerted family criticism and pressure was only brought to bear on the unfortunate Rosie. It was in relation to her that one can see fully the extent of familial pressure, and the extraordinary way in which the sisterhood could be almost simultaneously punitive and supportive.

The sisterhood had not been called into play during Rosie's marriage to Dyson Williams. They condoned it, despite his lack of prospects, and commented on his illness. But only Kate seems to have had an idea of how difficult he was during his illness, and she alone seems to have offered Rosie support. It was during her widowhood and the second marriage, the time when Rosie was transgressing the sexual norms appropriate for a woman of her class, that the sisterhood became active.

During the time that Rosie was wandering around Europe in the role of a 'merry widow', she often thought her sisters might know something about her many affairs—and rather feared the consequences of their knowledge. In view of the fact that some of her liaisons were with men whom some of the family knew, this fear was well founded. And indeed the family did have some idea of what was happening, some sisters threatening to drop her if she became the subject of an open scandal.

Mary Playne was one of these. She made her position clear when Rosie went to Longfords to convalesce after her attack of scarlet fever.[26] At this time, Rosie was trying to decide whether or not to marry George Dobbs. She was feeling intensely pressured as George knew all about her past, and she feared that he might use this knowledge against her, or divulge it to her sisters. At the same time, they did not greatly approve of George, and so in the end she told the two sisters who mattered most to her, Kate and Beatrice, that she and George had been lovers in order to overcome their opposition and to make them welcome him into the family. The sisters acknowledged George, but never thought much of him. Within a few months, however, he was the recipient of their sympathy and concern—as they became aware of the enormity of Rosie's behaviour after marriage.

Beatrice did not record the full details of Rosie's heinous behaviour in her diaries, but she certainly recorded her own and the general family response to it.

Another tragedy of a worse kind is the torture of George Dobbs. Mad or bad is his wife or both. She never had any good: now she is developing positive evil. We look on—all of us—middle aged women and men with consternation, shame and disgust and with pity for the young man whose life is being wrecked; we even feel some remorse that we did not warn him that she was 'dangerous'. But he had already had intimate relations with her and naturally enough we grasped at the chance that marriage with a man she seemed to love might transform her.[27]

The sisters did more than merely 'look on with consternation', as Rosie's account of that traumatic episode shows. It was they who arranged for her to be seen by a panel of 'mental specialists', and they who threatened her with incarceration in an asylum and with the loss of her children. George's action in going straight to Maggie Hobhouse was an unequivocal statement of his inability to cope and of his desire for familial intervention. This came with great force, and it is scarcely surprising that Rosie subsequently found it rather hard to forgive George for visiting the wrath of her sisters upon her.

But the Potter sisters did not only enforce obedience and bring pain. Having shown their power, and cowed Rosie completely, they then proceeded to offer her support. At their suggestion, Rosie and George went away for a few weeks holiday to try and patch up their marriage while Maggie Hobhouse, whose suggestion the holiday had been, took Pat and his nurse down to Hadspen to stay with her. Noel was away at boarding school, but the sisters kept an eye on him too.

This situation, in which the sisters drew the limits of freedom, enforced obedience to social norms—and then provided help in keeping to these limits, seems to encapsulate the structure and the operation of the sisterhood. It was unequalled in its criticism and its harshness at times but it could also show compassion and offer help when it saw it as needed. In Rosie's case this was in part clear even before the débâcle. As we have seen, both she and George rejected Pat almost from the moment he was born. Some of the sisters tried to make up for this lack of parental affection to the baby. Kate and Maggie visited him regularly, brought or sent toys, and generally seem to have gone out of their way to supply some of the attention which he did not receive from his mother.

At the same time it is interesting to see that the Potter sisters concentrated their punitive powers on each other. When it came to others, especially to brothers-in-law, who could be seen to be hurting members of the sisterhood, they did not act in concert. In part this is simply a reflection of the prevailing sexual double standard. Thus while Daniel Meinertzhagen was assumed by many members of the family to have other women while he neglected Georgie, nothing was ever said about this. Even in regard to Willie Cripps, who took his mistress home and made his wife receive and entertain her, there was not a unanimity of condemnation. Beatrice, although she understood the strain Willie had had to cope with in his life with Blanche, found his behaviour after he met Giulia Ravogli intolerable. In her view, his pushing of her onto Blanche and his behaviour with her in front of the family was not only distasteful, but even went so far as to make him almost into Blanche's murderer. She hoped for a bit that his apparent grief after Blanche's death might reform him, but when this did not happen, she decided to cut him permanently.[28] The rest of the family was less definite.[29] After Blanche's death, Willie ceased to visit or to be visited and he was rarely mentioned by anybody. Whereas Alfred Cripps remained an integral part of the family, Willie ceased to be one. Several members of the family continued to see him occasionally—and to rely on him for medical assistance. Thus when one of the Meinertzhagen girls had been told she needed an abdominal operation, Willie was referred to for confirmation. Similarly when Daniel Meinertzhagen was in the terminal stages of the kidney disease from which he died in 1910, a visit from Willie gave the family a great sense of re-assurance.[30] Mary Playne, who had been one of the two sisters to attend Blanche's funeral, also kept in contact with Willie and more especially with his children.[31]

While the behaviour of the Potter sisters reflects a double standard of sexual morality, it also points to the ways in which all of them as women were caught within this situation. They were appalled by Rosie's behaviour, and decided to punish her for it. At the same time all of them, and indeed Rosie herself, recognized that they could not ignore the situation. The reputation of the other sisters was threatened by Rosie's behaviour, and they acted as much to protect themselves as to limit her. Their own respectability and standing within the community was at risk if Rosie's behaviour resulted in an open scandal, and hence they took upon themselves the task of policing her sexual relations. When it came to their brothers-in-law, they were not at risk in the same way. The flagrant immorality of men was accepted within the respectable society in which the Potter sisters lived and a wronged sister, although pitiable in herself, posed no threat to the others. Moreover the sisters were themselves powerless to do anything about their brothers-in-law. Daniel and Willie were heedless of them and their ideas and they had no way in which to enforce their views or their values. Mary Playne was very well aware of this, and pointed out to Beatrice that the sisters should maintain contact with Willie in order to be able to help Blanche's children. He would behave as he chose, flaunt or marry his mistress, and ignore them all.[32] They were abso-lutely powerless to influence or to threaten him in any way. The much vaunted moral pre-eminence of women in the late nineteenth and early twentieth centuries was a very limited thing, providing them with the need to enforce social ideas of correct behaviour on other women, but leaving them powerless to deal with the many iniquities perpe-trated by men. In the very act of carrying out their moral duty as

regards Rosie, the Potter sisters were illustrating their own circum-
scribed position within the broader social framework. They were not
free to ignore her delinquencies and so they carried out the prescribed
role for them all. Women were to a very large extent the people who
enforced morality in the nineteenth century—but only on other
women. The Potter sisters simply carried this out within a particular
familial context, and in a style which they devised for themselves.

XII

Conclusion

THE lives and experiences of the Potter sisters, as one sees them from their diaries and letters, provide us with information and insight into a fascinating group of women. What is immediately evident from this is the range of personalities, talents, abilities, and eccentricities exhibited by this quite remarkable family. But the individual tales, more particularly the family sorrows and tragedies, offer insight into something broader than a tale of private misery. They suggest something about the tensions, problems, and crisis points inherent in particular family structures and centring on the role of women within these structures.

Their large and luxurious homes, equipped as they were with every comfort and tended by armies of servants, did not prevent the Potters from experiencing devastating domestic misery and distress. While they were in truth the mistresses of their homes, the lives of the Potters, as of women in other social classes during their time, were organized not around their own desires and wishes, but around those of their husbands and children. Although they were not required to provide physical labour for their families, their lives were as much dedicated to family service as were those of poorer and humbler women of their day. Moreover, as we have seen, their dedication and service to husbands and children were rarely rewarded and they were left to face the hardships of old age without the care or concern of those to whom they had dedicated their own lives.

That this should have been so was partly a result of the devaluation of women which accompanied their legal disabilities and their social inferiority. But it was a result also of the failure amongst most of the Potters to arouse in their children the personal devotion which resulted in care and concern. It is perhaps ironic that Georgie, the least devoted mother of all and the one who left most responsibility to a nanny, should have been the one sister who was offered real devotion and care in her final days. Her charm was rewarded by her children in a way in which the self-sacrifice and constant care offered by Lallie or Mary to their children was not. It is clear that the Potters were not the stuff of which lovable wives and mothers are made. Criticism of them abounds in the memoirs of their children and in the recollections of their descendants, most of it echoing the sense others had of their lack of charm, tact, and femininity and of the capacity to make domestic life relaxing and comfortable for others and for themselves. Some of the sisters, as their siblings and their children recognized, exhibited a range of intellectual, administrative, and political skills which had nothing to focus on in domestic life, but would have been a great boon in the public arena. Indeed, what emerges with most force from this study of the Potters is the extent to which they were a group of exceptional women bound to lives which did not suit them. Apart from Beatrice, they were not the stuff from which great pioneering women were made. They lacked the ambition, the religious fervour, and the single-mindedness evident amongst the great Victorian women like Florence Nightingale or Mary Carpenter. They did not criticize or rebel against the expectations imposed on them by their class and their sex, but they demonstrated only too clearly how difficult it was for some women to fulfil these expectations. Public life offered an outlet for a few, but it could only be engaged in by those able to free themselves from domestic and familial duties—that is, by those with small families or those whose families had grown up. Moreover the public arena was itself a narrow one, offering only philanthropic work or the chance to support the political objectives of husbands or other friends and relatives. This range did not suit the talents or interests of all the sisters.

The Potters were very much aware that their lives did not meet their own or their society's expectations. They saw this as their children did, as the result of their personal failings. Beatrice alone saw it as having some connection with the broader context of the legal and social situation of women. The Potters do not seem to have discussed the complex and problematical nature of family life, nor did they ever complain of their subordination to their husbands within the family. Lallie's story is in some ways the most poignant within this framework, and her solitary last years spent miserably asking herself where she had gone wrong provide a graphic illustration of the costs a woman might have to face for devoting herself entirely to her duty as she and the society around her saw it. Lallie could not and would not countenance any deviation from the prescribed role for Victorian women. She set herself in opposition to her favourite sister, Kate, both when Kate wished to withdraw from Society life and when she wanted to enter into an unconventional relationship with Leonard Courtney. Yet Kate's self-assertion brought happiness and fulfilment, while Lallie's conformity brought misery and despair. Lallie also offers the clearest example of a woman whose great abilities and organizing talents were wasted within the confines of family life. The political acumen noted by others, the inclination and ability to lead and to take charge, were all wasted within domestic life where, if anything, they proved disruptive and uncomfortable. Yet her dedication to that life meant that her involvement in public matters was minimal as all she did was to offer political support to Robert Holt and do her bit to support the establishment of district nursing. The last years of her life were sad, even tragic—but the underlying point is not just one of personal suffering: rather, it is a tragedy of wasted abilities.

This study of the Potter sisters serves finally as a reminder of the narrowness and rigidity of the framework in which late Victorian women lived. The family and social networks, the sisterly bonds, the interest in social and political development which have been studied so extensively in recent years show some of the strategies women developed to cope with their lives. The 'widening sphere' of public and political activity which has also received so much attention recently was for the most part confined to single women of means. For most women life was structured around and dominated by family demands and considerations. Even for the wealthiest and most privileged of women, the ordinary constraints of womanhood had to be reckoned with and life within these constraints could be a difficult matter.

Notes

I. *Introduction*

1. Beatrice Webb, Diaries, 11 Feb. 1924.
2. Beatrice Webb, *My Apprenticeship*, Cambridge, 1979, pp. 2–5.
3. See P. J. Waller, *Democracy and Sectarianism: A Political and Social History of Liverpool*, Liverpool, 1981, pp. 15–31, 72–4, 494.
4. See G. P. Gooch, *Life of Lord Courtney*, London, 1920.
5. Stephen Hobhouse, *Margaret Hobhouse and Her Family*, privately printed, 1930, pp. 84–9, and Henry Hobhouse, *Memoir*, London, 1927.
6. Webb, Diaries, 13 June 1937.
7. Georgie Meinertzhagen, *From Ploughshare to Parliament*, London, 1908.
8. See Lee Holcombe, *Victorian Ladies at Work*, Newton Abbot, 1973, and Martha Vicinus, *Independent Women: Work and Community for Single Women, 1870–1914*, London and Chicago, 1985.
9. See Patricia Hollis (ed.), *Women in Public: The Women's Movement, 1850– 1900*, London, 1979 and F. K. Prochaska, *Women and Philanthropy in Nineteenth-Century England*, Oxford, 1979.
10. Barbara Caine, 'Beatrice Webb and the "Woman Question" ', *History Workshop Journal*, 14 (1982), 23–43.

II. *The Potter Family*

1. Webb, *Apprenticeship*, p. 43.
2. Dobbs Papers, R. Dobbs, 'Confidential Autobiography', p. 8.
3. Lawrencina Potter, Journal, 27 June 1858.
4. Ibid., 2 Oct. 1864.
5. Passfield Papers, II I (1) 7, Richard Potter to Margaret Potter, 14 Jan. 1879.
6. Webb, *Apprenticeship*, p. 3.
7. Passfield Papers, II I (1) 220, Beatrice Potter to Mary Playne, 30 Apr. 1889.
8. The most detailed summary of Potter's business interests is in the obituary notice, 'Death of Mr. Richard Potter, "A King of Men" ', *Gloucestershire Chronicle*, 9 Jan. 1892. This was included in Mary Playne's privately printed memorial pamphlet, 'To My Sisters', 1892. See also Webb, *Apprenticeship*, pp. 3–5.
9. Booth Papers, University of London MS 797/I/5111, Charles Macaulay to Mary Booth, 13 Feb. 1871.
10. Webb, *Apprenticeship*, p. 40.
11. Herbert Spencer, *Autobiography*, London, 1894, I, p. 427.

12. Jeanne Mackenzie, *A Victorian Courtship: The Story of Beatrice Potter and Sidney Webb*, London, 1979, p. 5.

13. Dobbs Papers, Richard Potter to Rosie Potter, 19 May 1883.

14. Passfield Papers, II I (1) 129, Maggie Potter to Beatrice Potter, n.d.

15. Potter Papers, Maggie Potter to Richard Potter, 28 Sept. 1873.

16. Webb, *Apprenticeship*, p. 7.

17. Ibid., p. 11 and Webb, Diaries, 26 Nov. 1889, pp. 1118–31.

18. Webb, *Apprenticeship*, p. 7.

19. Sir Daniel Gooch, *Memoirs and Diary*, ed. R. Burdett Wilson, Newton Abbott, 1972, pp. 111–12. I am indebted to Nicholas Meinertzhagen for this reference.

20. See A. W. Currie, *The Grand Trunk Railway of Canada*, Toronto, 1957, pp. 115–23 and pp. 202–45, and E. T. MacDermot, *History of the Great Western Railway*, London, 1964, II, pp. 1–25.

21. Dobbs Papers, Rosalind Dobbs, 'Confidential Autobiography', p. 3.

22. Booth Papers, University of London MS 797/I/5223, Charles Macaulay to Mary Booth, 20 Aug. 1875.

23. Ibid. 5115, Charles Macaulay to Mary Booth, 21 Feb. 1875.

24. Ibid. 5199, Charles Macaulay to Mary Booth, 20 Dec. 1874.

25. Belinda Norman Butler, *Victorian Aspirations: the Life and Labour of Charles and Mary Booth*, London, 1972.

26. Booth Papers, University of London MS 797/I/5199.

27. Holt Papers, 920 Dur 11/8/16, Mary Playne to Lallie Holt, Dec. 1883.

28. Webb, *Apprenticeship*, p. 8.

29. *The Diaries and Letters of Marie Belloc Lowndes*, ed. Susan Lowndes, London, 1971, p. 244.

30. Interview with Kitty Muggeridge, 6 Mar. 1983.

31. Malcolm Muggeridge recalls Beatrice Webb telling him how she had to keep 'all those women' away from her father's sick bed. Interview with Malcolm Muggeridge, 6 Mar. 1983.

32. Webb, *Apprenticeship*, pp. 12–13.

33. Ibid., p. 11.

34. Spencer, I. p. 311.

35. Dobbs Papers, Richard Potter to Rosie Potter, 17 Apr. 1883.

36. Dobbs Papers, R. Dobbs, 'Confidential Autobiography', p. 12.

37. Passfield Papers, II I (1) 32, Richard Potter to Beatrice Potter, 2 Sept. 1884.

38. L. Potter, Journal, 27 June 1858.

39. L. Potter, *Laura Gay*, 2 vols., London, 1856. The novel was published anonymously by Hurst and Blackett. Lawrencina did not repeat this experiment.

40. Dobbs Papers, K. Muggeridge, 'Notes on Lawrencina Potter'.

41. Ibid.

42. L. Potter, *Laura Gay*, I, p. 147.

43. L. Potter, Journal, 27 June 1858.

44. Ibid., 18 July 1864.
45. Ibid., 29 Dec. 1864.
46. Ibid., 15 July 1865.
47. Dobbs Papers, R. Dobbs, 'Confidential Autobiography', pp. 6–7.

III. *The Early Years of the Potter Sisters*

1. Spencer, I, p. 427.
2. Dobbs Papers, R. Dobbs, 'Confidential Autobiography', p. 19.
3. Webb, *Apprenticeship*, p. 39.
4. Ibid., pp. 39–41. See also Mary Girouard, *The Victorian Country House*, New Haven and London, 1979, pp. 27–9.
5. Girouard, pp. 34–7.
6. Dobbs Papers, R. Dobbs, 'Confidential Autobiography', pp. 14–23.
7. Courtney Collection, vol. 6, 57, Mary Playne to Kate Courtney, 1 Oct. 1896. See also Webb, *Apprenticeship*, pp. 18–21, 152–7.
8. Ibid., p. 12.
9. See Alfred Cripps, *Memoir of Theresa*, privately printed, 1893, p. 18.
10. Booth Papers, University of London MS 797/I/3327. Mary Booth to Charles Booth, 19 Sept. 1884.
11. See Carol Dyhouse, *Girls Growing Up in Late Victorian and Edwardian England*, London, 1981, pp. 3–39.
12. Holt Papers, 920 Dur 39/2/9, Lallie Potter to Lawrencina and Richard Potter, 13 Dec. 1862.
13. L. Potter, Journal, 27 June 1858.
14. Dobbs Papers, R. Dobbs, 'Confidential Autobiography', p. 17. See also James Walvin, *A Child's World: A Social History of English Childhood, 1800–1914*, Harmondsworth, 1982, pp. 45–60.
15. Webb, *Apprenticeship*, p. 58.
16. Dobbs Papers, Rosie Dobbs, 'Confidential Autobiography', p. 6.
17. A. Cripps, p. 21.
18. Dobbs Papers, R. Dobbs, 'Confidential Autobiography', p. 23.
19. Passfield Papers, II I (1) 49, Lawrencina Potter to Beatrice Potter, 20 July and II I (1) 154 and 155, Beatrice Potter to Lawrencina Potter, n.d.
20. H. Spencer, II, p. 42.
21. Webb, *Apprenticeship*, p. 27.
22. Passfield Papers, II I (1) 145, Beatrice Potter to Lawrencina Potter, 26 Feb.
23. Webb, *Apprenticeship*, p. 26.
24. Passfield Papers, II I (1) 142, Beatrice Potter to Lawrencina Potter, 30 July (probably 1865).
25. Passfield Papers, II I (1) 51. Lawrencina Potter to Beatrice Potter, 3 Aug. (1870).
26. Dobbs Papers, R. Dobbs, 'Confidential Autobiography', pp. 33–4.
27. Webb, Diaries, 13 Mar. 1874, p. 39. See also Norman and Jeanne

Mackenzie (eds.), *The Diary of Beatrice Webb*, 4 vols. (London, 1982; 1983; 1984; 1985), II, p. 17.

28. Webb, *Apprenticeship*, pp. 10–11.
29. Dobbs Papers, R. Dobbs, 'Confidential Autobiography', p. 34.
30. Ibid., p. 78.
31. Ibid., p. 35.
32. Dyhouse, pp. 130–80. See also J. Gillis, *Youth and History: Tradition and Change in European Age Relations, 1770 to the Present*, New York, 1981.
33. For the history of girls' education in Victorian England, see Josephine Kamm, *Hope Deferred: Girls' Education in English History*, London, 1965; Rita McWilliams-Tullberg, 'Women and Degrees at Cambridge University', in M. Vicinus (ed.), *A Widening Sphere*, Bloomington and London, 1977, and Barbara Stephen, *Emily Davies and Girton College*, London, 1928.
34. Passfield Papers, II I (1) 3, Richard Potter to Beatrice Potter, 5 Mar. 1875.
35. Dobbs Papers, Correspondence between Richard Potter and Rosie Potter, 1883.
36. Holt Papers, 920 Dur 39/2/9, Lallie Potter to Lawrencina and Richard Potter, 13 Dec. 1862.
37. Holt Papers, 920 Dur 39/2/12, Lallie Potter to Lawrencina Potter, 10 May 1861.
38. Cf. Dyhouse, pp. 46–7.
39. Holt Papers, 920 Dur 39/2/10, Lallie Potter to Lawrencina Potter, just dated Saturday 20.
40. Holt Papers, 920 Dur 39/2/9–31.
41. Holt Papers, 920 Dur 39/2/29, Lallie Potter to Lawrencina Potter, 13 Dec. 1862.
42. Holt Papers, 920 Dur 39/2/14, Lallie Potter to Lawrencina Potter, 14 June 1861.
43. Holt Papers, 920 Dur 39/2/30, Lallie Potter to Lawrencina Potter, 7 Feb. 1863. See also British Library of Political and Economic Science, Courtney Collection, 29, Kate Courtney, Diaries, 1905–6, p. 128.
44. Webb, Diaries, 27 Mar. 1875. See also Mackenzie, *Diary of B. Webb*, I, p. 20.
45. Passfield Papers, II I (1) 111, Theresa Potter to Beatrice Potter, spring 1875.
46. Webb, Diaries, 19 Sept. 1875. See also Mackenzie, *Diary of B. Webb*, I, p. 21.

IV. *Coming Out and the Social Season*

1. Webb, *Apprenticeship*, p. 45.
2. Ibid., pp. 45–9.
3. L. Potter, Journal, 2 Oct. 1864.
4. For the Season, see Leonore Davidoff, *The Best Circles: Society, Etiquette and*

the Season, London, 1973, pp. 37–58. Hilary Evans and Mary Evans, *The Party that Lasted One Hundred Days: The Late Victorian Season*, London, 1976, and Stella Margetson, *Victorian High Society*, New York, 1980, pp. 60–5.

5. Webb, Diaries, 3 Aug. 1874. See also Mackenzie, *Diary of B. Webb*, I, p. 18.
6. Webb, Diaries, 18 Dec. 1875. See also Mackenzie, *Diary of B. Webb*, I, p. 23.
7. Webb, *Apprenticeship*, p. 81.
8. Passfield Papers, II I (1) 112, Theresa Potter to Beatrice Potter, spring 1873.
9. Passfield Papers, II I (1) 106, Theresa Potter to Beatrice Potter, 1873.
10. Dobbs Papers, Richard Potter to Rosie Potter, 25 Feb. 1883.
11. Passfield Papers, II I (1) 106, Theresa Potter to Beatrice Potter, 1873.
12. Passfield Papers, II I (1) 107, Theresa Potter to Beatrice Potter, 1873.
13. Webb, *Apprenticeship*, p. 81.
14. Maggie Potter to Beatrice Potter, 1878, quoted in S. Hobhouse, *Margaret Hobhouse*, p. 57.
15. Ibid., p. 49, Maggie Potter to Lawrencina Potter, Oct. 1874.
16. Passfield Papers, II I (1) 131, Maggie Potter to Beatrice Potter, Nov. 1878.
17. See S. Hobhouse, *Margaret Hobhouse*, pp. 75–83, for the Egyptian trip.
18. Maggie Potter to Beatrice Potter, quoted ibid., p. 83.
19. Florence Nightingale, 'Cassandra' in Ray Strachey, *The Cause: A Short History of the Women's Movement in Great Britain*, repr. London, 1978, pp. 395–418.
20. Passfield Papers, II I (1) 128, Maggie Potter to Beatrice Potter, 25 Nov. 1873.
21. Meinertzhagen Papers, Georgie Meinertzhagen to Daniel Meinertzhagen, 20 Apr. 1876.
22. Courtney Collection, vol. 21, Kate Courtney, Diaries, first entry dated just 1875.
23. For a history of the Charity Organisation Society, see Helen Bosanquet, *Social Work in London, 1869–1912*, repr. Brighton, 1973. For the work of women in the COS, see also Anne Summers, 'A Home from Home: Women's Philanthropic Work in the Nineteenth Century', in Sandra Burman (ed.), *Fit Work for Women*, London and Canberra, 1979.
24. Passfield Papers, II I (1) 120, Margaret Potter to Richard Potter, n.d.
25. Webb, *Apprenticeship*, p. 65.
26. Webb, Diaries, 24 Mar. 1874.
27. H. and M. Evans, pp. 10–21.
28. Webb, *Apprenticeship*, p. 49.
29. Dobbs Papers, Richard Potter to Rosie Potter, 4 Apr. 1883.
30. Webb, Diaries, 16 Mar. 1884.
31. Ibid., 8 Mar. 1885.
32. Ibid., 10 Dec. 1886. See also Mackenzie, *Diary of B. Webb*, I, p. 191.

V. *Courtship and Marriage*

1. See P. Jalland, 'Victorian Spinsters: Dutiful Daughters, Desperate Rebels and the Transition to the New Woman', in Partricia Crawford (ed.), *Exploring Women's Past*, Melbourne, 1983, pp. 129–72.
2. Conversation with Belinda Norman Butler, 10 Feb. 1983.
3. Holt Papers, 920 Dur 11/8/25, Mary Playne to Lallie Holt, n.d.
4. Courtney Collection, vol. 3, 108, Blanche Cripps to Kate Potter, 6 Aug. 1882.
5. Webb, *Apprenticeship*, p. 11.
6. This is the amount stipulated in the marriage settlements drawn up for Maggie and for Theresa, the only two which seem to be extant.
7. Richard Meinertzhagen, *Diary of a Black Sheep*, London and Edinburgh, 1964, p. 45.
8. Courtney Collection, vol. 3, 85, Richard Potter to Kate Potter, 13 Aug. 1882.
9. Courtney Collection, Vol. 21, Kate Courtney Diaries, 1881, p. 55.
10. Holt Papers, 920 Dur 39/2/129, Lallie Potter to Lawrencina Potter, n.d.
11. Ibid.
12. Passfield Papers, II I (1) 5, Richard Potter to Beatrice Potter, 6 Aug. 1878.
13. Booth Papers, University of London MS 797/I/5129, Charles Macaulay to Mary Booth, 13 July 1873, but cf. John Lord, *Duty, Honour, Empire: The Life and Times of Colonel Richard Meinertzhagen*, London, 1971, p. 33.
14. Potter Papers, Maggie Potter to Richard Potter, 28 Sept. 1873.
15. Booth Papers, University of London MS 797/I/5130, Charles Macaulay to Mary Booth, 20 July 1873.
16. Courtney Collection, vol. 21, Kate Courtney, Diaries, 1909–10, p. 120.
17. Webb, Diaries, 2 June 1905. See also Mackenzie, *Diary of B. Webb*, II, p. 346.
18. See M. Jeanne Peterson, *The Medical Profession in Mid-Victorian London*, Berkeley, 1978.
19. Davidoff, p. 24.
20. J. A. and Olive Banks, *Feminism and Family Planning*, Liverpool, 1965, p. 76.
21. Plarr's *Lives of the Fellows of the Royal College of Surgeons*, London, 1930, I, pp. 295–6.
22. F. H. Cripps, *Life's a Gamble*, London, 1957, p. 12.
23. Passfield Papers, Beatrice Webb, Diaries, original MS 4, fo. 88, Mary Playne to Beatrice Potter n.d. (Beatrice inserted several letters pertaining to Theresa's engagement into her diary).
24. Ibid., fo. 92, Georgie Meinertzhagen to Beatrice Potter, 11 Sept.
25. Holt Papers, 920 Dur 11/8/1, Mary Playne to Lallie Holt, 26 Sept.
26. Webb, Diaries, 13 July 1933.
27. See S. Hobhouse, *Margaret Hobhouse, pp. 84–7, and the Dictionary of National Biography*.

28. Courtney Collection, vol. 21, Kate Courtney, Diaries, 1881, p. 63.

29. Ibid., p. 71.

30. Ibid., Jan. 1882, p. 77.

31. Courtney Collection, vol. 3, Kate Potter to Leonard Courtney, 16 May 1882.

32. Courtney Collection, vol. 3, Leonard Courtney to Kate Potter, 17 May 1882.

33. Courtney Collection, vol. 3, Leonard Courtney to Kate Potter, 18 May 1882.

34. For details of Leonard Courtney's career, see G. P. Gooch, 25 ff.

35. Courtney Collection, vol. 3, Kate Potter to Leonard Courtney, 19 May 1882.

36. See B. Caine, 'Beatrice Webb', pp. 24–8.

37. See Dennis Judd, *Radical Joe: A Life of Joseph Chamberlain*, London, 1977, and Richard Jay, *Joseph Chamberlain: A Political Study*, Oxford, 1981.

38. Webb, Diaries, 16 Mar. 1884. See also Mackenzie, *Diary of B. Webb*, I, p. 111.

39. Webb, Diaries, 16 Mar. 1884. See also Mackenzie, *Diary of B. Webb*, I, p. 111.

40. Webb, Diaries, 16 Mar. 1884. See also Mackenzie, *Diary of B. Webb*, I, pp. 111–12.

41. Ibid., 19 Dec. 1886.

42. Dobbs Papers, R. Dobbs, 'Confidential Autobiography', p. 68.

43. Ibid.

44. Ibid., pp. 75–6.

45. Ibid., p. 78.

46. Ibid., p. 76.

47. Passfield Papers, II I (1) 219, Beatrice Potter to Mary Playne, n.d.

48. Holt Papers, 920 Dur 11/8/12, Mary Playne to Lallie Holt, 14 May 1888.

49. Courtney Collection, vol. 23, Kate Courtney Diaries, 1886–8, 7 Feb. 1888, p. 213.

50. Webb, *Apprenticeship*, pp. 216–57, 346–95.

51. Webb, Diaries, 14 Feb. 1890.

52. See Jeanne Mackenzie, *A Victorian Courtship*, pp. 99–105.

53. Holt Papers, 920 Dur 11/7/35, Kate Courtney to Lallie Holt, 9 Jan. 1892.

VI. *Married Life*

1. See Erna Reiss, *The Rights and Duties of Englishwomen*, Manchester, 1934, and Lee Holcombe.

2. See Mary Beard, *Women as Force in History*, repr. New York, 1962, pp. 87–105.

3. See Barbara Caine, 'Woman's "Natural" State: Marriage and the 19th Century Feminists', *Hecate*, 3 (1977), 84–102.

4. J. S. Mill, 'The Subjection of Women', in Alice Rossi (ed.), *John Stuart Mill and Harriet Taylor, Essays in Sex Equality*, Chicago, 1970.

5. Holt Papers, 920 Dur 1, Holt Family Diaries, vol. 4, 5 Oct. 1868.

6. Webb, Diaries, 28 Nov. 1901 and 29 Apr. 1903.

7. Dobbs Papers, R. Dobbs, MS. autobiographical fragment, 'My First Marriage'.

8. G. Meinertzhagen, *A Bremen Family*, London, 1912, Preface.

9. See particularly comments she made on the family after giving a family party for her nieces and nephews in 1937. Webb, Diaries, 13 June 1937.

10. See the comments in her Diaries on Arthur Playne, 15 July 1878, on Henry Hobhouse, 13 Feb. 1882, on Alfred Cripps, 2 Sept. 1882, on Leonard Courtney, 15 Oct. 1882, on Robert Holt, 29 Apr. 1903 and on Daniel Meinterzhagen, 27 July 1910.

11. Ibid., entry dated Apr. 1918, p. 3594.

12. Courtney Collection, vol. 24, Kate Courtney Diaries, 30 Aug. 1888.

13. Ibid., 15 Mar. 1883.

14. See Webb, Diaries, 19 Oct. 1900, 16 Nov. 1900, and the handwritten inserts which follow these on pp. 2042–50. See also her summing up on 31 Dec. 1902.

15. Ibid., 13 July 1892.

16. Ibid., 8 Dec. 1913.

17. Holt Papers, 920 Dur 39/2/57, Lallie Potter to Lawrencina Potter, 18 Aug. 1867.

18. Passfield Papers, II I (4) 87, Mary Playne to Beatrice Potter, 1883.

19. Potter Papers, Maggie Hobhouse to Mary Playne, 30 Dec. 1901.

20. Quoted in S. Hobhouse, *Margaret Hobhouse*, p. 20.

21. S. Hobhouse, *Forty Years and an Epilogue: An Autobiography*, London, 1951, p. 17.

22. Webb, Diaries, 29 Aug. 1903.

23. R. Meinertzhagen, p. 99.

24. Meinertzhagen Papers, Georgie Meinertzhagen to Daniel Meinertzhagen, 25 July (1876).

25. Passfield Papers, II I (1) 29, Richard Potter to Beatrice Potter, 30 Aug. 1884.

26. Meinertzhagen Papers, Georgie Meinertzhagen to Daniel Meinertzhagen, 8 Aug. (1878).

27. Passfield Papers, II I (1) 219, Blanche Cripps to Beatrice Potter, 11 Feb. (1877).

28. See W. Harrison Cripps, *Cancer of the Rectum: Its Pathology, Diagnosis and Treatment*, London, J. A. Churchill, 1880. Two drawings are illustrated in Plate 10. (See further the List of Plates.)

29. W. Harrison Cripps, *Ovariotomy and Abdominal Surgery*, London, J. A. Churchill, 1898. This carries a dedication 'to B.H.C. in affectionate acknowledgement for the illustrations and invaluable help in its prepara-

tion'. In the sketch of her sisters which Rosie appended to her Autobiography, she commented that after having done these microscopic
drawings for Willie, Blanche's trees 'often looked like gigantic cancers'.
Dobbs Papers, R. Dobbs, 'Description of My Sisters'.

30. Webb, Diaries, 2 June 1905.
31. Cripps Papers, Blanche Cripps Diary, 8–9 Sept. 1900.
32. Webb, Diaries, 2 June 1905.
33. Dobbs Papers, R. Dobbs, MS autobiographical fragment, 'My First
    Marriage'.
34. Dobbs Papers, Dyson Williams to Rosie Williams, 18 Dec. (1886).
35. Dobbs Papers, Dyson Williams to Rosie Williams, 21 July 1890. Kate, who
    was closest to Rosie at this time, refers frequently to Dyson's 'difficult
    temper' in her diaries in the 1890s.
36. Dobbs Papers, R. Dobbs, 'My First Marriage'.
37. Webb, Diaries, Christmas Day, 1893. See also Mackenzie, *Diary of
    B. Webb*, II, p. 42.
38. Dobbs Papers, R. Dobbs, typescript, 'My Second Marriage', p. 41.
39. Dobbs Papers, R. Dobbs, MS, 'My Last Testament'.
40. Dobbs Papers, R. Dobbs, typescript, 'An Autobiography', p. 41.
41. Ibid., pp. 8–11.
42. Ibid., p. 32. Rosie wrote about this episode in her life many times. There
    are more than a dozen manuscript accounts—written in her children's
    school exercise books as well as short typed fragments which replicate the
    account in the main typescript, 'An Autobiography'.
43. Ibid., pp. 26–7. See also Gillian Tindall, *The Born Exile: George Gissing*,
    London, 1974, pp. 166–7, and Pierre Coustillas, *London and the Life of
    Literature in Late Victorian England: the Diary of George Gissing*, Brighton,
    1978, Introduction. I am indebted to Margaret Harris for the Gissing
    references.
44. Dobbs Papers, R. Dobbs, 'An Autobiography', p. 25.
45. Malcolm Muggeridge, *Chronicles of Wasted Time*, London, 1973, II,
    pp. 266–7.
46. Passfield Papers, Webb/Mac, Sec A i Playne, 99, Beatrice Webb to Mary
    Playne, n.d.
47. Rosie hinted at this in the typescript she had made of her autobiography.
    Dobbs Papers, R. Dobbs, 'An Autobiography', p. 37. The episode was
    recounted in much more detail in several identical manuscript versions
    written on scraps of paper and in old school exercise books. See also
    Webb, Diaries, May 1900 and 12 June 1900.

VII. *Domestic Life and Motherhood*

1. Holt Papers, 920 Dur 39/2/82, Lallie Holt to Lawrencina Potter, n.d.
2. Holt Papers, 920 Dur 11/10/1–2, Theresa Cripps to Lallie Holt, n.d.

3. Booth Papers, University of London MS 797/I/3471, Mary Booth to Charles Booth, 15 July 1891.

4. Passfield Papers, II I (1) 99, Blanche Cripps to Beatrice Potter, 31 July (1877).

5. Passfield Papers, II I (1) 131, Maggie Potter to Beatrice Potter, n.d. (Nov.1878).

6. Passfield Papers, II I (1) 123, Theresa Potter to Beatrice Potter, n.d.

7. Holt Papers, 920 Dur 39/2/130, Lallie Holt to Lawrencina Potter, n.d.

8. Holt Papers, 920 Dur 39/2/82, Lallie Holt to Lawrencina Potter, n.d.

9. See Patricia Branca, *The Silent Sisterhood: Middle Class Women in the Victorian Home*, London, 1975, p. 74.

10. Ibid., pp. 114–38.

11. J. A. Banks, *Prosperity and Parenthood*, Liverpool, 1955.

12. Cf. F. B. Smith, 'Sexuality in Britain, 1800–1900: Some Suggested Revisions', in M. Vicinus (ed.), *A Widening Sphere: Changing Roles of Victorian Women*, London and Bloomington, 1977, pp. 182–98.

13. For a discussion of the conservatism of the medical profession on the question of contraception, see Angus McLaren, *Birth Control in Nineteenth Century England*, London, 1978, pp. 116–40.

14. Hobhouse Papers, Henry Hobhouse Accounts, 1877–98.

15. Webb, Diaries, 20 June 1896. See also Mackenzie, *Diary of B. Webb*, II, p. 97.

16. See Mackenzie (eds.), *The Diary of B. Webb*, I, p. 354.

17. Maggie Potter to Beatrice Potter, n.d. quoted in S. Hobhouse, *Margaret Hobhouse*, p. 60.

18. Meinertzhagen Papers, Georgie Meinertzhagen to Daniel Meinertzhagen, 23 July (1879).

19. Meinertzhagen Papers, Georgie Meinertzhagen to Daniel Meinertzhagen, 28 Aug. (1879).

20. Passfield Papers, II I (1) 93, Mary Playne to Beatrice Potter, n.d.

21. See Anna Davin, 'Imperialism and Motherhood', *History Workshop Journal*, 5 (1978), 9–65, and Jane Lewis, *The Politics of Motherhood*, London, 1980.

22. F. B. Smith, *The People's Health, 1830–1900*, London, 1979, p. 21.

23. Ibid., pp. 17–27.

24. For his ideas on the importance of antisepsis, see Harrison Cripps, *Ovariotomy*, particularly 'Preparation of Abdominal Section', pp. 62–6.

25. This subject was treated powerfully by George Moore in *Esther Waters*, London, 1894. See also George D. Sussman, 'The Wet Nursing Business in Nineteenth-Century France', *French Historical Studies*, 9 (1975–6), 304–30.

26. Booth Papers, University of London MS 797/I/3230, Mary Booth to Charles Booth, 1879.

27. Holt Papers, 920 Dur 11/10/5, Theresa Cripps to Lallie Holt, 3 Aug. 1885.

28. Passfield Papers, II I (1) 137, Kate Potter to Beatrice Potter, 1873.

29. Passfield Papers, II I (1) 134, Maggie Potter to Beatrice Potter (1879).
30. Holt Papers, 920 Dur 39/2/100, Lallie Holt to Lawrencina Potter (1871).
31. S. Hobhouse, *Margaret Hobhouse*, pp. 111–12.
32. Cripps Papers, B. Cripps, Diaries for 1881–2. See also Holt Papers, 11/8/23, Mary Playne to Lallie Holt, n.d.
33. J. Lord, p. 34.
34. Conversation with John Booth, 4 Apr. 1983.
35. Beatrice Mayor, 'One Family of Ten', p. 44. I am grateful to Lady Theresa Rothschild for showing me an extract of this unpublished work of her mother's.
36. Potter Letters, Maggie Hobhouse to Mary Playne, 1906.
37. Hobhouse Papers, Arthur Hobhouse to Maggie Hobhouse, 11 Nov. Maggie's comment was written on the letter.
38. A. Cripps, p. 57.
39. Ibid., p. 70.
40. Ibid., pp. 70–1.
41. Dobbs Papers, R. Dobbs, 'My First Marriage', p. 14.
42. Conversations with Kitty Muggeridge, 6–9 Mar. 1983.

VIII. *Family Life*

1. Erna Reiss, pp. 50–96. See also David Roberts, 'The Paterfamilias of the Victorian Governing Class', in Anthony S. Wohl (ed.), *The Victorian Family*, London, 1978, pp. 59–81.
2. Holt Papers, 920 Dur 1/6, Holt Family Diaries, 9 June 1886.
3. Maggie Hobhouse to Henry Hobhouse, 29 Aug. (1880) in S. Hobhouse, *Margaret Hobhouse*, pp.91–2.
4. Potter Letters, Maggie Hobhouse to Henry Hobhouse, 23 July 1883.
5. Blanche Harrison Cripps, Diaries, Dec. 1879.
6. Ibid., 26 Aug. 1898.
7. Ibid., 1898, see particularly 26 Feb. to 19 Mar., and 2 June.
8. Ibid., 6 July 1898.
9. Ibid., see particularly 'Summary' for 1899.
10. Conversation with Mrs E. Lee, 22 May 1984.
11. Courtney Collection, vol. 24, Kate Courtney Diaries, 1910, p. 120, and conversations with Lady Rothschild, 2 Mar. 1983.
12. Conversations with Lady Rothschild, 2 Mar. 1983, and with Kitty Muggeridge, 7–10 Mar. 1983.
13. C. Dyhouse, pp. 5–30.
14. A. Cripps, p. 56.
15. S. Hobhouse, *Margaret Hobhouse*, p. 107.
16. Ibid., p. 110.
17. Ibid., p. 142.
18. Potter Letters, Maggie Hobhouse to Mary Playne, 1 Nov. 1889.

19. See M. Vicinus, *Independent Women*, pp. 121–62.

20. Hobhouse Papers, Maggie Hobhouse to Rachel Hobhouse, 1901.

21. Beatrice Mayor, p. 41.

22. Meinertzhagen Papers, Georgie Meinertzhgen to Betty Meinertzhagen, 21 May 1908.

23. Barbara Drake, *Women in the Engineering Trade*, London, 1918, and *Women in Trade Unions*, London, 1921.

24. Conversation with Lady Rothschild, 2 Mar. 1983.

25. See William Cecil Whetham and Catherine Durning Whetham, *The Family and the Nation: a Study in National Inheritance and Social Responsibility*, London, 1909 and *Heredity and Society*, London, 1912.

26. Holt Papers, Dur 1/5, Holt Family Diaries, 25 July 1881.

27. Holt Papers, Dur 11/8/8, Mary Playne to Lallie Holt, n.d.

28. R. Meinertzhagen, p. 65.

29. Hobhouse Papers, Henry Hobhouse Account Books.

30. Lee Holcombe, *Victorian Ladies at Work* and M. Vicinus, *Independent Women*, *passim*.

31. Holt Papers, Dur 11/8/22, Mary Playne to Lallie Holt, n.d.

32. Dobbs Papers, R. Dobbs, 'Memories of Noel'.

33. Ibid.

34. R. Meinertzhagen, p. 102.

35. Margaret Booth, Diary, 4 Nov. 1914. I am grateful to John and Antonia Booth for showing me their mother's diaries.

36. R. Meinertzhagen, p. 102.

37. Ibid., pp. 158–68.

38. Ibid., p. 163.

39. Ibid., p. 129.

40. Dobbs Papers, R. Dobbs, 'An Autobiography', p. 38.

41. Ibid., p. 39.

42. Dobbs Papers, R. Dobbs, 'Last Confession 1926', p. 1.

43. Conversation with Kitty Muggeridge, 7 Mar. 1983.

44. Conversation with Kitty Muggeridge, 7 Mar. 1983.

45. Hobhouse Papers, Maggie Hobhouse to Arthur Hobhouse, 4 Oct. 1907.

46. Passfield Papers, 4 II g 77, Maggie Hobhouse to Beatrice Webb, n.d.

47. Conversation with Niall Hobhouse, 26 Feb. 1983, and Hobhouse Papers, Arthur Hobhouse, letters for 1902–3; see also Frances Spalding, *Vanessa Bell*, London, 1983, p. 161.

48. Beatrice Mayor, p. 26. See also Booth Papers, University of London MS 797 I/4176, Mary Booth to Charles Booth, 22 Oct. 1902.

49. Conversation with John Booth, 5 Apr. 1983.

50. Dobbs Papers, R. Dobbs, Autobiographical Fragments.

51. Webb, Diaries, 12 Sept. 1929.

52. Hobhouse Papers, Betty Russell (née Holt) to Maggie Hobhouse, 2 Apr. 1919.

53. Holt Papers, Dur 1/7, Holt Family Diaries, 10 Nov. 1897.

54. Holt Papers, Dur 11/17/10–15, Eliza Holt to Lallie Holt, 1900–1.

55. Holt Papers, Dur 11/17/8, Eliza Holt to Lallie Holt, Sept. 1900.

56. I am indebted to George Holt for this account. See also Webb, Diaries, 29 Apr. 1903.

57. Ibid., 29 Apr. 1903 and 29 May 1906; Holt Papers, Dur 11/17/21–3, Eliza Holt to Lallie Holt, n.d.

58. 'Memorandum of a Conversation held at 52 Ullet Road on 4 August 1902', in the possession of George Holt. Those present were Lallie Holt, Betty, Molly, and Robert Holt's brother, Philip Holt. Robert Holt was not present and only very reluctantly accepted the settlement negotiated between his brother, his oldest son, Dick and Lallie, Betty and Molly.

59. Holt Papers, Dur 11/17/21, Eliza Holt to Lallie Holt, 25 Aug. (1902).

60. Holt Papers, Dur 1/8. Holt Family Diaries, 27 Nov. 1902 and Jan. 1903.

61. Webb, Diaries, 29 May 1906.

62. Ibid., 9 Mar. 1923.

IX. *Public Life*

1. See P. Hollis (ed.), pp. 223–75.

2. See F. K. Prochaska, pp. 222–30.

3. See M. Vicinus, *Independent Women*, pp. 10–45 and *passim*.

4. See Catherine Hall, 'The Early Formation of Victorian Domestic Ideology', in Sandra Burman (ed.), *Fit Work for Women*, London, 1979, pp. 15–32, and Sandra Delamont and Lorna Duffin (eds.), *The Nineteenth Century Woman: Her Cultural and Physical World*, London, 1978; cf. Prochaska, pp. 21–46, and pp. 222–30 and Davidoff, pp. 20–36.

5. Holt Papers, Dur 1/4–5. See also Anne Holt, *A Ministry to the Poor*, Liverpool, 1936, and Margaret Simey, *Charitable Effort in Liverpool in the Nineteenth Century*, Liverpool, 1951.

6. S. Hobhouse, *Margaret Hobhouse*, pp. 84–7.

7. Alfred Cripps, pp. 73, 81–3.

8. Webb, Diaries, 28 Nov. 1901.

9. Courtney Collection, vols. 21–37, Kate Courtney's Diaries from 1883 until 1915 provide a detailed account of all her charitable and political work.

10. Margaret Cole, *Beatrice Webb*, London, 1945, pp. 33–4, 56–67 and Webb, Diaries, 20 May 1900 and 1 Jan. 1901.

11. Letter to E. R. Pease, quoted in Norman and Jeanne Mackenzie, *The First Fabians*, London, 1971 p. 193.

12. Webb, Diaries, 31 Dec. 1909. See also Cole, pp. 89–109, and A. M. McBriar, *Fabian Socialism and English Politics, 1884–1918*, Cambridge, 1962, pp. 263–79.

13. See Margaret Cole, pp. 126–34.

14. G. Meinertzhagen, *From Ploughshare to Parliament, passim* and T. Swinels, *Manchester Streets and Manchester Men* (first series), Ilkley, n.d. pp. 249–51.

15. L. Potter, *Laura Gay*, I, p. 147.

16. L. Potter, Journal, 28 Mar. 1857.

17. See Ray Strachey, p. 279.

18. Courtney Collection, vol. 23, Kate Courtney Diaries, 1886, p. 215.

19. Courtney Collection, vol. 24, Kate Courtney Diaries, 1888–90, p. 8.

20. Ibid., p. 121.

21. Courtney Collection, vol. 29, Kate Courtney Diaries, 1897–1900, p. 139.

22. *Gloucestershire Chronicle*, 6 Oct. 1923, p. 7.

23. Holt Papers, Dur 1/6, Holt Family Diaries, 20 May 1889.

24. Hobhouse Papers, Yarlington to Hobhouse, 19 Nov. 1889.

25. 'An Appeal Against Female Suffrage', *Nineteenth Century*, 25 (June 1889), pp. 788–92. See also Brian Harrison, *Separate Spheres*, London, 1978, pp. 115–17.

26. See B. Caine, 'Beatrice Webb and the "Woman Question" ', *History Workshop Journal*, 14 (1982), 33–5.

27. Courtney Collection, vol. 27, Kate Courtney Diaries, 1892–4, p. 55.

28. Courtney Collection, vol. 35, Kate Courtney Diaries, 1908–10, p. 136.

29. B. Caine, 'Beatrice Webb', pp. 34–5, and N. Mackenzie (ed.), *The Letters of Sidney and Beatrice Webb*, Cambridge, 1978, II, pp. 362–3.

30. Webb, Diaries, 4 Aug. 1906.

31. B. Caine, 'Beatrice Webb', pp. 36–7.

32. Courtney Collection, vol. 36, Kate Courtney Diaries, 1912, pp. 21, 55–7, 73, and Webb, Diaries, 3 Nov. 1914.

33. Anne Summers, pp. 33–6.

34. Gloucester Record Office, Ace. M14, *A Short History of the Gloucester Training College of Domestic Science* (third edn.), n.d., p. 2.

35. Ibid., see also Carol Dyhouse, 88 ff.

36. Gloucester Record Office, Ace. M14, *A Short History of the Gloucester Training College of Domestic Science*, p. 7, and Records of Training, the Gloucester Training College of Domestic Science.

37. Records of Training, Gloucester Training College of Domestic Science.

38. *A Short History of the Gloucester Training College of Domestic Science*, p. 7.

39. Gloucester Record Office, Minutes of the Gloucester Education Committee, 1903–14.

40. See Brian Abel-Smith, *A History of the Nursing Profession*, London, 1960, Celia Davies (ed.), *Rewriting Nursing History*, London, 1980, Lee Holcombe, *Victorian Ladies at Work*, Newton Abbot, 1973, pp. 68–96, and M. Vicinus, *Independent Women*, pp. 85–120.

41. Florence Nightingale, 'On Trained Nurses for the Sick Poor', in L. R. Seymer (ed.), *Selected Writings of Florence Nightingale*, New York, 1954, p. 314. This piece was originally published in *The Times* in 1876.

42. Lee Holcombe, pp. 89–92.

43. Liverpool Record Office, Reports of the Liverpool District Nursing Association, 1890–1906. All reports show the exclusively male membership of the committees. See also Margaret Simey, pp. 129–30 for the exclusion of women from mainstream charity work in Liverpool.
44. Report of the Liverpool District Nursing Association, 1906, p. 18.
45. Gloucester Record Office, Minutes of the Stroud and Nailsworth District Nursing Association.
46. Ibid., meeting of 28 Feb. 1898.
47. S. Hobhouse, *Margaret Hobhouse*, pp. 202–10.
48. Ibid., p. 227.
49. Webb, Diaries, 15 May 1915.
50. Ibid.
51. Mrs Henry Hobhouse, *I Appeal Unto Caesar*, London, 1917. But see Jo Newberry, 'Russell as Ghost Writer: A New Discovery', *Russell: Journal of the Bertrand Russell Archives*, 15 (1974), 19–23. I am grateful to Jo Newberry for sending me this article.
52. Courtney Collection, vol. 37, Kate Courtney Diaries, 1915, p. 26. See also Gertrude Bussey and Margaret Timms, *The Women's International League for Peace and Freedom*, London, 1965, pp. 17–21, and Lea B. Costin, 'Feminism, Pacifism, Internationalism and the 1915 International Congress of Women', *Women's Studies International Forum*, 5 (1984), 301–15.
53. S. Hobhouse, *Margaret Hobhouse*, pp. 228–30.
54. John Lord, p. 154.
55. See Margaret Cole, p. 141.
56. Ibid., p. 143.
57. Passfield Papers, Beatrice Webb, Seaham Division Newsletters.
58. M. Cole, p. 142.
59. Webb, Diaries, 9 Feb. 1921.

X. *Old Age and Death*

1. But see Howard Chudacoff, 'The Life Course of Women: Age and Age Consciousness, 1865–1915', *Journal of Family History*, 5 (1980), 214–92 and Peter N. Stearns, 'Old Women: Some Historical Observations', *Journal of Family History*, 5 (1980), 44–57.
2. J. S. Mill, 'The Subjection of Women', in Alice Rossi (ed.), *John Stuart Mill and Harriet Taylor, Essays in Sex Equality*, pp. 172–3.
3. Webb, Diaries, 29 Apr. 1903.
4. Courtney Collection, vol. 32, Kate Courtney Diaries, 4 June 1906.
5. Ibid.
6. Webb, Diaries, 29 May 1906.
7. Blanche's Diaries for 1905 deal extensively with her painting, her Shakespeare translations, and her attempt to refurnish the holiday house. They give no indication of her intention to commit suicide.
8. Blanche's death certificate states, as the cause of death, 'suffocation.

Strangulation by hanging when suspended with bandage placed round neck. Suicide. Temporary insanity following fits'. There is a very full description of the whole scene in Webb, Diaries, 2 June 1905.

9. Ibid.
10. Ibid., 5 Oct. 1929. See also Mackenzie, *Diary of B. Webb*, IV, p. 197. The name of Mrs Westby is omitted in Beatrice's Diaries.
11. Webb, Diaries, 29 May 1906, Courtney Collection, vol. 32, Kate Courtney Diaries, 4 June 1906.
12. Webb, Diaries, 18 Oct. 1916 and 9 Mar. 1923.
13. Hobhouse Papers, bundle called Mrs Hobhouse's Seances. This is a large bundle of papers carefully collected by Maggie and Anne Grant. I am grateful to Christopher Clay for alerting me to them and to Niall Hobhouse for locating them.
14. Potter Papers, Maggie Hobhouse to Georgie Meinertzhagen, 8 Oct.
15. Webb, Diaries, 25 Apr. 1902.
16. Leonard Courtney, *Diary of a Churchgoer*, London, 1902. See also Courtney Collection, vol. 9, 96-7, Lallie Holt to Georgie Meinertzhagen, n.d., and 98, Lallie Holt to Leonard Courtney, 27 Dec. 1904.
17. Webb, Diaries, 5 May 1890 and 29 Apr. 1903.
18. Ibid., 22 May 1893. I have been unable to find any trace of Theresa's book on spiritualism.
19. B. Mayor, pp. 39–42.
20. Webb, Diaries, 15 June 1906. See also Mackenzie, *Diary of B. Webb*, III, p. 39.
21. Ibid., 18 June 1899. See also Mackenzie, *Diary of B. Webb*, II, p. 161.
22. Ibid., 1 Apr. 1931.
23. Ibid., 14 Nov. 1915.
24. Ibid., 2 June 1905.
25. Courtney Collection, vol. 32, Kate Courtney Diaries, 24 June 1905.
26. Holt Papers, 920 Dur 1/9, Holt Family Diaries, 24 May 1906.
27. Webb, Diaries, 29 May 1906.
28. Courtney Collection, vol. 32, Kate Courtney Diaries, 4 June 1906.
29. Passfield Papers, II 4 C 93, Mary Playne to Beatrice Webb, 20 Aug. 1907.
30. Diary of Margaret Booth, 29 Oct. 1914.
31. Webb, Diaries, 3 Nov. 1914.
32. Ibid., 2 July 1916.
33. Quoted in S. Hobhouse, *Margaret Hobhouse*, p. 221.
34. Ibid., p. 222.
35. Ibid., pp. 245–56.
36. Dobbs Papers, R. Dobbs, Diary of the Great War.
37. Dobbs Papers, R. Dobbs, Diary Since I Last Saw Noel, p. 3.
38. R. Dobbs, London, 1920.
39. S. Hobhouse, *Margaret Hobhouse*, pp. 257–60, and Hobhouse Papers, Mrs Hobhouse's Seances.

40. Webb, Diaries, 21 Dec. 1920.
41. Quoted in S. Hobhouse, *Margaret Hobhouse*, pp. 274–5.
42. Hobhouse Papers, Maggie Hobhouse to Konradin Hobhouse, 30 Jan. 1921.
43. Webb, Diaries, 9 Feb. 1921.
44. Ibid., 21 Dec. 1921. See also Mackenzie, *Diary of B. Webb*, III, p. 375.
45. Ibid., 9 Feb. 1921. See also Mackenzie, *Diary of B. Webb*, III, p. 376.
46. Ibid., 16 Mar. 1921.
47. Ibid., 17 Nov. 1922.
48. Dobbs Papers, R. Dobbs, Continuation War Diary, Nov. 1918.
49. Webb, Diaries, 11 Aug. 1923.
50. Ibid., 12 Oct. 1923.
51. Ibid., 11 Aug. 1923.
52. Ibid., 6 Mar. 1929.
53. M. Cole, p. 164.
54. Webb, Diaries, 23 Jan. 1930.
55. Ibid., 27 Mar. 1931.
56. Ibid., 5 Oct. 1929.
57. Conversations with Kitty and Malcolm Muggeridge, 6–9 Mar. 1983.
58. Dobbs Papers, R. Dobbs, Travel Diaries.
59. Conversations with Kitty Muggeridge, 6–9 Mar. 1983.
60. Conversations with Malcolm and Kitty Muggeridge, 6–9 Mar. 1983.
61. Dobbs Papers, R. Dobbs, Autobiographical Fragments.
62. M. Muggeridge, I, pp. 88–9, 158–9, II, pp. 265–7.
63. Conversations with Kitty Muggeridge, 6–9 Mar. 1983.
64. Dobbs Papers, R. Dobbs, World War II Diaries.

XI. *The Sisterhood*

1. This abbreviation for the family of Richard Potter was used frequently by the sisters, especially by Beatrice. See e.g. Webb, Diaries, 10 July 1936.
2. There was considerable bitterness amongst Lallie's daughters at the discrepancies between their inheritance and that of their brothers, particularly their eldest brother who, they believed, had deprived them of money intended for them by their uncle, Philip Holt. Holt Papers, 920 Dur 14/4/1–19.
3. Webb, Diaries, 12 June 1900.
4. Courtney Collection, vol. 22, Diary for 1885, p. 73. See also vol. 23, 2 Sept. 1884, p. 4. Theresa was also at Georgie's during the miscarriage and the two of them nursed her through it.
5. See the Diaries of Margaret Booth, 1910–14.
6. Potter Papers, Maggie Hobhouse to Mary Playne, 1906.
7. Francis Galton, *English Men of Science*, London, 1874, pp. 34–5.
8. Mary Booth commented to her husband on this point. See Booth Papers,

University of London MS 797/1/3237, Mary Booth to Charles Booth, Jan. 1880.

9. Alfred Adler, *Understanding Human Nature*, New York, 1927, pp. 152–3.
10. Courtney Collection, vol. 3, 29, Kate Potter to Leonard Courtney, 25 May 1882.
11. Holt Papers, 920 Dur 11/8/25 and 11/10.
12. Passfield Papers, II I (1) 85, Mary Playne to Beatrice Potter, 15 July 1883.
13. Dobbs Papers, R. Dobbs, 'My First Marriage', p. 14.
14. See Alfred Adler, pp. 149–50.
15. Conversations with Kitty Muggeridge, 6–8 March 1983. See also Malcolm Muggeridge, I, pp. 137–9.
16. Webb, Diaries, 22 May 1893.
17. Ibid., 21 June 1893.
18. A useful collection of recent research is in Michael Lamb and Brian Sutton-Smith (eds.), *Sibling Relationships: Their Nature and Significance Across the Life Span*, London, 1982.
19. Webb, Diaries, 12 June 1900.
20. Ibid., 22 June 1905.
21. Ibid., 21 Dec. 1920.
22. Ibid., 11 Aug. 1923.
23. See particularly the 'Note, February, 1920' appended to the earlier entry in Beatrice's diary dealing with Rosie's marital problems, and chiding herself for 'uncharitableness and lack of reasoning sympathy' with her youngest sister. Webb, Diaries, May 1900.
24. Conversation with Kitty Muggeridge, 7 Mar. 1983. See also K. Muggeridge and R. Adam, *Beatrice Webb*, London, 1968, pp. 1–4.
25. Passfield Papers, Webb/Mac sec A i Play, c 33, Beatrice Webb to Mary Playne (1 Aug. 1905).
26. Dobbs Papers, Rosie Williams to George Dobbs, n.d.
27. Webb, Diaries, May 1900.
28. Ibid., 5 Oct. 1905.
29. Ibid., 14 Oct. 1905.
30. Diary of Margaret Booth, 13 Apr. 1910 and Meinertzhagen Papers, Bardie Meinertzhagen to Georgina Meinertzhagen, 22 July (year not given).
31. Passfield Papers, II 4 C 2, c 29, Mary Playne to Beatrice Webb (5 June, 1905). Georgie had also been at the funeral.
32. Webb, Diaries, 14 Oct. 1905.

Select Bibliography

I. MANUSCRIPT SOURCES

(a) *In Libraries*

British Library of Political and Economic Sciences
  Courtney Collection
  Passfield Papers

Liverpool City Libraries
  Holt Papers

University of London Library
  Booth Papers

(b) *In Private Collections*

The Diaries of Margaret Booth, now held by Antonia Booth
The Papers of Rosalind Dobbs, now held by Kitty Muggeridge
The Diaries of Blanche Harrison Cripps, now held by Elsie Lee
The Hobhouse Papers, now held by Paul Hobhouse
'One Family of Ten', the autobiography of Beatrice Mayor, now held by Lady Theresa Rothschild
The Meinertzhagen Letters, now held by Daniel Meinertzhagen
The Potter Papers, now held by Christopher Clay as literary executor to Rachel Clay
The Diary of Lawrencina Potter, now held by Johnathon King

II. BOOKS AND ARTICLES BY OR ABOUT THE POTTERS AND THEIR IMMEDIATE ASSOCIATES

Caine, Barbara, 'Beatrice Webb and the "Woman Question"', *History Workshop Journal*, 14 (1982), 23–43.
Cole, Margaret, *Beatrice Webb*, London, 1945.
Courtney, Leonard, *Diary of a Churchgoer*, London, 1902.
Cripps, Alfred, *Memoir of Theresa*, privately printed, 1893.
Cripps, F. H., *Life's a Gamble*, London, 1957.
Drake, Barbara, *Women in the Engineering Trade*, London, 1918.
—— *Women in Trade Unions*, London, 1921.

Gooch, Sir Daniel, *Memoirs and Diary*, ed. R. Burdett Wilson, Newton Abbott, 1972.

Gooch, G. P., *Life of Lord Courtney*, London, 1920.

Harrison Cripps, W., *Cancer of the Rectum: Its Pathology, Diagnosis and Treatment*, London, 1880.

— *Ovariotomy and Abdominal Surgery*, London, 1898.

Hobhouse, Henry, *Memoir*.

Hobhouse, Mrs Henry, *I Appeal Unto Caesar*, London, 1917.

Hobhouse, Stephen, *Margaret Hobhouse and Her Family*, privately printed, 1930.

— *Forty Years and an Epilogue: An Autobiography*, London, 1951.

Lord, John, *Duty, Honour, Empire: The Life and Times of Colonel Richard Meinertzhagen*, London, 1971.

Mackenzie, J., *A Victorian Courtship: The Story of Beatrice Potter and Sidney Webb*, London, 1979.

Meinertzhagen, Georgina, *A Bremen Family*, London, 1912.

— *From Ploughshare to Parliament*, London, 1908.

Meinertzhagen, Richard, *Diary of a Black Sheep*, London and Edinburgh, 1964.

Muggeridge, Kitty and Adam, Ruth, *Beatrice Webb*, London, 1968.

Muggeridge, Malcolm, *Chronicles of Wasted Time*, 2 vols, London, 1973.

Potter, L., *Laura Gay*, 2 vols., London, 1856.

Spencer, Herbert, *Autobiography*, 2 vols., London, 1894.

Webb, Beatrice, *The Diary of Beatrice Webb*, ed. Norman and Jeanne Mackenzie, London and Cambridge, Mass., 4 vols., 1982–5.

— *My Apprenticeship*, London, 1924, repr. Cambridge, 1979.

— *Our Partnership*, ed. B. Drake and M. I. Cole, London, 1948.

Webb, Sidney and Beatrice, *The Letters of Sidney and Beatrice Webb*, ed. Norman Mackenzie, 3 vols., Cambridge, 1978.

Whetham, William Cecil and Durning, Catherine, *The Family and the Nation: A Study in National Inheritance and Social Responsibility*, London, 1909.

— and — *Heredity and Society*, London, 1912.

III. SECONDARY SOURCES

Abel-Smith, Brian, *A History of the Nursing Profession*, London, 1960.

Adler, Alfred, *Understanding Human Nature*, New York, 1927.

Banks, J. A., *Prosperity and Parenthood*, Liverpool, 1955.

— and Banks, Olive, *Feminism and Family Planning*, Liverpool, 1965.

Beard, Mary, *Women as Force in History*, repr. New York, 1962.

Bosanquet, Helen, *Social Work in London, 1869–1912*, repr. Brighton, 1973.

Branca, Patricia, *The Silent Sisterhood: Middle Class Women in the Victorian Home*, London, 1975.

Bussey, Gertrude and Timms, Margaret, *The Women's International League for Peace and Freedom*, London, 1965.

Butler, Belinda Norman, *Victorian Aspirations: The Life and Labour of Charles and Mary Booth*, London, 1972.

Caine, Barbara, 'Women's "Natural" State: Marriage and the 19th Century Feminists', *Hecate*, 3 (1977), 84–102.

Chudacoff, Howard, 'The Life Course of Women: Age and Age Consciousness, 1865–1915', *Journal of Family History*, 5 (1980), 44–57.

Costin, Lea B., 'Feminism, Pacifism, Internationalism and the 1915 International Congress of Women', *Women's Studies International Forum*, 5 (1984), 301–15.

Currie, A. W., *The Grand Trunk Railway of Canada*, Toronto, 1957.

Davidoff, Leonore, *The Best Circles: Society, Etiquette and the Season*, London, 1973.

Davies, Celia (ed.), *Rewriting Nursing History*, London, 1980.

Davin, Anna, 'Imperialism and Motherhood', *History Workshop Journal*, 5 (1978), 9–65.

Delamont, Sarah and Duffin, Lorna (eds.), *The Nineteenth Century Woman: Her Cultural and Physical World*, London, 1978.

Dyhouse, Carol, *Girls Growing Up in Late Victorian and Edwardian England*, London, 1981.

Evans, Hilary and Evans, Mary, *The Party that Lasted One Hundred Days: The Late Victorian Season*, London, 1976.

Gillis, J., *Youth and History: Tradition and Change in European Age Relations, 1770 to the Present*, New York, 1981.

Girouard, Mark, *The Victorian Country House*, New Haven and London, 1979.

Hall, Catherine, 'The Early Formation of Victorian Domestic Ideology', in Sandra Burman (ed.), *Fit Work for Women*, London, 1978.

Harrison, Brian, *Separate Spheres*, London, 1978.

Holcombe, Lee, *Victorian Ladies at Work*, Newton Abbot, 1973.

Hollis, Patricia (ed.), *Women in Public: The Women's Movement, 1850–1900*, London, 1979.

Holt, Anne, *A Ministry to the Poor*, Liverpool, 1936.

Jalland, P., 'Victorian Spinsters: Dutiful Daughters, Desperate Rebels and the Transition to the New Woman', in Patricia Crawford (ed.), *Exploring Women's Past*, Melbourne, 1983.

Jay, Richard, *Joseph Chamberlain: A Political Study*, Oxford, 1981.

Judd, Dennis, *Radical Joe: A Life of Joseph Chamberlain*, London, 1977.

Kamm, Josephine, *Hope Deferred: Girls' Education in English History*, London, 1965.

Lamb, Michael and Sutton-Smith, Brian (eds.), *Sibling Relationships: Their Nature and Significance Across the Life Span*, London, 1982.

Lewis, Jane, *The Politics of Motherhood*, London, 1980.

—— *Women in England, 1870–1950*, Brighton, 1984.

Lowndes, Marie Belloc, *The Diaries and Letters of Marie Belloc Lowndes*, ed. Susan Lowndes, London, 1971.

McBriar, A. M. *Fabian Socialism and English Politics, 1884–1918*, Cambridge, 1962.

MacDermot, E. T., *History of the Great Western Railway*, 3 vols., London, 1964.

Mackenzie, Norman and Jeanne, *The First Fabians*, London, 1971.

McLaren, Angus, *Birth Control in Nineteenth Century England*, London, 1978.

McWilliams-Tullberg, Rita, 'Women and Degrees at Cambridge University', in M. Vicinus (ed.), *A Widening Sphere*, Bloomington and London, 1977.

Margetson, Stella, *Victorian High Society*, New York, 1980.

Newberry, J., 'Russell as Ghost Writer: A New Discovery', *Russell: Journal of Bertrand Russell Archives*, 15 (1974), 19–23.

Nightingale, Florence, 'On Trained Nurses for the Sick Poor', in L. R. Seymer (ed.), *Selected Writings of Florence Nightingale*, New York, 1954.

Plarr, V. G., *Lives of the Fellows of the Royal College of Surgeons*, London, 1930.

Prochaska, F. K., *Women and Philanthropy in 19th Century England*, Oxford, 1979.

Reiss, Erna, *The Rights and Duties of English-Women*, Manchester, 1934.

Roberts, David, 'The Paterfamilias of the Victorian Governing Class' in Anthony S. Wohl (ed.), *The Victorian Family*, London, 1978.

Rossi, Alice (ed.), *John Stuart Mill and Harriet Taylor, Essays in Sex Equality*, Chicago, 1970.

Simey, Margaret, *Charitable Effort in Liverpool in the Nineteenth Century*, Liverpool, 1951.

Smith, F. B., *The People's Health, 1830–1900*, London, 1979.

Stearns, Peter N., 'Old Women: Some Historical Observations', *Journal of Family History*, 5 (1980), 44–57.

Stephen, Barbara, *Emily Davies and Girton College*, London, 1928.

Strachey, Ray, *The Cause: A Short History of The Women's Movement in Great Britain*, repr. London, 1978.

Summers, Anne, 'A Home from Home: Women's Philanthropic Work in the Nineteenth Century', in Sandra Burman (ed.), *Fit Work for Women*, London and Canberra, 1979.

Sussman, George D., 'The Wet Nursing Business in Nineteenth-Century France', *French Historical Studies*, 9 (1975–6), 304–30.

Tindall, Gillian, *The Born Exile: George Gissing*, London, 1974.

Vicinus, Martha (ed.), *A Widening Sphere: Changing Roles of Victorian Women*, London and Bloomington, 1977.

—— *Independent Women: Work and Community for Single Women, 1870–1914*, London and Chicago, 1985.

Waller, P. J., *Democracy and Sectarianism: A Political and Social History of Liverpool*, Liverpool, 1981.

Walvin, James, *A Child's World: A Social History of English Childhood, 1890–1914*, Harmondsworth, 1982.

POTTER FAMILY TREE

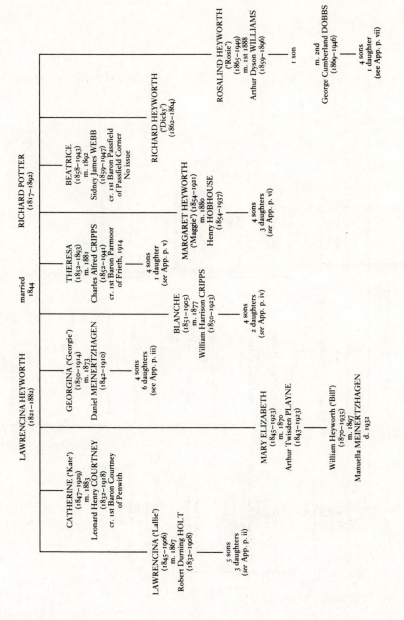

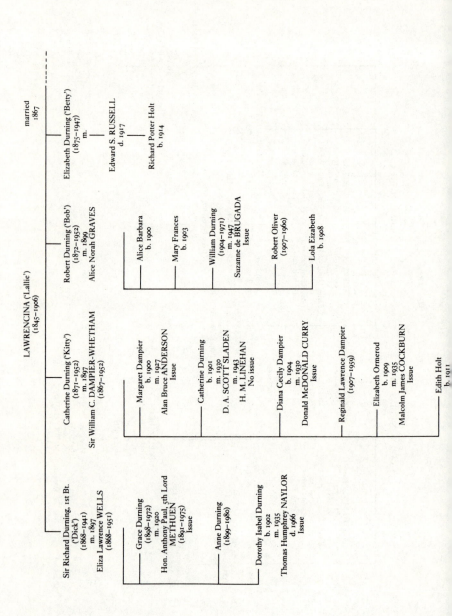

LAWRENCINA ('Lallie')
(1845–1906)

married
1867

Elizabeth Durning ('Betty')
(1875–1947)
m.

Edward S. RUSSELL
d. 1917

Richard Potter Holt
b. 1914

Robert Durning ('Bob')
(1872–1952)
m. 1899
Alice Norah GRAVES

Alice Barbara
b. 1900

Mary Frances
b. 1903

William Durning
(1904–1971)
m. 1947
Suzanne de BRUGADA
Issue

Robert Oliver
(1907–1960)

Lola Eizabeth
b. 1908

Catherine Durning ('Kitty')
(1871–1952)
m. 1897
Sir William C. DAMPIER-WHETHAM
(1867–1952)

Margaret Dampier
b. 1900
m. 1927
Alan Bruce ANDERSON
Issue

Catherine Durning
b. 1901
m. 1930
D. A. SCOTT SLADEN
m. 1943
H. M. LINEHAN
No issue

Diana Cecily Dampier
b. 1904
m. 1930
Donald McDONALD CURRY
Issue

Reginald Lawrence Dampier
(1907–1959)

Elizabeth Ormerod
b. 1909
m. 1935
Malcolm James COCKBURN
Issue

Edith Holt
b. 1911

Sir Richard Durning, 1st Bt.
('Dick')
(1868–1941)
m. 1897
Eliza Lawrence WELLS
(1868–1951)

Grace Durning
(1898–1972)
m. 1920
Hon. Anthony Paul, 5th Lord
METHUEN
(1891–1975)
Issue

Anne Durning
(1899–1980)

Dorothy Isabel Durning
b. 1902
m. 1935
Thomas Humphrey NAYLOR
d. 1966
Issue

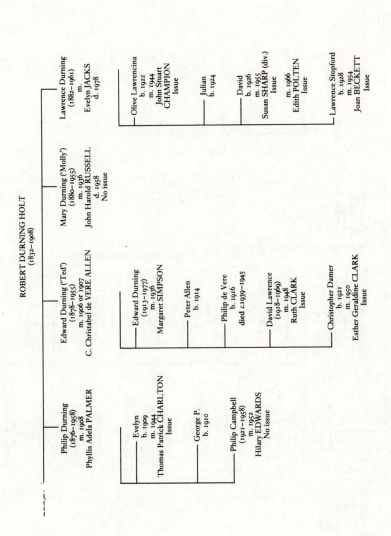

ROBERT DURNING HOLT
(1832–1908)

Philip Durning
(1876–1958)
m. 1908
Phyllis Adela PALMER

Edward Durning ('Ted')
(1878–1955)
m. 1906 or 1907
C. Chrisabel de VERE ALLEN

Mary Durning ('Molly')
(1880–1955)
m. 1936
John Harold RUSSELL
d. 1958
No issue

Lawrence Durning
(1882–1961)
m.
Evelyn JACKS
d. 1978

Evelyn
b. 1909
m. 1944
Thomas Patrick CHARLTON
Issue

George P.
b. 1910

Philip Campbell
(1921–1958)
m. 1952
Hilary EDWARDS
No issue

Edward Durning
(1913–1977)
m. 1936
Margaret SIMPSON

Peter Allen
b. 1914

Philip de Vere
b. 1916
died c.1939–1945

David Lawrence
(1918–1969)
m. 1948
Ruth CLARK
Issue

Christopher Damer
b. 1921
m. 1950
Esther Geraldine CLARK
Issue

Olive Lawrencina
b. 1922
m. 1944
John Stuart
CHAMPION
Issue

Julian
b. 1924

David
b. 1926
m. 1955
Susan SHARP (div.)
Issue
m. 1966
Edith POLTEN
Issue

Lawrence Stopford
b. 1928
m. 1954
Joan BECKETT
Issue

GEORGINA ('Georgie')
(1850–1914)

married
1873

(William) Hubert WARRE-CORNISH
(1872–1934)

Daniel
(1875–1898)

Barbara ('Bardie')
(1876–1963)
m. 1900
Bernard Harpur DRAKE
(1876–1941)
No issue

Colonel Richard
(1878–1967)
m. 1911
Armorel LE ROY-LEWIS
(div. 1919)
m. 1921
Annie Constance JACKSON
d. 1928

Margaret ('Margy')
(1880–1959)
m. 1906
George Macaulay BOOTH
(1877–1971)

George Frederick ('Fritz')
(1881–1962)
m. 1909
Florence MAXWELL-BARNES
d. c.1940
No issue

Lawrencina
(1883–1971)
m. 1906
(William) Hubert WARRE-CORNISH

Anne Margaret
b. 1921
m. 1946
Herbert John PAIN
(div.)
Issue
m. 1978
Robin ADAM

Daniel
(1925–1944)

Richard Randle
b. 1928
m. 1959
Gloria TAYLOR
(div.)
m. 1964
Susan DAY
(div.)
Issue
m. 1966
Gillian MORGAN
Issue

Daniel Macaulay
(1907–1962)
m. 1949
Joan B. F. GUTHRIE
d. 1962
No issue

Antonia ('Toni')
b. 1909

Georgina
b. 1912
m. 1934
Lionel BIRCH
Issue

John Sebastian Macaulay
b. 1913
m. 1957
Juno LIDDELL
(1930–1968)
Issue

Paulina
b. 1915
m. 1941
John C. ROTTON
Issue

Charles Zachary Macaulay
(1917–1984)

Laurencina ('Nell')
b. 1906

Francis Hubert
b. 1908
m. 1949
Angela Mary Alice GREEN

Hermione
(1910–1914)

Philip Amyas
b. 1912
m. 1944
Lucilla BLOW
Issue

Jane ('Jenny')
(1917–1990)

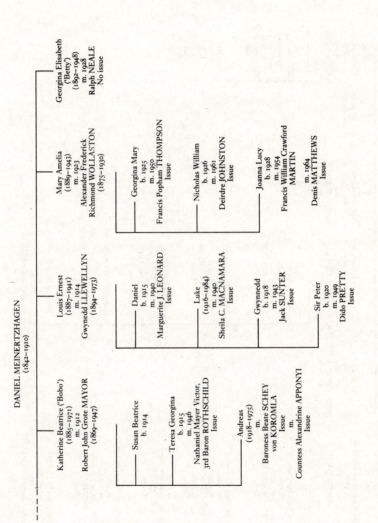

DANIEL MEINERTZHAGEN
(1842–1910)

Katherine Beatrice ('Bobo')
(1885–1971)
m. 1912
Robert John Grote MAYOR
(1869–1947)

Susan Beatrice
b. 1914

Teresa Georgina
b. 1915
m. 1946
Nathaniel Mayer Victor,
3rd Baron ROTHSCHILD
Issue

Andreas
(1918–1975)
m.
Baroness Beate SCHEY
von KOROMLA
Issue
m.
Countess Alexandrine APPONYI
Issue

Louis Ernest
(1887–1941)
m. 1914
Gwynedd LLEWELLYN
(1894–1973)

Daniel
b. 1915
m. 1940
Marguerite J. LEONARD
Issue

Luke
(1916–1984)
m. 1940
Sheila C. MACNAMARA
Issue

Gwynnedd
b. 1918
m. 1943
Jack SUNTER
Issue

Sir Peter
b. 1920
m. 1949
Dido PRETTY
Issue

Mary Amelia
(1889–1943)
m. 1923
Alexander Frederick
Richmond WOLLASTON
(1875–1930)

Georgina Mary
b. 1925
m. 1950
Francis Popham THOMPSON
Issue

Nicholas William
b. 1926
m. 1961
Deirdre JOHNSTON
Issue

Joanna Lucy
b. 1928
m. 1954
Francis William Crawford
MARTIN
m. 1964
Denis MATTHEWS
Issue

Georgina Elisabeth
('Betty')
(1892–1948)
m. 1928
Ralph NEALE
No issue

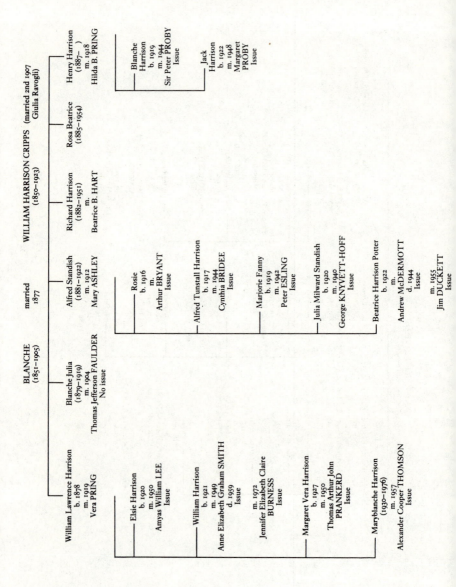

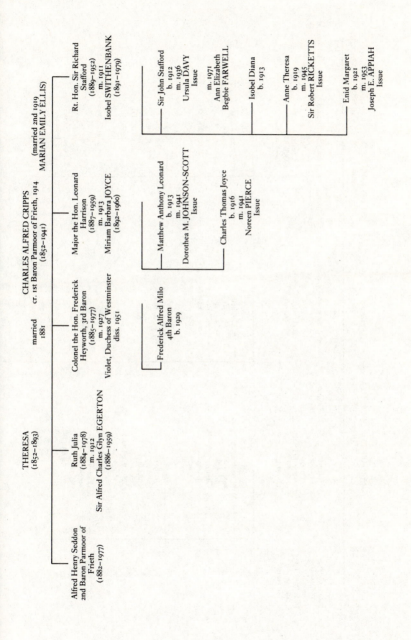

THERESA
(1852–1893)

CHARLES ALFRED CRIPPS
cr. 1st Baron Parmoor of Frieth, 1914
(1852–1941)

married
1881

(married 2nd 1919
MARIAN EMILY ELLIS)

Alfred Henry Seddon
2nd Baron Parmoor of
Frieth
(1882–1977)

Ruth Julia
(1884–1978)
m. 1912
Sir Alfred Charles Glyn EGERTON
(1886–1959)

Colonel the Hon. Frederick
Heyworth, 3rd Baron
(1885–1977)
m. 1927
Violet, Duchess of Westminster
diss. 1951

Major the Hon. Leonard
Harrison
(1887–1959)
m. 1913
Miriam Barbara JOYCE
(1892–1960)

Rt. Hon. Sir Richard
Stafford
(1889–1952)
m. 1911
Isobel SWITHENBANK
(1891–1979)

Frederick Alfred Milo
4th Baron
b. 1929

Matthew Anthony Leonard
b. 1941
m. 1941
Dorothea M. JOHNSON-SCOTT
Issue

Charles Thomas Joyce
b. 1916
m. 1941
Noreen PIERCE
Issue

Sir John Stafford
b. 1912
m. 1936
Ursula DAVY
Issue

Ann Elizabeth
Begbie FARWELL
m. 1971

Isobel Diana
b. 1913

Anne Theresa
b. 1919
m. 1945
Sir Robert RICKETTS
Issue

Enid Margaret
b. 1921
m. 1953
Joseph E. APPIAH
Issue

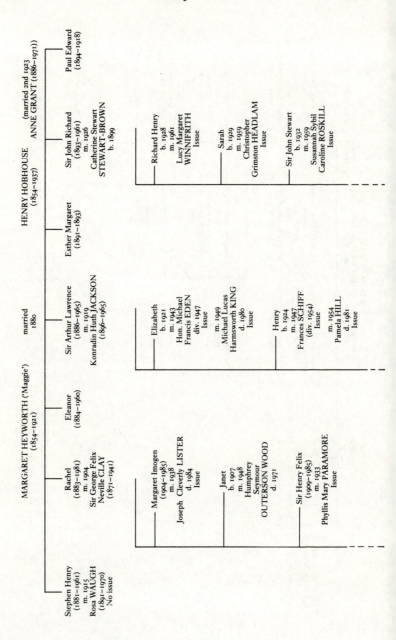

MARGARET HEYWORTH ('Maggie') (1854–1921)   married 1880   HENRY HOBHOUSE (1854–1937)   (married 2nd 1923 ANNE GRANT (1886–1971))

Stephen Henry
(1881–1961)
m. 1915
Rosa WAUGH
(1891–1970)
No issue

Rachel
(1883–1981)
m. 1904
Sir George Felix
Neville CLAY
(1871–1941)

Eleanor
(1884–1960)

Sir Arthur Lawrence
(1886–1965)
m. 1919
Konradin Huth JACKSON
(1896–1965)

Esther Margaret
(1891–1893)

Sir John Richard
(1893–1961)
m. 1926
Catherine Stewart
STEWART-BROWN
b. 1899

Paul Edward
(1894–1918)

Margaret Imogen
(1904–1985)
m. 1938
Joseph Cleverly LISTER
d. 1984
Issue

Janet
b. 1907
m. 1948
Humphrey
Seymour
OUTERSON WOOD
d. 1971

Sir Henry Felix
(1909–1985)
m. 1933
Phyllis Mary PARAMORE
Issue

Elizabeth
b. 1921
m. 1943
Hon. Michael
Francis EDEN
div. 1947
Issue

m. 1949
Michael Lucas
Harmsworth KING
d. 1986
Issue

Henry
b. 1924
m. 1947
Frances SCHIFF
(div. 1954)
Issue

m. 1954
Pamela HILL
d. 1981
Issue

Richard Henry
b. 1928
m. 1961
Lucy Margaret
WINNIFRITH
Issue

Sarah
b. 1929
m. 1959
Christopher
Grimston HEADLAM
Issue

Sir John Stewart
b. 1932
m. 1959
Susannah Sybil
Caroline ROSKILL
Issue

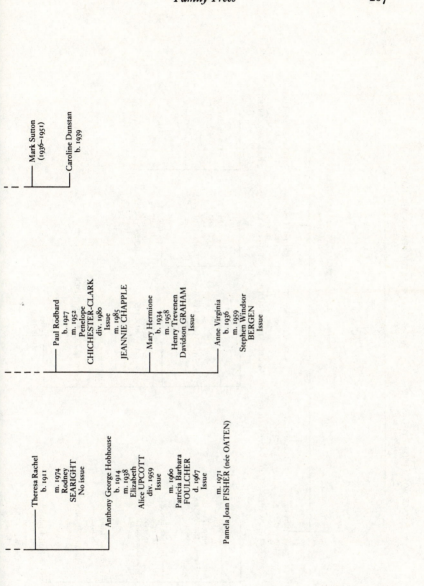

Mark Sutton
(1936–1951)

Caroline Dunstan
b. 1939

Paul Rodbard
b. 1927
m. 1952
Penelope
CHICHESTER-CLARK
div. 1980
Issue
m. 1985
JEANNE CHAPPLE

Mary Hermione
b. 1934
m. 1958
Henry Trevenen
Davidson GRAHAM
Issue

Anne Virginia
b. 1936
m. 1959
Stephen Windsor
BERGEN
Issue

Theresa Rachel
b. 1911
m. 1974
Rodney
SEARIGHT
No issue

Anthony George Hobhouse
b. 1914
m. 1938
Elizabeth
Alice UPCOTT
div. 1959
Issue
m. 1960
Patricia Barbara
FOULCHER
d. 1967
Issue
m. 1971
Pamela Joan FISHER (née OATEN)

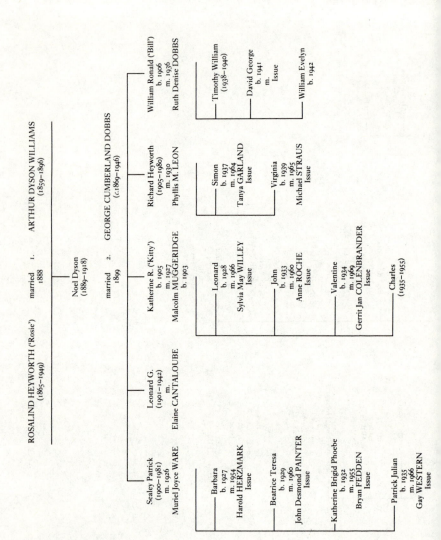

Index